D0959127

THE VAST UNKNOWN

Also by the Author

Triumph on Everest: A Photobiography of Sir
Edmund Hillary

Touching My Father's Soul: A Sherpa's Journey to
the Top of Everest (with Jamling Tenzing Norgay)

Everest: Mountain Without Mercy

Aama in America: A Pilgrimage of the Heart

Nepali Aama: Life Lessons of a Himalayan
Woman

Edited by the Author

Himalaya: Personal Stories of Grandeur,
Challenge, and Hope (with Richard C. Blum
and Erica Stone)

Ahead of Their Time: Wyoming Voices of
Wilderness (with Leila Bruno)

The
VAST
UNKNOWN

America's First Ascent of Everest

Broughton Coburn

CROWN PUBLISHERS

New York

Library of Congress Cataloging-in-Publication Data
Coburn, Broughton
The vast unknown: America's first ascent of Everest/
Broughton Coburn.—First edition.
        p.   cm.
Includes bibliographical references.
    1. American Mount Everest Expedition
(1963) 2. Mountaineering expeditions—Everest, Mount
(China and Nepal) 3. Mountaineers—United States—
Biography. 4. Everest, Mount (China and Nepal)—
Description and travel. I. Title.
        GV199.44.E85C64 2013
796.522095496—dc23   2012040986

ISBN 978-0-307-88714-6
eISBN 978-0-307-88716-0

Printed in the United States of America

Book design by Donna Sinisgalli
Map by David Lindroth, Inc.
Jacket design by Eric White
Jacket photography: Barry Bishop/National Geographic Stock

1 3 5 7 9 10 8 6 4 2

First Edition

For Didi

CONTENTS

Part II: The Vast Unknown

Part III: Cherishing Mystery

CAST OF CHARACTERS

MEMBERS OF THE EXPEDITION

Al Auten. Radio operator. A self-effacing Morse code expert from Denver. Played a critical role by carrying a load to the high camp on the West Ridge.

Barry Bishop. Polar researcher and adventurer from the Midwest. Directed *National Geographic*'s Committee for Research and Exploration. Teamed up with Lute Jerstad on the South Col. In 1963, Bishop's wife, Lila, was a twenty-eight-year-old from Cincinnati.

Jake Breitenbach. A Dartmouth math whiz and buddy of Barry Corbet, he dropped out to climb and guide in the Tetons. A peak in the Lost River Range of Idaho is named after him.

Barry Corbet. A brilliant, "supremely able-bodied" Dartmouth student, he moved to the Tetons and later became a beloved advocate for the disabled. Married Muffy French, a tantalizing redhead and East Coast debutante.

Dave Dingman. Expedition doctor, with Gil Roberts. A Dartmouth climber who guided in the Tetons. Climbed high on Everest and aided struggling climbers above and below the South Col.

Dan Doody. Expedition cinematographer and assistant to Norman Dyhrenfurth. A gaunt and awkward farm boy from Connecticut, he contracted thrombophlebitis.

Norman Dyhrenfurth. Leader. A Swiss American, he conceived and organized the expedition and filmed it, fulfilling a multigenerational destiny with Everest.

Dick Emerson. Sociologist and a climbing ranger in Grand Teton

National Park. From Salt Lake City. He oversaw expedition logistics and did sociology research.

Nawang Gombu. Diminutive friend and sidekick to Jim Whittaker and nephew of Tenzing Norgay from Darjeeling, India. He escaped from a Tibetan monastery to climb in northern India and Nepal.

Tom Hornbein. In charge of oxygen, and a West Ridge fanatic. A prominent anesthesiologist and researcher, he designed an oxygen mask as a navy doc.

Lute Jerstad. Lighthearted South Col climber and buddy of Barry Bishop. Actor, teacher, and veteran guide on Washington's Mount Rainier.

Jim Lester. The expedition psychologist. A nonmountaineer and accomplished musician, he conducted research on stress in isolated circumstances.

Maynard Miller. The team's glaciologist. An authority on Alaska's glaciers, he drilled ice cores and measured mass and movement of the Khumbu Glacier.

Dick Pownall. High school teacher and principal in Denver and a veteran Tetons guide. He was skilled and cautious. Climbed above the South Col with the second summit party.

Barry Prather. Suffered pulmonary edema on the South Col. A farm boy and Dartmouth climber, he was known for his size and strength.

Gil Roberts. The large-hearted and levelheaded medical director. A Stanford and air force surgeon, he had previously climbed in the Himalaya. No relation to Jimmy Roberts.

Colonel Jimmy Roberts. Transport officer. Retired from a career with the British army in India, he managed nine hundred porters and thirty-nine Sherpas with an English sense of order. Later developed "trekking" in the Himalaya.

Will Siri. Deputy leader and physiology researcher. He led an expedition to Mount Makalu, the world's fifth highest peak, in 1954.

James Ramsey Ullman. Expedition scribe and historian. Wrote several acclaimed books relating to mountains. Turned back the first day of the approach march.

Willi Unsoeld. Climbing leader. Legendary raconteur, ethicist, philosopher, professor, "metaphysician," and West Ridge climber. Married to Jolene.

Jim Whittaker. South Col climbing powerhouse, CEO of REI, and a legend in Pacific Northwest mountaineering circles, along with his twin brother Lou.

OTHERS

Bob Bates. Willi Unsoeld's counterpart in the Peace Corps in Nepal and a member of the 1938 American expedition to K2.

Nick Clinch. Amiable Palo Alto attorney, mountain historian, and leader of two American Himalayan expeditions, to Hidden Peak (1958) and Masherbrum (1960).

Jack Durrance. Dartmouth and Tetons climbing legend in the 1930s. Later a Denver physician.

Günter Oskar and Hettie Dyhrenfurth. Parents of Norman. Widely known in Europe as Himalayan explorers, they were awarded gold medals in the 1936 Olympics.

Glenn Exum. A legend in Tetons climbing and guiding, beginning in the 1930s. Partnered with Paul Petzoldt in the first guiding service in the Tetons.

Elizabeth "Liz" Hawley. Reuters correspondent based in Kathmandu and preeminent historian for Himalayan expeditions.

Sir Edmund Hillary. The first person to climb Mount Everest, with Tenzing Norgay, on May 29, 1953. He dedicated the rest of his life to providing assistance to the Sherpas.

Charles Houston. Veteran of 1938 and 1953 expeditions to K2. He became a noted high-altitude physiologist and was a director of the Peace Corps in India.

Chuck Huestis. While working as a vice president at Hughes Aircraft, developing the Syncom satellite, he acted as the expedition's impresario and fund-raiser.

Boris Lisanevich. Russian ballet veteran. Manager and master of ceremonies at Kathmandu's Hotel Royal.

Father Marshall Moran. Jesuit priest and founder of Nepal's premier private school. A dedicated ham radio operator.

Paul Petzoldt. The first person to guide a client in the Tetons of Wyoming, in the 1930s. Partnered in the first guide service with Glenn Exum, and founded the National Outdoor Leadership School.

Ron Rosner. Consular officer and third secretary of the U.S. Embassy in Kathmandu. Helped with expedition logistics and clearance of expedition equipment by Nepal's authorities.

Woodrow Wilson Sayre. Grandson of President Woodrow Wilson. He staged a bootleg, shoestring attempt on Everest in 1962, with three companions.

Ang Dawa Sherpa. Talented and persistent, he was assigned to Norman Dyhrenfurth, and carried supplies high on the South Col route. From Darjeeling.

Ang Pema Sherpa. A dedicated icefall load carrier, he was injured in a collapse of ice in the Khumbu Icefall while roped to Jake Breitenbach. From Khumbu, Nepal.

Kancha Sherpa. Mail runner. As a youth, followed trains of loaded yaks to Tibet, for trade. From Khumbu, Nepal.

Jolene Unsoeld. Met Willi Unsoeld while climbing at Oregon State University and married him. U.S congresswoman (D-WA) for six years.

Nanda Devi Unsoeld. Exuberant daughter of Willi and Jolene, she was named after Nanda Devi, a peak in the Himalaya of India that captivated Willi in 1949.

Sydney Wignall. Sneaked into Tibet in 1955 to climb a peak near the Nepal border and was apprehended by the Chinese for spying.

PREFACE

IN THE SPRING OF 1965, THE STUDENT BODY OF MY MIDDLE SCHOOL in Tacoma, Washington, was summoned to the assembly hall. A famous northwest climber named Willi Unsoeld was about to give a presentation. Mr. Unsoeld, we were told, had climbed Mount Everest two years earlier, as part of America's first official expedition to the mountain.

Unsoeld looked more rough-hewn than the school's usual speakers, but his callused hands grew animated and his laserlike eyes came alive as he spoke. His clarity and humor put us at ease as he slipped into a travelogue that took us far beyond our suburban comfort zone.

Transfixed, we watched projected color images of shaggy men with grizzled beards and blistering skin forging up impossibly steep Himalayan slopes. The glaciers and crevasses frightened us, and the summit of Everest glowed with an otherworldly aura. It was as if Unsoeld and his climbing partner, Tom Hornbein, had sneaked up to the top, brashly tagged the edge of outer space, and scrambled down without getting caught. Except that they *had been* caught. They were forced to spend a night in the open at nearly twenty-eight thousand feet—in what they called "the death zone," an elevation where even *plants* couldn't live.

We stared. An image of Unsoeld's feet filled the screen—revealing toes that had shriveled into grotesque, blackened stubs, the result of frostbite. When the lights came up, our speaker had a special surprise: a jar containing those very toes, preserved in formaldehyde. He brandished the jar as if it were an exotic treasure that he had gone into the Himalaya to seek, and had valiantly retrieved.

The more I learned about Unsoeld, the more curious I became about what drove him. His zany spirit seemed powered by a boundless curiosity and irrepressible joy. He also seemed to be on some sort of search—a pilgrimage, perhaps. But to where? For Unsoeld, who described himself to students as a "metaphysician," the mountains were his starting point. They were the doors and steeple of something much bigger: the realm of the sacred.

Later that year, a photo on the back cover of a magazine caught my eye. A peak that looked like Mount Everest—and its ragged West Ridge—rose in the distance. The foreground featured a well-tanned outdoorsman with boyish good looks. A sling across his chest was threaded with pitons and carabiners; glacier goggles were pushed onto his forehead, and he held a pair of leather work gloves. His name, I learned, was Barry Corbet, and he was a teammate of Willi Unsoeld and Tom Hornbein. His gaze seemed focused beyond the horizon.

When I moved to the Tetons of Wyoming in 1993, I was riveted by stories of Corbet's life there. Following a helicopter accident while shooting a ski film in 1968, he'd been paralyzed from the waist down. Undaunted, Corbet had jumped into every activity and sport he could imagine, setting out to become "the most active gimp who ever lived." His mountain-forged spirit—and experience as a climbing guide— inspired other disabled people. Then he took up kayaking. His free-wheeling, whitewater spirit carried him into advocacy, as editor of a magazine for the disabled, which he injected with heart and guts. Everest, for Corbet, had been useful practice for reaching even higher goals—from his wheelchair.

There were more where Unsoeld and Corbet and Hornbein came from. Everest Base Camp in 1963 was the scene of a convergence of scientifically curious, patriotic, entrepreneurial, and visionary men. They were spontaneous and single-minded, iconoclastic and spiritual, democratic and dogmatic, employed and poverty stricken— a cross-section of the peculiar spirit that defined America in the 1950s and '60s.

In the 1980s, I spent three years working in Nepal on the approach route to Everest. Over the past half century, the environmental and socioeconomic impact of climbing and tourism on this narrow valley has been nothing less than transformative. Nearly every day strings of porters and yaks—and more recently, helicopters—pass through the area en route to Everest.

The cusp of that transformation was 1963. It was in the early 1960s that the Sherpas took their first tenuous—and then bold and joyous—steps out of the twelfth century and into the twenty-first. Now many of them look back with nostalgia on their homeland from new homes in Kathmandu, Europe, or the United States.

The year 1963 was a historical sweet spot, a time when Everest was the province of tough men. But the memory of that era is fading. Globalization, economic expansion, competition, and technology have captured our attention. What happened to the basic human values of diligence, teamwork, compromise, and compassion—the traits that carried us through the Cold War, the space race, the civil rights movement, and the assassination of JFK?

Mount Everest would change the Americans who went to climb it. To some degree, it would also change America. Climbers and citizens were on a path of self-discovery, pushing the envelope of achievement and the boundaries of the human spirit. Everest was about to become America's mountain, at least for a moment.

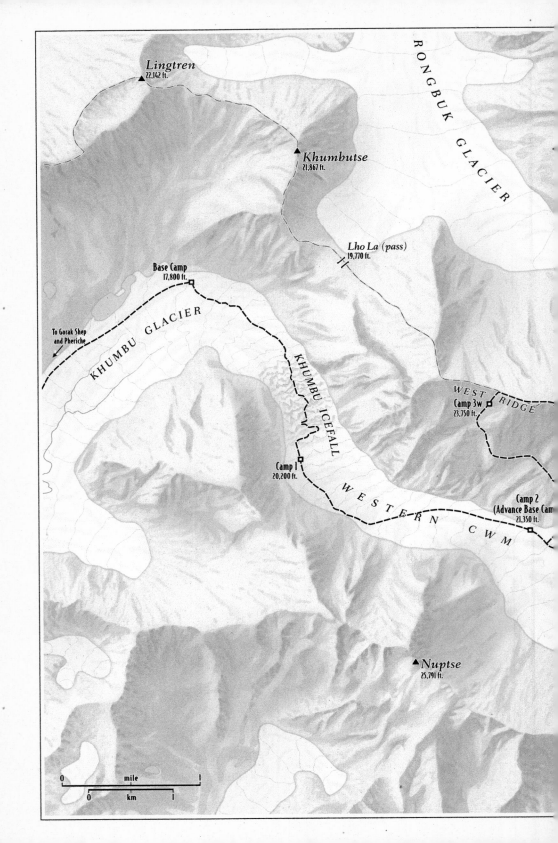

RONGBUK GLACIER

Lingtren
22,142 ft.

Khumbutse
21,867 ft.

Lho La (*pass*)
19,770 ft.

Base Camp
17,800 ft.

KHUMBU GLACIER

To Gorak Shep
and Pheriche

KHUMBU ICEFALL

WEST RIDGE

Camp 3w
23,750 ft.

Camp 1
20,200 ft.

WESTERN CWM

Camp 2
(Advance Base Camp
21,350 ft.

Nuptse
25,791 ft.

0   mile   1

0   km   1

EAST RONGBUK GLACIER

N O R T H   F A C E
(TIBET)

NORTHEAST RIDGE

Camp 4w
25,100 ft.

Yellow Band

W E S T

Hornbein Couloir

Camp 5w
27,250 ft.

R I D G E

Mount Everest
29,035 ft.

Yellow Band

Hillary Step

S O U T H W E S T   F A C E

▲ *South Summit*

Camp 6
27,450 ft.

K A N G S H U N G

Camp 3
22,900 ft.

SOUTH   COL

*Geneva
Spur*

Camp 5
26,000 ft.

F A C E
(TIBET)

Camp 4
24,900 ft.

L H O T S E   F A C E

Yellow Band

Lhotse ▲
27,890 ft.

Lhotse Shar ▲
27,503 ft.

PROLOGUE

Many years ago the great British explorer George
Mallory, who was to die on Mount Everest, was asked
why he wanted to climb it. He said, "Because it is
there." Well, space is there, and we're going to climb it,
and the moon and the planets are there, and new
hopes for knowledge and peace are there. And,
therefore, as we set sail we ask God's blessing on the
most hazardous and dangerous and greatest adventure
on which man has ever embarked.

> —PRESIDENT JOHN F. KENNEDY,
> RICE STADIUM, HOUSTON, TEXAS,
> SEPTEMBER 12, 1962, AT THE CLOSURE
> OF HIS "MOON SPEECH"

IN THE LATE AFTERNOON OF MAY 15, 1963, TOM HORNBEIN AND Willi Unsoeld found a level site to establish Camp 4 West, at twenty-five thousand feet above sea level directly below the West Ridge of Mount Everest. One vertical mile below their wind-scoured outlook, the cluster of tents at Advance Base Camp were visible as mere specks in the long glacial snowfield of the Western Cwm (pronounced *koom*). Unsoeld and Hornbein had committed themselves to an unusual and daunting challenge: climbing the legendary monolith by a new, un-mapped route and descending its far side over terrain they had never seen. They pitched their tent, anchored it with snow stakes, and climbed in.

Their tent was zipped and sealed, but the wind rattling the fabric gave them the sensation of dwelling inside a frantically panting lung. Despite the frigid temperatures, tight quarters, and cumbersome oxygen apparatus—they had just set up a single tank, with a T splitter dividing the life-giving gas between them—Unsoeld had a task to perform. He withdrew a blue hardbound diary from his pack and popped its robust cover snap. Cupping his hand around the flickering candle flame, he waved his ballpoint's nib in the fire to thaw out a moment's worth of ink.

Less than an hour earlier, a tiny space capsule named *Faith 7* had lifted off from Cape Canaveral, Florida, atop a massive Atlas rocket. Gordon Cooper, an astronaut with Project Mercury, was its sole passenger. This was the beginning of the longest space flight to date for an American: thirty-four hours and twenty minutes, a duration exceeding all five of the previous Mercury missions combined. While Unsoeld wrote in his diary, Cooper passed a hundred miles above Everest on the first of his twenty-two orbits.

Gordon Cooper slept intermittently during orbits ten through thirteen, awakening now and then to adjust the temperature of his spacesuit. He sang during orbits eighteen and nineteen—marveling both at the greenery of Earth and the miracle of beholding our gemlike planet from his perspective.

Unsoeld's diary was not intended as a keepsake or a volume of remembrances. He and the other twenty members of the 1963 American Mount Everest Expedition had been instructed by Dick Emerson, the team's sociologist, to carefully record their feelings and their constantly shifting estimates of success for each of the two Everest summit routes being attempted.

Jim Lester, the team's psychologist, had also secured a research grant; his would study the effects of stress and confinement. Increasingly, military assignments (such as nuclear submarine duty) entailed long isolation in stressful circumstances. The data from Everest would be useful to NASA, too, for extrapolating how astronauts might fare during prolonged space missions. No one cared, especially, if the results would be useful for mountain climbers.

Astronauts and climbers shared an existence at the edges of human possibility—breathing oxygen from pressurized containers, eating reconstituted food, and wearing specialized garments to protect them from hostile environments.

To be selected as an astronaut, Cooper had submitted to an array of physical and psychological exams that involved being heated, frozen, twirled in a centrifuge, placed in isolation, and sealed into a chamber where the pressure was reduced to simulate breathless altitudes.

The climbers of the 1963 American Mount Everest Expedition had tested and proved their stamina in the challenging playgrounds of the Rockies, Cascades, Sierras, and Shawangunks, where they'd executed many complicated ascents. And they had grudgingly submitted to a battery of psychological tests, administered not to determine if they were qualified for the expedition, but to collect baseline data for pioneering studies of human physiology, isolation, stress, and group dynamics.

These were uncommon men—hybrid scientist-adventurers—setting out not only to explore, but to fill in the blanks on the maps of worldly experience and academic knowledge. Mount Everest, and Earth orbit, offered starting points to push this quest into the vast unknown.

Still, there were differences between them. Cooper was on a prescribed path, with few decisions to make. The climbers, on the other hand, were still seeking a viable route, revising their logistics, and deciding their futures moment by moment.

"We agreed, sitting around our camp, thinking of Cooper up there," Tom Hornbein wrote, "that his fate was entirely in the hands of a bunch of technicians on the ground. At least we had a certain amount of control over our destinies."

Individual drive had gotten each man to this point, yet each was part of a team effort. Layers of infrastructure and supporters were impelling them from behind, offering their shoulders to lift them, and their arms to catch them when they landed. For Cooper and *Faith 7*, eighteen thousand servicemen had been stationed around the globe on twenty-eight ships, aboard 171 aircraft, and at far-flung earthbound bases. On Everest's West Ridge, Willi Unsoeld and Tom Hornbein were perched atop a pyramid of supplies that had been ferried to higher and higher camps by a team of nineteen other climbers, thirty-two Sherpas, and more than nine hundred Nepalese porters.

By now, those porters had descended to their valley villages. Most of the other climbers, waiting far below, were keen to leave the mountain and return home. The supplies of supplemental oxygen had been depleted. What remained at this moment was a slender margin for success—and a wide margin for error, bad luck, and failure. An ultimate question loomed: *Should they go for it?*

In Hornbein's and Unsoeld's minds, that question had been answered long before. They had released themselves from the worldly ties that bind feebler men. They had no choice but to climb upward.

The space program, and America, would go for it, too. It was the only answer that made sense to a youthful nation that had recently emerged victorious from the Second World War—a country that was preparing to enter John F. Kennedy's New Frontier of "unknown opportunities and perils." Technology, abundance—and uncertainty—awaited.

Five and a half years earlier—on October 4, 1957—a basketball-sized spacecraft known as *Sputnik,* the first artificial satellite to orbit the earth, was launched by the Soviets. The Space Age was officially born. America watched like a hovering, would-be parent, hoping to conceive and raise some *Sputnik*s of its own. At the very least, satellites promised to change the way we monitored the physical world and communicated with one another. And if the arc of space travel continued, who could say what we'd find on the moon, or even Mars? Here was a boundless new frontier, a new venue for the pioneer momentum that had efficiently settled America.

Sputnik's launch caught most Americans by surprise. The eerie *beep beep beep* that it broadcast from outer space—becoming louder as it passed overhead, then fading as it continued along its orbit—was the sound track to a suspicion that our adversaries might soon control an ominous and strategic high ground. The Soviet Union—and, by association, communism—had pulled off a propaganda coup, fueling visions that outer space might provide the venue for the next act in the Cold War. Space offered a frightening new artery for delivering weapons. It became easy to picture a celestial battle spiraling out of control, ending in the "mutually assured destruction" of the United States, the USSR, and perhaps the rest of the world.

Twenty-three months before Gordon Cooper's flight, cosmonaut Yuri Gagarin had become the first human launched into space. Then— nine months before *Faith 7*—the Soviets sent up *Vostoks* 3 and 4, a day apart. Each *Vostok* capsule held a single cosmonaut. They circled the earth sixty-four and forty-eight times, respectively, approaching within a few miles of each other while in orbit. Two more *Vostoks*, 5 and 6, were scheduled to lift off a month *after* Cooper's flight.

It appeared that the Soviets just might beat America to the moon.

America had to do something. The Cold War was ramping up. In 1961 America botched an invasion of the Bay of Pigs, and in 1962 the Soviets had delivered nuclear-armed missiles to Cuba. The United States was considering intervention in Vietnam. The civil rights move- ment was gathering steam, and in the first few months of 1963, Martin Luther King, Jr., was arrested and imprisoned in Birmingham, Ala- bama. Then the nuclear submarine USS *Thresher* sank in the Atlantic Ocean, killing all 129 crewmen. Even the Himalaya weren't immune to tension. China and India—along with the United States—remained on high alert following the brief Sino-Indian War that had erupted only seven months earlier, not far from Everest.

America—despite its trademark optimism—was struggling with loss, confusion, and an identity crisis. Who were we? No one was sure, exactly, but the world was watching, waiting to find out. Might the United States fall into second place as a world superpower?

In mountaineering circles, the United States lagged even farther be- hind. The British and Swiss had reached Everest's summit a decade earlier and basked in glory across Europe. But neither the Russians nor the Chinese had yet climbed Everest. The Americans had an opening, a narrow one, to beat them at something. Failure, of course, would mean global disgrace.

Mountain ranges and climbing had not, however, captured the attention of the American public. If someone had heard of Mount Everest at all, they probably knew that its summit had *already* been reached. And why go there, anyway? Adventure and risk? A picnic was as much wilderness as most people cared for. Driving a car to the Grand Canyon and staring over the edge was risky enough. Hike *into* the canyon? No way . . . have to get home and mow the lawn.

The United States was consumed with scrambling its way toward domestic and economic security. The country was busy rolling out the Interstate Highway System and putting the nightmares of World War II and Korea behind. Men wore suits with skinny ties, while women made finger sandwiches, molded Jell-O, and played bridge.

Nick Clinch, an avuncular Palo Alto attorney, had led expeditions to the Himalaya in 1958 and 1960—a time when the sport of mountain climbing had virtually no cultural acceptance. "If you met someone more than two miles from a trailhead," Clinch said of the 1950s, "they spoke German and carried a rope." Climbers, a miniature and broadly dispersed community, mostly knew or had heard of one another. They were welcoming to outsiders, but there simply weren't many who wanted to get in.

"Labeling oneself a climber mostly branded one as a screw-off and loser," Clinch went on. "From the Depression of the 1930s through World War II, a full generation of Americans had faced crises. After the war, people longed to settle down. They wanted stability and peace. Why seek out ways to be uncomfortable when America had won such a draining victory?"

Climbers existed on an oddly tilted plane. Everest and other summits represented freedom from the tethers of society and all its trappings. The mountains stood as vertical dreamscapes, as artists' stone blocks ready for sculpting into an ideal and pure world. For fleeting moments, the highest peaks might even reveal a glimpse of metaphysical understanding or spiritual grace. Peering down on the rest of the world, climbers saw material things through a rarified lens. They viewed cars as a means of reaching places without roads; golf clubs as metal that could be forged into pitons; mortgages and investments as useless distractions from high hills and wild places.

The 1963 American Mount Everest Expedition didn't enjoy even a fraction of NASA's funding or support. Everest had little to offer sponsors who were looking for productive applications in the fields of technology or defense—the forces driving the space program. A mountain like Everest was mostly a geological oddity, a feature of interest to surveyors and academics—but a long way from anywhere that mattered.

For some, however, it was a place to project their dreams. Never mind that twice as many people had died on the mountain as had reached the summit. It was as if this detail only made the mountain that much more attractive.

On the West Ridge, in deafening wind, Unsoeld wrote dutifully. The team's psychologist, Jim Lester, had asked the climbers to record their dreams while camped high on Everest. Unsoeld's entry seemed to reach simultaneously into the past and the future:

> I am helping a man clear a vacant lot of cars—to be used as
> a parking lot for approaching football game. He is husband of
> E——, an old girlfriend of mine. I watch her walk by in the
> street, and her feet are only ½ as long as the black slippers
> she wears.

His hand clumsy from the cold, Unsoeld closed the diary. He and Hornbein slept fitfully, awakened by turbulent gusts peeled by Everest's summit from the bottom of the jet stream. As morning dawned, the winds subsided. Now Unsoeld sang, reveling in the metaphysics of sky and snow and heavenly rock. The cathedral-like ramparts of the West Ridge, at once life threatening and life affirming, loomed above, and Unsoeld's songs and yodels resounded in supplication to them.

In the early morning of May 16, 1963, during Gordon Cooper's fifth Earth orbit, Willi Unsoeld and Tom Hornbein laced up their insulated boots and strode out from Camp 4W on a reconnaissance of the upper section of Everest's West Ridge. They were attracted to the steep and ragged line of the ridge itself, but knew that the Sherpas would not be able to carry loads safely up this highly technical route. After drifting onto the North Face of the mountain, they looked up at a narrow snow gully. It just might provide a suitable upward route and intersect with the West Ridge not far below the summit.

By the time Unsoeld and Hornbein returned to Camp 4W, climbers Barry Corbet and Al Auten had arrived, along with four Sherpas carrying fresh supplies of food and oxygen. They pitched two more tents on the site.

The next morning, Cooper and *Faith 7* reentered the atmosphere and splashed into the Pacific Ocean. The capsule was lifted by crane onto the deck of the USS *Kearsarge*. Cooper blew the capsule's hatch and stepped out to a hero's welcome, closing the final chapter of the Mercury program. Project Gemini was already under way, to be followed by Apollo. The United States and its youthful president had taken on the space race challenge. America was headed for the moon.

At virtually the same moment that *Faith 7* splashed down, Unsoeld and Hornbein crawled again from their tent at Camp 4W, this time stepping into pitch darkness, biting cold, and deafening wind gusts. Minutes earlier, fellow climber Al Auten had fought his way to the flap of their tent and shouted terrifying news: The gale-force winds had lifted two of the three tents—sheltering two climbers and the four Sherpas—and tumbled them off the ridge. The tents had begun sliding toward the glacier far below them, on the mountain's Tibetan side, before coming to rest 150 yards downslope. Miraculously, no one was hurt.

Unsoeld and Hornbein joined Auten in anchoring the remains of the battered tents to the mountainside. When morning broke, the West Ridge team retreated, through high winds, to Camp 3W.

None wanted to speak the obvious: The American effort to climb Everest's West Ridge would have to be abandoned.

But Tom Hornbein wasn't so sure. He spent a sleepless night rewinding and replaying their options, and awoke Unsoeld with a plausible solution: They would eliminate one of the high camps and make a single, last dash for the summit. It was a long shot, but if the planets aligned with their personal passions, it just might work.

Hornbein and Unsoeld were strong and ready. Barry Corbet, a young luminary of the ski world and hotshot mountain guide from the Grand Tetons of Wyoming, was also in top physical form.

Their bottled oxygen and food supplies were sufficient, however, for only two.

Auten offered to remain behind. "The two of you should go,"

Corbet insisted to Hornbein and Unsoeld. "For one thing, you've plugged harder on the route than any of us. You two have been climbing together, you know each other, and you'll make the strongest team. What's more," he said semiseriously, "you're both just about over the hump. This is my first Himalayan expedition; I'll be coming back."

Barry Corbet had long admired veterans Willi Unsoeld and Tom Hornbein for their exceptional climbing skills, but it was their ability to *make things happen* on a mountain that most impressed him.

Corbet also knew that events in the mountains can be shaped by forces beyond one's control. What he didn't know was that the course of his own life would soon change dramatically. Five years later, his parting words to Hornbein and Unsoeld would echo with poignancy.

Just a few days after Unsoeld recorded his dream in his journal—just as it seemed to have prophesized—his own feet would freeze, resulting in the amputation of nine of his toes. But he was lucky, or blessed, as were his twenty friends and fellow climbers. All but one of them, that is, who would never leave the flanks of Everest.

Whether they were aware of it or not, these men were consummating the diffuse but tenacious dreams of a cautiously hopeful nation. The route that had brought them to that point had been long and difficult—and the road ahead would be even more so.

Part I

Dragons at Play

Sheep don't get up these things.
Dragons get up these things.

—WILLI UNSOELD

Chapter 1

A Vertical Playground

*The mountains have no personality, good or bad. But
they influence us enormously. They are the topographic
yang of our planet, and cannot be denied. What to do
with them?*

—Barry Corbet, in the *Mountain Gazette*,
September 1972

A gemlike oasis of grass and trickling water graces Garnet
Canyon, an alpine cirque sheltered beneath Wyoming's 13,770-foot
Grand Teton. In August 1954, Tom Hornbein—a brilliant young rescue expert and seasonal ranger—was visiting the Teton Range for the
first time. He meandered upward through a dry alpine forest, traversed
steep meadows erupting in wildflowers, and entered Garnet Canyon.
With a climbing buddy, Hornbein was heading higher up to spend the
night in a cave, to be poised for an attempt on the 11,000-foot peak of
Red Sentinel the next day.

Short and already balding, with a slightly beaked nose, Hornbein
paused to cup water from the stream. From a distance, he might be
mistaken for a mountain gnome.

A bearded man wearing baggy shorts with oversized pockets came
bounding down the trail above. The man's Tyrolean hat bobbed up
and down, and his army rucksack swung from side to side on his back.
Fifty feet away, he stopped.

"Hoo—Tom Boy!" he shouted amiably. "How are you?"

Who is this guy? Hornbein wondered. "How'd you know my name!?" he said back.

"I'm Willi Unsoeld," the man said with a wink, explaining that he'd met Hornbein's climbing partner just above them. He was a climbing guide, but there were no guided clients in sight. As he spoke, his wiry beard stuck out in all directions, as if electrified. His twinkling eyes scanned the cirque, though part of his view seemed oddly directed inward.

Two days later, Unsoeld, the grizzled mountain man, and Hornbein, the thoughtful gnome, ran into each other again. Unsoeld described for Hornbein the route up "the Grand," pointing to the long, natural ledge known as Wall Street. He mapped out the path from the summit to the rappel point—the spot to fix an anchor for a hundred-foot vertical roped descent. Hornbein was deeply impressed. Here was a man, he thought, who was a part of the mountain; a guy who belonged here; a guy who already had a lifetime of experience and the exuberance to match.

Willi Unsoeld was fresh from a Himalayan expedition to Mount Makalu—his latest summit in a climbing career that had begun at the end of World War II. Growing up, Unsoeld filled his spare moments scrambling up and down peaks in the Cascades, Selkirks, Tetons, and Yosemite Valley—with a climbing partner if he could find one, alone if not. Equally comfortable on snow and rock, he felt especially at home in the jagged peaks of the Tetons, which were quickly becoming a premier place to find summer guiding jobs for serious (and generally cash poor) climbers. Sooner or later most climbers, fulfilling an unexplainable destiny with high peaks and wild places, seemed to find themselves in the Tetons. A number of them never quite found their way out.

A few weeks later, Barry Corbet and Jake Breitenbach, two young climbers from the Pacific Northwest, rested at the same oasis in the Garnet Canyon cirque. Both were in the prime of youth, able to jog uphill while wearing a loaded pack. Corbet was solid and angular, yet gentle and graceful. Breitenbach was all sinewy muscle, topped with a shock of Dennis the Menace blond hair and a mischievous grin to go with it. They squatted to collect water from the stream, luxuriating in the warm smell of lichens, alpine flowers, and pine trees.

A rustling in the bushes nearby startled them. A hairy, bearded man burst into the clearing, Bigfoot style. Willi Unsoeld.

Unsoeld's appearance was not entirely a surprise. A few days earlier, Corbet and Breitenbach had navigated Corbet's battered 1948 Hudson to the Tetons from Dartmouth College in New Hampshire, where they were both studying. Even before they arrived in Wyoming, they'd heard descriptions of the exceptionally strong and notoriously chimerical figure known as Willi Unsoeld.

"Have you seen my missing clients?" Unsoeld asked the young men, with his customary sense of irony. Unsoeld's guided charges had gone off ahead of him down the trail. This gave him an opportunity to refresh himself at the stream and charm the lads with a few short tales about life and near-death in the Tetons. Then he sprang from his rocky perch, released a quick yodel, and, in a series of joyful leaps toward the valley floor, disappeared.

"The contact was strong," Corbet recounted, "and the taste of it lasted. The way Unsoeld looked at me—it was as if I was hypnotized. I couldn't look to the left or to the right. I had to look right into his eyes."

Over an industrious six days, fueled partly by their chance meeting with Unsoeld, Breitenbach and Corbet climbed six of the Tetons' highest and most difficult peaks. In the evenings, they attended the nightly campfires beside Jenny Lake, the jewellike centerpiece of Grand Teton National Park. Unsoeld's twisting, humorous yarns about battling the demons of gravity transfixed them, delivered with an intensity so robust that he seemed to vibrate. And they devoured tales from other legendary characters of the Tetons—men with huge calves and poet beards—who converged on the campfire seemingly from nowhere. Like a celebrating band of oversized elves, they invoked the deities of the hills in an unscripted ritual of song and communion—as a way to immunize themselves from the sleepwalking of mainstream American culture.

Their heads swam with mountain-sized dreams of never-attempted routes, and with a way of *being* in the mountains that was ethical and pure, where they could lose themselves—lose their *selves*, really—and no longer cling to their egos or to the earth. They had joined a quest for meaning, but at the same time they were amused by the ephemeral nature of such a quest. They were born to wander and to search.

Like acolytes, Corbet and Breitenbach absorbed gentle guidance from Dick Emerson, the first climbing ranger for Grand Teton National Park—or any national park, for that matter. Tall and sensible, Emerson had climbed more routes and knew more of the crannies in the park than Breitenbach and Corbet thought humanly possible. During his early years in the Tetons, Emerson found some of the new and "difficult" routes so easy—compared to the daunting descriptions he had heard—that he initially feared he had lost his way.

Corbet and Breitenbach also listened to the quiet wisdom of veteran guide Dick Pownall, who had climbed the Grand Teton more than one hundred times. Pownall had preceded Willi Unsoeld as one of the original guides hired onto the fledgling guide service. His smooth features and self-effacing manner belied an inexplicable, near-silent command over his clients. He executed climbing moves on vertical rock with similar effortlessness.

The Tetons guides were part of a new tradition that was redefining the art and science of mountaineering—in America at least. It began during summers in the 1930s when an oxlike Tetons climber, Paul Petzoldt, and his skinnier colleague (and eventual competitor) Glenn Exum climbed in the Alps. They were surprised and a little baffled to watch the European guides loop a rope around their clients' waists and simply haul them up difficult sections of a climb—offering no instruction in either climbing techniques or rope handling. For the descent, the guides lowered their clients like deadweights, rather than teaching them how to rappel on their own. Exum and Petzoldt wondered what was going on. The European guides, they surmised, feared losing business if the general public were to catch on and learn their skills.

Maybe climbers would appreciate mountaineering even more if they could *participate* in its challenges, Exum and Petzoldt thought. They began to envision a thoroughly new approach to guiding high peaks.

After World War II, Exum and Petzoldt established a guide

service in the Tetons and headquartered it at a repurposed Civilian Conservation Corps campsite on a wooded moraine near Jenny Lake. They framed their lessons and climbs around the ideals of initiative, interdependence, responsibility, skill development, and the strength to overcome obstacles. Here was the model for a totally new—and distinctly American—guiding tradition.

The Teton guides aspired to do more than just climb and lead. They took pride in teaching, in savoring the outdoors, and in sharing it with others. Willi Unsoeld remarked on seeing the light of awareness dawn in the eyes of his clients as they learned to appreciate "the sublime intricacy of the minute structure of a great peak." A guide is uniquely privileged, he felt, to catalyze relationships between people and mountains, to witness the human soul synchronize with the mood of the mountain. Being able to play a role in this experience should be ample reward for any guide.

Unsoeld's vitality was infectious, and some guides puzzled over what sort of mountain-spirit alchemy sustained him. "He was a pied piper, and his harmonica was his pipe," one guide said. "Willi even played tunes going *up* the trail, when most people are breathless. He would come dragging out from a climb of the Grand, long after dark, with a wet, exhausted group of clients who could barely walk—and he'd be playing his harmonica while everyone sang. He never seemed to have a bad day, never complained, never said a bad word about anyone." Barry Corbet and Jake Breitenbach quickly took notice: Unsoeld and some of his fellow guides were more than just teachers and route finders. They were in the business of changing lives.

Corbet's and Breitenbach's apprenticeship in the world of climbing and guiding in the Tetons was part initiation, part therapy. "This new life offered the possibility of growing up sane," Corbet said. He was raised in a repressive family environment, and now he had new kin. "It's not enough to say that I admired these people. I loved and admired their families, their lifestyles, and their aspirations." Corbet saw in Unsoeld, especially, a level of intellectual curiosity that he hadn't found in his college peers.

And in Corbet and Breitenbach, guide service owner Glenn Exum saw something he didn't often see. With his trademark bone-crushing handshake, he hired them on. In the late 1950s, simply having a strong desire to do the job was a primary qualification. By that measure, Corbet and Breitenbach were overqualified. When Exum learned of the peaks they had knocked off within only a few days, he knew that, like Willi Unsoeld, they would excel as guides.

Strong and sensitive, Jake Breitenbach was a Nordic archetype with blue eyes that seemed to glow with light drawn from the Wyoming sky. Dartmouth classmate Pete Sinclair regarded him as the most lovable person he knew, and—like many others—was enlivened by Breitenbach's cherubic, generous grin and with the endearing way he brushed the shock of straight blond hair from his eyes. At the same time, his eyes carried a wistful, far-off look, raising curiosity about what was going on inside his head. It was as if his personal code of ethics was doing battle with the competitive, material world. In daily life, he exhibited what one guide called a "radical innocence."

Breitenbach felt it was dishonest to take a shortcut or the easy way out of a situation if it involved compromising one's standards. He belonged in the high hills, where he could challenge himself on his own terms. "In the mountains," he explained, "I know what is expected of me." If someone ever wondered if a route or a peak could be climbed, he would quietly wander off—without ceremony—and try it, simply to enjoy the pure physical creativity of climbing.

Barry Corbet would soon become another legend in the Tetons. "He reminded me of George Mallory," one guide said, referring to the brilliant, driven Brit who was lost high on Everest in 1924. "Barry was well spoken, considerate, good-looking, a man among men. His sheer talent on rock made him someone I wanted to climb with."

"The mountains provided an arena," Corbet reflected, "where a social loner like me could express some sense of positive identity. The mountains represented freedom from the pressures of being adolescent in what I considered to be a very dumb world." Mountains were more consistent, and reliable, than humans and their constructs.

Corbet reportedly had the highest IQ, at that time, of any incoming Dartmouth freshman, and he was an astute geology student. He appreciated geology as the ultimate hard science, while it also resonated on a tactile, personal level. He discerned artistic patterns in rock formations, and terms such as "scalometric anisotropy"—referring to the property of directional-differential hardness—rolled easily from his tongue, like poetry.

One afternoon near the Jenny Lake ranger's cabin, Corbet was free climbing on a massive boulder. He maneuvered his way down and stepped back onto the asphalt of the park path to consider a new route.

A tourist walked up. "Where did this boulder come from, anyway?" the man asked tentatively.

"It's what we call a 'glacial erratic.'" Corbet said. "It was carried down by the glacier and left here." Finally, he could put part of his geology education to work.

"So . . . where did the glacier go?"

Corbet responded with a straight face. "Back to get more."

Breitenbach and Corbet got to know each other at Dartmouth, where they bonded as climbing and drinking buddies. In Wyoming their friendship grew, and they began to wonder whether it might actually be possible to make a living outdoors, doing what they loved. In the 1950s, it wasn't easy to sustain a path between a society-driven life of achievement and a simpler, earth-centered existence in the mountains. But angst about work, study, and relationships hung over them. "Jake and I shared a manic-depressive tendency," Corbet said, "and we jollied each other through many of the highs and lows." While climbing, it was mostly highs.

In the Tetons, mountaineers, guides, clients, and park staff mingled in a refreshingly classless society. There was a place for everyone. Some of the older climbers and guides were World War II veterans and had come to the Tetons to forget the war and to reaffirm their trust in nature, the world, and themselves. Some were well-to-do; some lived in perpetual poverty. Others were bouldering experts, preferring, like chess masters, to work obsessively on "technical problems." Many were students, headed for careers in the sciences or academics.

In the mountains, guiding was virtually the only job that paid. But guiding came with great responsibility. The clients routinely put their lives in the hands of the guides. Willi Unsoeld especially enjoyed helping guided climbers overcome their fears; his banter and contagious grin could reliably lure dedicated flatlanders off their couches and into the mountains. He'd assure them that, first off, the guides *never* fell. With slightly exaggerated sincerity he'd add that, if a guide ever *did* fall, his first responsibility would be to reach up to his chest—while in midair—and rip off his "guide's badge."

"Climbing and guiding is a process of discovery," Barry Corbet said, "not a deliberate development. It requires a rock-solid platform of steadiness and a deep, inner reservoir that you discover within yourself. Clients routinely asked for, and got, the impossible. And they got it right when it was needed."

The Grand Teton rises abruptly to a point 7,500 vertical feet above the broad valley of Jackson Hole. Its summit rocks are blocky and skewed—distorted by eons of tectonic uplift fighting for command over the forces of erosion. Adding to the geological drama, the Snake River meanders close to the base of the mountain, as if threatening to undermine the whole affair. The proximity of river and mountain makes the scene one of the most photographed natural vistas in America.

Climbs of the Grand began at the Guides Camp, a tidy but ramshackle collection of tent platforms near Jenny Lake (intentionally situated out of view of tourists and canoeists) that housed the guides and their assorted, generally offbeat guests. Climbing parties averaged four to a guide. After midmorning introductions, everyone shouldered packs and headed up the trail, ascending at a leisurely one thousand vertical feet per hour. The guides taught the clients how to walk without wearing themselves out, setting a "rest step" pace that relies on balance and rhythm more than muscles.

The groups paused for lunch in Garnet Canyon, then arrived at the Lower Saddle around 5 p.m., tired and sore. At this high camp, climbers could nab a few hours of sleep before their predawn departure for the summit.

For dinner, everyone packed in a can of soup. Assorted Campbell's classics, chili con carne, and unlabeled dehydrated mixtures (along with asparagus tips or corned beef hash, if either was lying around) were dumped into a single stewpot and swirled together on a two-burner Coleman stove. *"Mmmm—warm and re-hydrating!"* the guides had trained themselves to proclaim as they taste-tested it.

Unsoeld called the concoction a "sacrificial feast," and not just because of the effort required for the clients to pack their cans to the Lower Saddle. "Psycho-internally speaking," he said, "it required an even greater degree of sacrifice to face the prospect of digesting the meal itself."

The simple quality of *patience*, Willi Unsoeld came to realize, was a guide's most important attribute. In an article in the *American Alpine Journal*, he outlined the guide's role when attending to clients at the Lower Saddle:

> With supper out of the way (either internally or otherwise), the next job is to secure the party for the night. In the old days this used to be accomplished quite literally by simply stuffing them into bags and covering the bundles with a great tarpaulin, which was then rocked down around the edges. Thus secured, the members were virtually incapable of movement until freed by the guide next morning. . . . One night I was jerked back rudely from the edge of sleep by a gurgling cry from a client who had succeeded in tucking his wad of chewing tobacco into his cheek long enough to whisper, "Guide, oh guide! Where do I spit?!" Ah, well—some people sneer at the climber's hat as being merely decorative.

After sunset, Unsoeld would blink Morse code signals with a flashlight down to his wife and best friend, Jolene, in the valley below. Jolene was assertive and self-sufficient, and was the first woman he met who wore GI army pants. He immediately fell in love. They went on to time the birth of their children so as to least interfere with the summer guiding season.

At 3 a.m., Unsoeld would rouse his party. The group downed cups of tea and set out in the dark, often without headlamps: The guides could navigate the trail in darkness. Dawn would break in silent chromatic splendor just as the group reached the base of the Upper Exum

Ridge—named for Glenn Exum himself. The guide would free climb up the ridge's rocky outcrops, then belay the first client behind him.

"A running fire of stimulating comment must be introduced as the party nears its psychological limit," Unsoeld stressed. This included downplaying the degree of difficulty of the pitches that the clients peered up at in terror—until they were up and over them, at which point they were complimented on the exquisite technical moves they had just pulled off.

The parties usually "topped out" at 11 a.m., hugged, took photos, then descended a short distance to the edge of a sheer hundred-foot rappel down the face of a cliff. When rappelling, Unsoeld often let loose a wailing scream—*"EEEAAAAahhhhh!!!!"*—adding to the effect as he zipped down the rope at near free-fall speeds.

Each climb with Unsoeld was embellished with scenic side trips and zestful showmanship (LIFE BEGINS AT 10,000 FEET was emblazoned on his parka). Once, on the summit of the Grand, Unsoeld watched a thunderstorm approach. He hurried his party to the steep rappel point, expedited them down the cliff, and instructed them to crawl into the overhang beneath it as far as they could. Huddled against the back wall, the party saw lightning strike as Unsoeld rappelled. He froze to the rope, swinging in midair in front of the clients—electrified but uninjured. It was a perfect showcase for Willi Unsoeld.

The climbing parties usually made it back to the shores of Jenny Lake, muscles aching, before dark. Glenn Exum wanted the clients to have the time of their lives, and most of them did.

On their days off, the guides tried to scale new, unclimbed routes. On one of those outings, Unsoeld and his wife, Jolene—a powerful climber in her own right—drifted off-route in search of unexplored terrain. They inadvertently climbed a new route on the Grand that they dubbed "Unsoeld-Unsoeld Direct," which was also the first ascent of the Grand's North Ridge by a woman.

One night, Willi Unsoeld didn't return from a solo climb of Mount Owen, the Tetons' second highest peak. Glenn Exum knew well that Unsoeld was not a reliable route finder (he wanted to explore and appreciate the mountains more than actually reach their summits). Exum promptly led packhorses up to Surprise Lake to look for him. At dawn, just as Exum was about to call in Dick Emerson and the park rangers to stage a formal rescue—or body recovery—Unsoeld came sauntering down the mountain, playing his harmonica.

At the time, Barry Corbet and Jake Breitenbach had no inkling that seeds were being planted that would germinate in hopes and dreams, and converging destinies, on the other side of the world—alongside Unsoeld and other legends of the Tetons.

In the early 1960s, mountaineering in America and the climbers on its forefront were gaining modest recognition. But it would take someone with a global vision—a European—to place American climbers on the international stage.

In the summer of 1939, just such a candidate first appeared on the scene. Norman Dyhrenfurth, a young Swiss climber and filmmaker, had motored out to the Tetons with two Harvard students to climb the Grand. Dyhrenfurth's solid frame and chiseled, Teutonic features typecast him as either a mountaineer or a surfing instructor—a cousin of one of the Beach Boys, perhaps.

Guide service co-owner Paul Petzoldt watched with fascination from the Grand's summit as Dyhrenfurth and a student deftly traversed the upper pinnacle of the mountain's difficult East Ridge. When they met, lower down on the mountain, Petzoldt immediately offered Dyhrenfurth a summer guiding job.

Dyhrenfurth, however, was due back in New York City for work with a small motion picture company. The world's mountains were where his heart was, and making movies offered opportunities to return to them and climb. Restricting himself to the Tetons, a small range, would be too confining. But Dyhrenfurth clearly saw, through a European lens, that the Tetons were the nursery for an embryonic clan of innovative and spirited American mountaineers.

Chapter 2

From Dartmouth Dorms
to Teton Tents

*We stand today on the edge of a New Frontier—the
frontier of the 1960s, the frontier of unknown
opportunities and perils, the frontier of unfulfilled
hopes and threats.*

—JOHN F. KENNEDY'S ACCEPTANCE SPEECH
FOR THE 1960 DEMOCRATIC PRESIDENTIAL
NOMINATION

IN 1936, A HANDSOME YOUNG DARTMOUTH STUDENT NAMED JACK
Durrance founded the Dartmouth Mountaineering Club. Talented as
a climber and daring by reputation, Durrance sketched no maps of
his ascents on the peaks of New England. Two decades later, it fell to
Barry Corbet and Jake Breitenbach and other student climbers to de-
duce his routes—by following chips in the rock where Durrance had
placed and withdrawn pitons.

In New England, few peaks or routes defeated the young Dartmouth climbers who followed Durrance. On weekends, they braved
wicked-cold weather and evaded irate farmers to reach the cliffs they
sought. They moved even faster on snow, and grew proud of their abilities to mix the specialized disciplines of snow and rock climbing in the
same outing. Barry Corbet often led.

"Barry could do whatever he put his mind to," his roommate said.
"In the center of campus he looked at Webster Hall, and decided that

the three-inch-deep decorative ledge—which circles the building about six feet above the ground—would have to be traversed. The ledge slopes downward; to remain on it, he had to grip the outer edge with his toes. He made it all the way around."

The Dartmouth climbers rappelled from the top of Bartlett Tower, an eighty-foot-tall stacked-stone monolith, and practiced rescues by placing a hapless underclassman in a litter, then lowering him from the tower on primitive manila ropes. Their inspiration for these stunts came partly from the humorous (but technically precise) bible for the sport of "buildering": *The Night Climbers of Cambridge,* written in 1937 under the pseudonym of Whipplesnaith.

As the Dartmouth boys made harder and harder climbs, they expanded their horizons beyond the Eastern Seaboard—toward distant Wyoming. Again, it was the maverick loner Jack Durrance who had led the way. In 1939, Durrance climbed a new route up a peak called Devils Tower in Wyoming's remote northeast. This magnificent solitary butte was formed of volcanic rock extruded into a gargantuan stump of hexagonal columns, and was used as a filming location by Steven Spielberg in 1977's *Close Encounters of the Third Kind.* Durrance kept moving west and "put up" several new routes in the Tetons—routes so technically puzzling and ambitious that some climbers wondered if they'd ever be repeated.

Corbet and Breitenbach couldn't wait to find out. They followed several of his routes, including a challenging climb of the Lower Exum Ridge of the Grand Teton. On the crux move—a nearly insurmountable obstacle on the route's Black Face—Corbet removed a noble souvenir: one of Durrance's hand-forged iron pitons. He later presented it to the legendary climber in Denver, where Durrance was practicing medicine. Until then, Durrance had been their invisible Chuck Yeager— inspiring them as the high-flying test pilot did the astronauts—to push every limit and keep their focus trained on success.

The Tetons had become the Dartmouth climbing clan's untamed, vertical playpen—a proving ground for the skills they'd honed on the primordial rocks of New England. During the summers of the 1950s, Jackson Hole hosted one of the greatest concentrations of Dartmouth students outside of New Hampshire.

Corbet chose to drop out of the college, but not because he lacked ambition. The university simply didn't offer him enough mental or physical challenges, and he wanted to be outdoors. Breitenbach, a year ahead of him, also left before graduating, partly out of resentment toward a professor who wouldn't accept his proof for a math problem, which he swore was perfectly valid.

In the early summer of 1959, Corbet and Breitenbach again piled their gear into Corbet's Hudson, and left Dartmouth for the last time. Windows rolled down, speeding along on two-lane roads, they joined the last generation to migrate west before the construction of the Interstate Highway System. They relished the mystique of just *being* in the West—it had a wistful, organic smell, an embracing sky, and a courageous, iconoclastic attitude all its own. "The first time we came out west," said one climber who was recently transplanted from the East, "even *Nebraska* was exciting."

The road was calling them even farther, and Breitenbach and Corbet decided to take a detour via Alaska. After hooking up with two other elite mountaineers, they climbed a new route up the South Face of Mount McKinley. They fought back altitude sickness and reached the summit, exhausted.

Back in the Tetons, even nonclimbers wanted to hear more about their exploits. Corbet and a McKinley teammate developed a slide show titled *To Get Away from Tidal Waves*—their standard response to people who asked why they climbed mountains.

In the 1960s, Barry Corbet was in his prime. He exemplified a type of physical specimen that he'd one day refer to—with a mixture of respect and nostalgia—as "supremely able-bodied." Corbet had become a role model for many younger Teton climbers, though he turned to senior guide Dick Pownall for his own inspiration.

Among other firsts, Dick Pownall had pioneered—in 1949, with two companions—the first direct ascent of the North Face of the Grand Teton. They'd topped out on the summit well after dark, seventeen hours after their climb began. Pownall accomplished a first while descending, too: The standard route down from the top of the Grand was treacherous and slippery. Pownall discovered a more dramatic but arguably safer shortcut: straight down over a cliff, via "the Pownall

Rappel." For sixty years, this hundred-foot drop has been taken by virtually all guided parties, saving an hour of tedious meandering.

At that time modern climbing harnesses, made of nylon belts and webbing sewn together with industrial stitching, were just being developed. Pownall was curious about such innovations, but he and his colleagues preferred the original rappelling technique that used no webbing or hardware at all: Climbers anchored the rope above them, then passed it between their legs, around the butt, across the chest, over the shoulder, and across the back. It was uncomfortable, but convenient. The Tetons are prone to afternoon thunderstorms, and they needed to be able to descend with alacrity. (Even when Pownall made a reunion climb of the Grand in 2002, at the age of seventy-five, it took some cajoling by his climbing companions to get him into a harness.)

In the summer of 1952, Dick Pownall and Glenn Exum guided seventeen teenage boys from a dude ranch on a climb of the Grand. Pownall, bringing up the rear, was accompanied up the trail by a pair of dogs: Irish setter and black Labrador mixes. The dogs made it all the way to the Lower Saddle, at 11,600 feet.

When the party departed for the Grand's summit before sunrise, Exum and Pownall tied up the dogs. They divided the teenagers into two groups, and took two different routes. "The dogs didn't like it," Pownall recalled. "They barked and whined and carried on to such an extent that we couldn't leave them. So Glenn and I returned to the Saddle and got them."

Each guide took a dog. Glenn coaxed his hound all the way, boosting it over rocks and ridges when he had to. Pownall carried his dog in his rucksack, its head sticking out the top. On the summit, the dogs went wild with joy.

Pownall found inspiration, himself, from national park climbing ranger Dick Emerson. The composure with which Emerson handled almost any situation led one guide to describe him as "a good candidate for sainthood." He was conscientious and analytical, as if preternaturally attuned to the sorts of details and signs that can foreshadow accidents.

Emerson had seen his share of accidents, and worse. During his senior year in high school, World War II broke out. Fibbing about his age—he was mature-looking and polite, even as a youth—he applied to join the army. Standing at the train station in Salt Lake City en route to enlist, he met fellow recruit Dave Brower, a large man from the Bay Area who knew the Sierras of California as well as anyone at the time. (Brower would later become an executive director of the Sierra Club and found Friends of the Earth.)

When he learned that Emerson had been a competitive ski jumper, Brower urged him to sign up with the Tenth Mountain Division: the ski troops. The Tenth Mountain was rumored to be the only unit of the U.S. Army in which the average IQ of the enlisted men was higher than that of the officers. It also suffered the greatest number of casualties of any division in the war; Emerson lost buddies before he even learned their names. But their brotherhood, cemented by the bonds of being mountaineers as well as soldiers, long outlasted the brutal losses they suffered. Nearly two thousand of the Tenth Mountain veterans—a quarter of the troops who survived—ended up working in skiing-related industries in the Rockies, Cascades, and Sierra Nevada, and they established sixty ski areas in North America.

In 1958, a new guide had arrived on the Tetons scene: Barry Corbet's tall, bookish Dartmouth classmate Dave Dingman—the only one of the Tetons Dartmouth climbers to graduate from the place. Here was another legend in training, some suspected. Earlier that summer, Dingman had climbed a difficult route on Mount McKinley, and was about to head off for the Andes. His training for a career in surgery and internal medicine seemed to be the only thing slowing him down.

Before starting med school, two years earlier, Dingman had joined a friend on a road trip to the Tetons. Arriving in Dingman's two-door Ford on a snowy June day, they pitched their canvas tent near Jenny Lake. As they huddled inside to keep warm, someone shook the fabric. It was Glenn Exum.

"Would you boys like to make a little money?"

"Sure thing," they chimed.

Exum assigned them to porter a cumbersome army tent—the kind normally transported in a vintage green military truck—to the Lower

Saddle. "It was heavy as hell, and we hauled it up there in multiple trips. Then we had to set it up." Dingman was hooked. It was tough work, but the job had initiated Dingman into both climbing and the Tetons.

In the early 1960s, American climbing was fragmented into a handful of barely connected locales: Yosemite, in California; the Cascades of Oregon and Washington; the Tetons of Wyoming; the Front Range of Colorado; and the Shawangunks in upstate New York. Little information flowed between these regions.

Advances in techniques and equipment boosted Yosemite—with its aesthetically arranged solid granite cliffs—from a provincial enclave to a world-class climbing venue. Yosemite's influence (and some of its better climbers) began to show up in the Tetons, too. The old-school climbing techniques of the Tetons were about to undergo what some regarded as exciting cross-fertilization. Others saw it as painful change.

Yosemite climbers brought with them a decimal system for rating climbs by their degree of difficulty, and they introduced an elevated level of safety and protection known as "Yosemite Standards." These standards stressed the placement of "bombproof" protection in the event of a fall. Aluminum "nuts" were developed for jamming in cracks in the rock, and "dynamic" (stretchy) ropes were introduced that could comfortably catch bigger falls.

In combination with improved techniques, these innovations meant that climbers could climb more confidently. This allowed them to make increasingly difficult moves and take on routes previously considered risky or impossible. Leading-edge climbers could finally discover the true limits of their abilities—by extending themselves until they (safely) fell.

Dave Dingman had passed Glenn Exum's test: He set up the bulky army tent on the Lower Saddle, at 11,600 feet. Exum took him on board as assistant guide on the Grand. Dingman soon found himself climbing "free"—unroped—alongside Willi Unsoeld and Dick Pownall. "We would put the clients to bed on the Lower Saddle," he said, "and spend most of the night climbing in the dark—doing crazy stuff I'd never dream of doing again."

Crazy dreams made these men. They were hardwired to do things they sensed they might never do again. Individually, each was remarkable. As a team, they just might "knock off" anything they set their collective minds to. How could they harness those dreams and channel that talent?

The dream-filled, "supremely able-bodied" legends of the Tetons— Unsoeld, Corbet, Breitenbach, Pownall, Emerson, and Dingman— had all the makings of a team. Their champion—and the foundation for their leadership—would appear in the form of that charismatic but little-known figure, originally from Switzerland, who had climbed in the Tetons in the late 1930s: Norman Dyhrenfurth.

Chapter 3

A Distant Vision

*In all recorded history, probably the sagest bit of advice
ever offered man was the ancient admonition to "know
thyself." As with individuals, so with nations. Just as a
man who realizes that his life has gone off course can
regain his bearings only through the strictest self-
scrutiny, so a whole people, become aware that things
have somehow gone wrong, can right matters only by a
rigidly honest look at its core of collective being, its
national purpose.*

—"We Must Climb to the Hilltop,"
a 1960 speech by Senator John F.
Kennedy

NORMAN DYHRENFURTH WAS ON A MISSION THAT WAS DRIVEN BY HIS
love of mountaineering, the lure of the Himalaya, and a rich family
history. By the late 1930s, Dyhrenfurth was barely out of his teens—
but his feet were already planted on two continents, straddling some
of the world's most spectacular mountain ranges. Soon he would be
moving between three continents.

His parents, Professor Günter Oskar Dyhrenfurth and his wife,
Hettie, had moved from Germany to Austria in 1923, when Norman
was five. Two years later they moved again—this time to Switzerland,
where they became citizens. The Himalaya, however, exerted a near-
mystical pull, and Günter became known in Europe as an expert on
the geography and geology of the range. After leading two Himalayan

expeditions, Günter and Hettie were awarded gold medals (the Prix Olympique D'Alpinisme) in the 1936 Summer Olympics in Berlin. The pageantry of the event was spellbinding; Norman recalled an incident when an officer entered a room and saluted: *Heil Hitler!* When Norman didn't return the salute, the officer approached him. Young Norman simply flashed his Swiss passport. The year before, Norman had worked for filmmaker Leni Riefenstahl, who had been hired to film the Olympics.

Günter and Hettie were Lutherans, but Hettie was half Jewish, by Nazi rules. In 1936, Hettie went to the United States on a lecture tour and showcased her adventures on the Himalayan peak of Kanchenjunga, the world's third highest. (For two decades Hettie held the world's altitude record for women.) Norman followed her there in 1937.

Hettie and Norman Dyhrenfurth found America to be welcoming. Norman taught skiing in New England, and was soon exploring North America's mountain ranges. He intended to return to Switzerland, but German submarines had sunk Allied ships, and the Swiss Legation in Washington advised its citizens living in the United States not to return to Switzerland, at least for the time being. He signed up for U.S. Army Officer Candidate School and applied for a post at Fort Benning, in Georgia. "I bunked with two excellent, officer-material colored men," Dyhrenfurth said. "They became my good friends—but I couldn't be seen walking into town with them." His military service would allow him to become a U.S. citizen without giving up his Swiss citizenship.

Norman's father had long dreamed of climbing Everest. He'd even planned an expedition for 1914, but World War I intervened. Dyhrenfurth senior continued to climb through late middle age, but Everest permits were being granted only to the British, and he diverted himself by studying and writing about the mountain. It thus fell to Norman Dyhrenfurth to take on the family destiny with Everest.

For nearly a century, the British had been trying to build an exclusive claim to the mountain. This incremental effort began in 1856, when British surveyors identified the Himalayan summit of "Peak XV" as the planet's tallest feature. During the Great Trigonometric Survey of India in 1856, they measured its height with remarkable accuracy (all from outside Nepal's borders), and named it for George Everest, a former surveyor general of India.

Until 1950, the British were the only ones to stage expeditions to Everest. They fielded seven teams—including one rather odd solo adventurer—during the 1920s and '30s alone. Nepal's borders were closed during those decades, and the only route of access was through Tibet, on Everest's northern side. The isolationist Tibetans didn't want the Europeans traipsing through their hinterlands, but they warily regarded British India as an exception. Despite their history of colonialism, the Brits might prove handy as a protector against the ambitions of the Chinese.

Before the 1950s it was mainly Brits, anyway, who took any interest in climbing mountains. In the late 1800s, mountaineering had come into vogue as a recreation for a hardy few among the leisure class—those who regarded mountain air and rigorous physical training as a healthful pursuit, potentially rich in meaning and symbolism.

In the 1920s, the UK sponsored costly, well-provisioned expeditions to the northern side of Everest. These were staged out of Darjeeling, a hill station of the British Raj. The third British expedition, in 1924, ended when George Leigh Mallory—one of Britain's leading rock climbers—disappeared with fellow climber Andrew Irvine in the mist below Everest's summit. Rather than damping enthusiasm, these daring excursions only fueled more speculation in Europe as to whether a mountain as tall as Everest could be climbed at all—even with the help of supplemental oxygen.

Four more British expeditions in the 1930s were unable to answer that question. George Mallory's teammates Edward Norton and Howard Somervell came within nine hundred feet of the summit in 1924, setting an altitude record that would remain unbroken for twenty-eight years.

By the late 1940s, the British had relinquished their rule over India. They had also lost the race to reach the North Pole. And the South Pole. They needed Everest as a trophy, to ease them into colonial retirement. Conveniently, in 1950 the Himalayan kingdom of Nepal opened its doors to outsiders for the first time. Gaining permission to stage expeditions to Everest suddenly became easier, especially for the non-British. And an approach from the south would be faster than through Darjeeling and Tibet.

The Brits had the motivation, the climbers, and plentiful private funding from the Royal Geographical Society and the Alpine Club. Distressingly, the Swiss had already secured exclusive permits for 1952 and planned two Everest expeditions from the Nepal side in both spring and fall. The Brits would have to wait until 1953—after the Swiss had climbed it, in likelihood.

During the spring Swiss expedition, Raymond Lambert and Tenzing Norgay (then known as Tenzing Bhotia, linking him by name to his ancestry in Bhot, or Tibet) came tantalizingly close to the summit. They were turned back only eight hundred vertical feet short of the top—done in by sheer exhaustion and a broken oxygen apparatus. For all their efforts, they had reached only one hundred feet higher than Norton and Somervell had in 1924.

Fall is a less desirable season for climbing than spring. The days are colder and shorter. But the Swiss saw the fall of 1952 as their last chance before the British would utilize their spring, 1953 permit for the mountain. (His Majesty's Government of Nepal allowed only one Everest expedition at a time; the spring of 1954 had already been given to the French.)

Norman Dyhrenfurth was invited to join the Swiss team in the fall of '52 as their photographer and filmmaker. But his permission to enter Nepal was delayed, and he languished in New Delhi for days, baking in the heat. When a visa was finally granted, he was told that he could enter Nepal only at Biratnagar, a town on the country's southeast border with India. Dyhrenfurth flew to Patna, rode clattering steam trains northward to Nepal, then raced over the rumpled Himalayan foothills on trails that had been traversed by only a handful of foreigners before him. After two weeks of fording streams and crossing passes, he caught up with the Swiss team just below Everest Base Camp.

The climbing was difficult. On October 31, 1952, an avalanche swept down the Lhotse Couloir, a steep, snowy chute below the South Col at twenty-six thousand feet. Three Sherpas were injured, and

Mingma Dorje, one of the stronger Sherpas and the father of three children, was killed. The team buried Mingma on a glacial moraine at twenty-two thousand feet, directly below the mountain.

Winter was approaching, and temperatures dropped to minus forty degrees Fahrenheit. The team reached the South Col on November 19, 1952, fighting a dangerous wind chill. "The noise of the rattling tent is like machine gun fire," one climber reported. "I can't remember any time in my life when I came closer to being driven mad."

The Sherpas refused to climb higher, or even stay where they were, and they descended. Three others, including Tenzing Norgay, made a try for the top, but ascended only a few hundred vertical feet before admitting that winter had indeed overtaken Everest. As the expedition leader put it, they had been "purged from the mountain."

The Swiss team retreated to lower elevations. Dyhrenfurth sat near a stupa and looked back at the mountain, wondering if he would ever see it again. "The great peak had been a terrible antagonist, but now we felt we were taking leave of a good friend," he said. At the Buddhist monastery of Tengboche, nested on a moraine at thirteen thousand feet, he gazed about at the high peaks, rhododendron forests, and chanting monks, suffused by a sensation that he had lived there in a previous lifetime.

"I was deeply moved and close to tears," Dyhrenfurth wrote, "as James Hilton's Robert Conway must have felt when turning his back on Shangri-la."

Dyhrenfurth was taking leave of a fairy-tale landscape, where people lived off the land, in harmony with the forests, fields, and pastures that nourished and sheltered them. The eighteen-day trek back to Kathmandu, and civilization, seemed all too short. In 1952, few foreigners had walked this path. Each day melded into the next as they seemed to float along on the trails, descending into layers of clouds that hugged the valley bottoms, drifting through earth-toned villages suspended in time.

The great mountain had cast its spell. Like others who'd been touched by Everest, Dyhrenfurth wasn't sure he could readjust to his previous life. "As much as I long to be back with my family," he wrote, "the thought of all the problems which await me at the University of

California, and the nervous strain encountered in making a living, worries me quite a lot. How long will it take to get back into the swing of things? In my tent I lie awake, reliving the past five months in my mind and trying to plan ahead for the future."

He returned to his job as director of the UCLA Film School's Theatrical Arts Division after six months of unpaid leave. But on his third day back in his office, Dyhrenfurth stared out the window. The desk was piled high with unfinished business: letters to be answered, committee meetings, budgets to be prepared, students to be counseled, films to be completed. The windows were open wide, and the California sun shined brightly. "Yet the air felt stuffy," he said. "Everything seemed to close in on me. The thought of returning to this kind of life filled me with dread. Telephones kept ringing, typewriters made infernal noises, and students stuck their heads through the window to ask unanswerable questions."

Dyhrenfurth wasn't sure the university was the right place for creative filmmaking, anyway. A bit of casual inquiry confirmed what he suspected: There were virtually no academics employed by the motion picture industry.

The Brits were ready to go. In 1953, an unclimbed Everest awaited them, and they simply didn't want to lose it. (The Indians and the Swiss were back in the permit queue, now behind them.) Their detailed plans would need to be executed with precision; they could even call up their army, if necessary. Indeed, they did so in the form of Lieutenant Colonel John Hunt, a competent climber with a solid background in military leadership.

In the spring of 1953, buoyed along as if by divine right, the British pulled it off. John Hunt's expedition delivered two citizens of the British Empire to the summit: Edmund Hillary from New Zealand and Tenzing Norgay from India. It was a smashing coronation gift for Queen Elizabeth II, who was crowned four days later.

The 1952 Swiss team sent congratulatory messages to the British climbers. Magnanimously, Hunt replied with a telegram acknowledging that Switzerland had paved the way: TO YOU ONE HALF THE GLORY!

The veil of mystery cloaking Everest was lifting. Several days after the 1953 British expedition departed Base Camp, an Indian Air Force plane flew over the mountain and took the first detailed images of its topography, including the alluring West Ridge. Along with Hillary's and Tenzing's summit photos, the pictures were snapped up by the international press.

Dyhrenfurth, now a U.S. citizen, spent much of 1954 as a Fulbright Scholar in Italy. While in Europe, as in Nepal and India, he was surprised and somewhat disturbed to overhear critical comments about Americans.

"In the eyes of Europeans—and many Asians—we are like big children without a cultural background or a clear understanding of their needs and aspirations," he wrote. "We are only interested in dollar profits or buying allies for our crusade against World Communism. The Europeans and Asians refuse to believe that we are idealists who are deeply and sincerely concerned with the recovery or the prosperity of less fortunate, war-torn countries."

In 1950s Europe, politics and sports were entwined. France appointed Maurice Herzog, leader of the first team to climb Annapurna, as minister of youth and sport. Russia was bent on proving that communism, as a superior form of government, produced the finest athletes, and they provided the budgets to make it happen. Soviet teams had won a number of world championships—even in ice hockey, which for decades had been Canada's domain. In 1954, the American press paid little attention to international sporting events, but Russia's domination profoundly impressed the rest of the world. In 1956, the Russians took most of the medals in the Summer and Winter Olympics. In 1960, they won both Olympics again.

The fifties bracketed the golden decade of Himalayan climbing. At the beginning of 1950, none of the world's fourteen 8,000-meter peaks (those higher than 26,247 feet) had been climbed. By 1961, thirteen of the "eight thousanders" had been scaled—but only one of them, Hidden Peak, by Americans. The United States had largely missed out.

Dyhrenfurth was confounded by America's ambivalence toward Himalayan climbing. Surely, the symbolic importance of these peaks could not be lost on a nation regarded as a superpower. "I was in Italy when the news of the Italian conquest of K2, the world's second highest mountain, hit the press," he said. "Its effect was electrifying, and can only be compared to the winning of a major battle—or even an entire war."

Opportunity, excellence, perseverance, and success were at the heart of the American dream. Dyhrenfurth was fully invested in it; where was everybody else? The question, he realized, held the key to its own answer. If no natural-born American was going to stage an attempt on Everest, he would have to put an expedition together himself.

Chapter 4

Entering the Arena

The fact remains that the first American go at Everest
will be an event. If we succeed, it will be a feather in
our cap, a booster to our prestige, a refutation beyond
argument of our detractor's taunt that we are a nation
gone soft and gutless. If we do not, we will at least have
entered the arena, joined the rest of the world in one of
its great enterprises, abandoned our "isolationism" in
mountaineering, as we have long since in other fields.
　　It is still there. It always will be. And it is time we
had a look for ourselves.

　　　　　　—EVEREST EXPEDITION PROPOSAL PREPARED
　　　　　　　BY NORMAN DYHRENFURTH

IN EARLY JUNE 1960, MEMBERS OF THE SWISS EXPEDITION TO NE-
pal's forbidding Dhaulagiri were recuperating in Kathmandu. Norman
Dyhrenfurth had been the cameraman on the trip, and he didn't want
to return home without applying for permission to lead an expedition
to Mount Everest. An American expedition.

　　Dyhrenfurth hopped into a "tiger taxi"—an Ambassador cab
painted with bright orange stripes, the better to scare villagers from
its path—to Singha Durbar, a sprawling former palace and the head-
quarters of His Majesty's Government. What he learned displeased
him: Permission for Everest had already been granted for the spring of
1961 to *another* American, William Hackett. In the 1950s, Hackett had

conceived the idea of climbing the highest peak on every continent. He had completed five and wanted to add Everest to his list.

Dyhrenfurth worked briefly with Hackett on combining their efforts into a joint expedition. But Hackett's funding never materialized, and the permit lapsed. Dyhrenfurth wrote to the Nepal government, asking for the spring of 1962. India had secured the permit for that season. The spring of 1963, however, was available. He resubmitted his application.

Mail delivery from Nepal is unreliable, but the postal stars aligned. On May 10, 1961, Dyhrenfurth received a letter from His Majesty's Government. He had been granted the Everest permit for the spring of 1963.

The first (and enduring) challenge would be to raise the funds for an expedition—a task that author James Ramsey Ullman, invited to join the team as its historian, described as "only slightly less difficult than soliciting funds for the erection of a statue of Karl Marx on the White House lawn."

Nick Clinch, who had led two Himalayan expeditions, told Dyhrenfurth wryly: "You won't even have to climb the mountain; you'll deserve a medal just for raising the dough. On Masherbrum in 1960 I was prepared to sell myself to the devil—but the devil wasn't buying."

To get the funds flowing, Dyhrenfurth would have to capture the public's imagination. Large expeditions from Russia, China, India, and Europe were routinely and liberally anointed with support from their governments. Dyhrenfurth would have to wing it and appeal to private donors and corporate sponsors. *Fine,* he thought. The bureaucracy (and political hierarchy among candidate climbers) of a state-sponsored expedition wouldn't suit American mountaineers, anyway.

Dyhrenfurth submitted a proposal to the Explorers Club, a venerable New York City institution dedicated to adventure, scientific research, and the hosting of well-lubricated member soirees. The Club had limited resources to support ventures outside its hallowed doors (in the early 1960s its membership was open only to men), but its blessing and imprimatur might help springboard the fund-raising efforts.

Dyhrenfurth needed to squarely address one annoying reality:

Everest had *already* been climbed. He was aware that he would have to hitch his appeal to something more unusual and dramatic than merely plodding upward in the footsteps of the British and Swiss.

America, Dyhrenfurth knew, needed a public relations fix. President Kennedy had witnessed the prestige earned by the Soviets when Yuri Gagarin became the first human to journey into outer space and orbit the earth, in 1961. Kennedy was determined that the United States catch up. Partly due to JFK's dedication, Project Mercury was on the launching pad. Its first astronaut, Alan Shepard, was scheduled to lift off a month after Gagarin's orbits.

Public relations was something Dyhrenfurth could do. His sunny, well-modulated manner and persuasive delivery were ideal for raising money. He had cohosted a weekly program on KPOC-TV in Los Angeles titled *Expedition!* that featured exotic destinations, and it gave him cachet as a television personality.

To make his expedition unique, Dyhrenfurth boldly proposed to knock off not just Everest, but its neighboring, interconnected peaks, Lhotse and Nuptse, for a "Grand Slam." For a well-equipped expedition with the goal of climbing three peaks, he calculated they would need $186,000.

Dyhrenfurth approached corporations, foundations, and government agencies, and even placed newspaper ads inviting contributions from individuals. *Life* magazine came forward with a semi-sizable sum of $2,500—a large enough indication of interest to breathe modest life into the dream.

As interest grew and donations dribbled in, so did the need for management and accounting. Chuck Huestis, vice president of the Hughes Aircraft Company in Southern California, had heard Dyhrenfurth speak. From that moment, Huestis yearned to play a role in getting Americans onto the slopes of Everest—with a hope that he might even see the mountain himself.

Huestis had spent the previous few years with Hughes developing the Syncom communications satellite. Dyhrenfurth was intrigued. He had touched on the realm of outer space himself while shooting dozens of films for the air force on the development of the Atlas rocket. Huestis, an armchair mountaineer, was just what the expedition needed:

an organized, irrepressible, well-connected big thinker. Dyhrenfurth brought him on board, and Huestis started off by setting up a non-profit corporation. With his tireless secretary—in the era before word processing—he crafted hundreds of letters seeking product donations and sponsorships from companies making everything from cameras to carabiners, from long underwear to short skis. To add flair to his fund-raising junkets, Huestis had access to the company plane: a Convair Liner the size of a DC-3.

They tried every angle to build a buzz. Dyhrenfurth even approached the popular CBS television program *I've Got a Secret,* in which contestants are challenged to ferret out a guest's unusual life secret. He was turned down. "I'm afraid that until the expedition has actually *climbed* Mount Everest," the show's executive producer responded, "there's no 'secret' in our definition of the term. We have never yet programmed as a 'secret' somebody who was *going* to do something."

No harm in asking. Dyhrenfurth kept going, and in a letter to U.S. senator Warren Magnuson (D-WA), he expanded his pitch. "I believe the time has come to obtain the whole-hearted endorsement and support of the President of the United States. In 1952, the President of Switzerland gave us a warm send-off. The Duke of Edinburgh was the Patron of the British Everest Expedition of 1953. . . . Nobody seems to question the why of golf, baseball, football, horse racing."

In the summer of 1961, Dyhrenfurth filmed an expedition installing the world's first nuclear isotope–powered weather station in the Canadian Arctic. Late that August he was heading to Washington, D.C., and wrote to President Kennedy directly, proposing that the Everest team place one of these stations on the South Col, at twenty-six thousand feet in the shadow of the mountain's summit. The facility would enhance the scientific prestige of the United States in Asia, he stressed, and "prove dramatically this country's intent to use atomic energy for the economic and social well-being of mankind." He offered to meet with the president or a senior member of the staff.

His timing could not have been worse. The Soviets had just demanded that Allied forces be removed from West Berlin, and they had coerced East Germany into erecting a concrete barrier separating West and East Germany: the Berlin Wall. Dyhrenfurth received an apologetic phone call from a White House staffperson. His proposal warranted careful consideration, he was told, but the president had just ordered 148,000 guardsmen and reservists back to active duty, and was swamped with conferences.

Only three weeks earlier, on August 6, 1961, the Soviets had launched *Vostok 2*, which had orbited the earth seventeen times with a cosmonaut on board. This was especially discomforting in view of the failure—while Dyhrenfurth was in Washington—of the first launch in the Ranger program, the United States' unmanned mission to get close-up images of the moon. The next five *Ranger* launches, between 1961 and '64, would also fail.

And on August 30, 1961, Soviet premier Nikita Khrushchev announced the end of a three-year nuclear testing moratorium. Two months later, the Soviets detonated one of the most powerful nuclear weapons ever devised, equivalent to ten times the explosives used in World War II combined.

Dyhrenfurth's weather station idea would be a tough sell in any case: As humble as it sounded, the device could have been the flashpoint for a diplomatic row in South Asia. Nepal, surprisingly, had no objection to the idea of installing a nuclear-powered device on its highest mountain. But the South Col of Mount Everest was situated precisely on the border between Nepal and China. Mao Tse-tung would surely disapprove of a nuclear-powered *anything* positioned so close to the People's Republic.

This was an awkward time in U.S. history. Tears in the fabric of America's self-confidence were beginning to show, and the world seemed to be looking for symptoms of American inadequacy. An expedition to Everest might not be the safest bet for resurrecting this perception. The country couldn't afford to invest in any more false starts and misdirected ventures. Success on the mountain wasn't assured. The Swiss had failed twice in 1952, and in 1960 the Indians came up short of the summit by 700 feet. In 1962, after spending three hypoxic nights at 27,600 feet, the Indians were again beaten back by wind and weather—this time just 400 feet below the top.

Dyhrenfurth's venture could go haywire in a variety of ways, and the White House cautiously sidestepped making an endorsement. But he had a powerful intuition that it would succeed and that America would prevail. It *had* to prevail. Risk and uncertainty weren't obstacles. They were good old American virtues. Uncertainty was a necessary ingredient for success.

The expedition's greatest risk, Dyhrenfurth knew, was not of injury or even loss of life. It was of shame. If America tried and failed, heroism would dissolve into hubris. The whole venture would be recorded as just another pathetic, lowercase footnote in the annals of climbing history. He knew plenty of those.

Chapter 5

Acceptance and Invitations

*By all pragmatic standards climbing mountains is
"useless." That, indeed, is one of its glories: that it
needs no end or justification beyond itself—like a
sunset, a symphony, or like falling in love.*

—James Ramsey Ullman, in *Americans on
Everest*

Muffy French, a vivacious redhead, rolled into Jackson
Hole, Wyoming, in a forest green 1956 Thunderbird—the model with
nautical portholes on the sides. The license plates spelled MUFF.

Muffy came from money. She could have "come out" as a debutante in New York, where she grew up. But she'd declined, regarding
the social scene as a cattle market legitimized by boring parties with
overprivileged people. "Women were supposed to wear poodle skirts,
fuss with their hair, and fall in love with their vacuum cleaners," she
said. "It was awful. My friends and I wanted to live by what was important to us, not what was important to anyone else—especially not
our parents. We wanted to be outdoors, skiing and climbing."

It was August 1959, and Muffy had driven to the Tetons to visit
her brother Bob French—another of Glenn Exum's favorite guides.
She had done some climbing before arriving at Jenny Lake, but Bob
thought she would enjoy climbing school. She signed up. Barry Corbet, a climber Bob respected, would be the guide.

"It was hard not to look at him," Muffy said of Corbet. "I thought
him very handsome. We said a few words, then our group climbed into

the boat to cross Jenny Lake. One of the clients asked Corbet how he spelled his last name. It's hard to explain, but when he said it was spelled with one *t*, I was privately relieved. Somehow I knew it would be *my* name—and I liked that spelling better."

Corbet was tall and squarely built, and Muffy saw that he moved with an elegant strength. The gleam in his eyes betrayed a love of wild places and rugged challenges. His quiet, knowing manner made her curious about what it was he knew, and where he had been.

But Corbet was as shy and inexperienced as he was charismatic. He was known around the Guides Camp for his "Corbet control," betraying little interest in women. But his grin was infectious, and he was patient with his charges. "During the knot-tying session I had trouble mastering the ring bend, and he stayed with me until I got it," Muffy recalled. She had intended to remain in Jackson Hole for only a few days. But Corbet saw her again, and invited her to join a climbing party he was leading up the Grand Teton.

"It was a beautifully clear day, with the smell of conifers and lichen-covered rocks warmed by the sun," Muffy recalled. "At the Lower Saddle, Barry decided that our party should depart for the summit early because of the joy of climbing in the moonlight. Everyone agreed. He got us up at two in the morning, and fed us breakfast. I was the first to notice that the moon—which had been bright and beautiful when we arose—had taken a nosedive into Idaho. He had miscalculated its path across the sky. Everyone went back to bed for a few hours."

They reached the summit and descended to Jackson without incident. But it was late August in Wyoming, and a cold front settled in. Muffy delayed her departure for several days.

"One thing led to another and, during that long, snowy week, everyone saw a lot of each other." Muffy had dated skiers and climbers before, so she was familiar with loners like Corbet. She considered herself one, too.

California would offer milder weather for fall climbing, so Corbet invited Muffy to join him there. They hopped into his Hudson—she sensed that he viewed her T-bird as an embarrassing extravagance—and left town with her dog, Furry, in the backseat.

Muffy, like the mountains, allowed Corbet to open up and breathe. They were married that December—an event they sanctified by walking through an arch of ice axes held by relatives and climbing friends. Back in Jackson Hole, they began to build an A-frame mountain chalet they called the Alp Horn, and manage it as a guest lodge. The sitting area was scented with wet ski boots and melted ski wax, and a piano stood near the fire. In the winter they skied and taught skiing at Snow King, the town hill. "My husband and I learned to ski there," one local said. "Barry Corbet had godlike status, at least when it came to skiing. He skied with fluid perfection, feet glued together— dazzling in all ways."

During the summer, Muffy altered and stitched the pants that the climbers wore, sewing loops and pockets for their hardware— unintended precursors to cargo pants. They weren't part of the "beat" generation, exactly, which was more of an urban tribe. Theirs was a smaller and more diffuse group of educated youth of the 1950s who simply didn't care for society's demands or its obsession with success and material accumulation.

Muffy's father and stepmother expressed concern about Corbet's future as a provider. Corbet drafted a letter defending his lifestyle and worldview. "Returning to school holds no terrors for me, but the whole delightful plan seems to break down when I ask myself what I want to learn. You suggest mining engineering and forestry. I don't pretend that my contribution to the world is very great, but it can be. Who is to say that becoming a mining engineer would make me more useful?"

At the same time he was defending his ideals, Corbet was finding that jobs in the climbing world were seasonal and scarce. Even his boss, Glenn Exum, spent his winters teaching high school music. Exum felt that guiding was a fine summer diversion, but the guides should have another life. Plus, Jackson Hole wasn't turning into quite the lifestyle utopia Corbet and Muffy and their friends had envisioned. In the early sixties, a series of deaths befell the Tetons climbing and skiing community. One climber died in a fall. A ranger broke through the ice of Jenny Lake. An avalanche buried a skier not far from a maintained ski hill. A client fell while descending the Grand. And Dave

Dingman's buddy—the one he'd come west with—was smothered in an avalanche.

"Every week or two I would hear of another death," Muffy said. "It was like a war."

In 1961—as if to refute these senseless losses—Muffy gave birth to their son, Jonathan. Their youthful, adventurous lifestyle was transitioning to Life, Part Two.

They weren't the only ones. Jake Breitenbach was close behind. Breitenbach had fled a suburban upbringing and a drumbeat of questions from his parents about what he intended to do with his life. The Tetons was his answer, and when he arrived in Wyoming he found others who had come to the same conclusion. He met a tall blond woman named Lou McGraw—a climber who shared his quiet, intellectual pursuit of meaning and ethics. They were married in the late winter of 1960, after snowplows cleared a path to the Chapel of the Transfiguration, a tiny log church in the heart of Grand Teton National Park. Breitenbach ran a small restaurant called the White Cupboard but soon found it to be more of an anchor around his neck than a springboard for more adventures.

Norman Dyhrenfurth had received hundreds of imploring letters from mountaineers who had heard about the American expedition, but he turned his initial sights on the Tetons. Barry Corbet and Jake Breitenbach were among the strongest and most dedicated guides in Exum's service. Dyhrenfurth wrote to invite them but provided few details, if only because he wasn't sure how, or even whether, the expedition would come together. They intended to depart in early February 1963, he said, and make a summit attempt no later than May. Four months in the Himalaya. More likely five.

Corbet was astonished by the invitation, and honored. But the decision wasn't a simple one. His son was a year old, and some construction remained to be done on the Alp Horn. Corbet was reluctant to leave his new family buried beneath an avalanche of unfinished tasks and responsibilities.

Breitenbach didn't respond immediately. He was torn about whether to accept, without knowing exactly why. He worried that he might not be able to summon up the single-minded devotion and gung ho team spirit that he sensed the venture would demand. Besides, he and his wife were sinking more money in their restaurant than they were taking out. It might not be fair (or financially prudent) to disappear for that long.

But the sheer rapture of climbing a large mountain was hard to turn down. If their wives went for it, perhaps Breitenbach and Corbet could place their fledgling family lives on hold—for just a little while.

Dyhrenfurth made a point of talking to the climbers' wives, whenever he could, to get their clearance. "A European wife would never consider telling her husband, 'No you can't go.' But American wives have done this." Muffy urged Corbet not to pass up the chance. And Breitenbach's wife encouraged him to go as well. Opportunities might arise outside their confined valley, and why not in the Himalaya? Plus, it might not be so bad to have two testosterone-fueled, unemployed adventurer-philosophers out of the house during the dreary spring "mud season."

Dyhrenfurth also tracked down the precocious former Exum guide Dave Dingman at the University of Maryland in Baltimore, where he had begun a residency in general surgery. Dyhrenfurth's invitation placed the young doctor in a bind.

"The offer came during an intense time in my career. I spoke to the professor and expected him to say, 'Forget it. What do you want to be: a doctor or a mountaineer?' Instead, he saw it as a once-in-a-lifetime opportunity and said that I should go—and that he'd arrange a slot for me when I returned."

Maturity, and interpersonal harmony, would be critical to the team's success. Perhaps Dyhrenfurth could replicate the rare camaraderie and selflessness shared by the climbers on an American ascent of Masherbrum in 1960. The members of that team were from similar socioeconomic backgrounds—equals with few rivalries, dedicated to a common purpose. It was led by the affable and chronically helpful Nick Clinch, who recognized that his primary role as overall leader was to raise funds and coordinate logistics. When they arrived at base camp, he deferred to his coleader on the climbing decisions. Throughout, the members climbed with team success in mind, not the fulfillment of individual goals.

One of those Masherbrum vets, Willi Unsoeld, was a natural choice for Everest. But Unsoeld had just taken on a two-year job with the Peace Corps in Nepal, as deputy director. He might not be granted leave so early in his assignment. His boss, climbing legend Bob Bates, would likely want to tag along, too—advancing age be damned. In 1938, Bates had made an attempt on Pakistan's K2, the world's second highest peak.

The Corps' founding director, Sargent Shriver (President Kennedy's brother-in-law), had recruited Bates to direct the first volunteer group in Nepal, in 1961. Shriver promptly asked Bates whom he would like as his deputy director.

"Willi Unsoeld," Bates replied without hesitation. He explained that Unsoeld was teaching religion and philosophy at a college in Oregon. "He's a beloved cult figure out there. Tough as they come, physically, but very spiritual, too." Unsoeld personified the rugged, spirited, Northwest archetype for Kennedy's new American ethic. In his Democratic nomination acceptance speech, the president had described a dynamic, forward-looking nation, one setting out on a "new frontier" characterized by citizens who demonstrated sacrifice, goodwill, persistence, and vigor. Willi Unsoeld was that citizen, and Nepal was the perfect place for him to showcase those qualities.

If the Peace Corps would release him from duty, Unsoeld figured, he could join the expedition. Plus, he'd made a pact with Masherbrum buddies Hornbein and Emerson: All three of them would go to Everest, or none of them. He didn't want to disappoint them.

Unsoeld was already a seasoned Asia hand, too—the veteran of three Himalayan expeditions. The first of these, in 1949 when he was twenty-two, grew into an inadvertent pilgrimage. For Unsoeld, the Himalaya held secrets of a spiritual as much as a geographical nature—secrets that might yield answers to his abiding questions about humanity and the planet.

———

With a climbing buddy, Unsoeld stood on the margin of Route 66 outside of Los Angeles. Their thumbs were cocked in an eastward direction, their fingers clutching a hand-lettered sign that read SWISS ALPS. (The Alps were only halfway to their actual destination, but they agreed to accept a ride going that far.) Unbeknownst to the drivers speeding past, this was the main contingent of the so-called Anglo-American Himalayan Expedition of 1949.

The borders of Nepal bracket some of the most enchanting peaks in the Great Himalayan Range, and none of them had been climbed. But the kingdom wouldn't open its doors to the outside world until 1950. India would have to suffice. Unsoeld had been captivated, anyway, by photos revealing the exquisite beauty of the Indian Garhwal, an imposing chain of mountains to the west of Nepal. He especially longed to behold the sacred Nanda Devi massif—one of the more sensuous collections of rock and snow in the range.

"Initial preparations for this trip were kept to a minimum since the possible success of the undertaking was considered much too unlikely to warrant much expenditure of energy," Unsoeld wrote in a light-hearted account that bounced along in the tone of the fictional *Ascent of Rum Doodle*. Their plan was to meet another climber in Zurich, warm up in the Alps, then make their way to India. "Dragging along a 60-pound pack did little to enhance the attraction of a clean-cut rock climb," Unsoeld said about hauling their Himalaya-bound gear through Europe, "but we hoped through such grinding discipline of body and spirit that we would profit from the conditioning later on." After working in an iron foundry in Sweden, they cadged first-class passage on a freighter that crossed the Red Sea, bound for the subcontinent.

Bombay was an exotic, vibrant gateway to the Orient. The ancient aroma of the city—a blend of firewood smoke, dung, and incense—drifted out to their ship as it approached. When the boat docked, they were quickly initiated into the chaos and color of India. They rode third-class trains and buses (while fending off monkeys trained to clamber through the open windows to steal personal effects) to the pilgrimage town of Rishikesh, near the headwaters of the sacred Ganges River.

Their loads had swelled to eighty pounds each. From Rishikesh they trekked fifty miles to the holy hamlet of Badrinath, on a path thronged with devout Hindu pilgrims. Some of their fellow travelers had been on the road for weeks or months, respectfully inchworming to their destination by means of body-length prostrations.

At Badrinath, the three climbers lodged in the basement grotto of a local temple as guests of a leading priest of the valley. The holy man considered it his duty to escort them to the base camp of the 21,640-foot peak they had selected to climb: Nilkanta, the Blue Throated One, another name for the wrathful Hindu deity Shiva.

From Nilkanta's base camp the climbers spied a straightforward route to the Col, at eighteen thousand feet, "but our style of life across India and the foothills had begun to take its toll," Unsoeld wrote. "Constant attacks of dysentery ['my shit was flying a yard out my ass'] and the lack of protein in our steady diet of fried stuffs from the bazaars had reduced our vitality." The snow deepened as they ascended, and they covered the final three hundred feet to the Col by performing a butterfly swimming stroke through chest-deep powder. They camped for the night before realizing they had brought neither food nor sleeping bags, having initially planned to descend the same day.

"This night on the Col must have been one of the most beautiful in our experience," Unsoeld wrote. "Perfectly clear with a full moon sheathing the region in shadowed silver—though the cold was too intense and our exhaustion too complete to allow such scenery to register consciously." They decided to retreat. One of the climbers returned to Europe.

Drained and emaciated, Unsoeld and his buddy arrived at Mussoorie, a hill station of the British Raj. Their mountain pilgrimage had been life altering, and at times heavenly. Their descent and return to the world of mortals was now skirting hell. American Christian missionary Ernie Campbell found them slumped against the closed doors of a shop in the local bazaar.

"You need help," Campbell said, and took them to his home. After some rehydration and home cooking—in one sitting, they finished off an entire tin of army surplus peanut butter—they improved.

Ernie Campbell was trained as a pastor, yet he didn't advocate conversion. He felt he'd been sent to India to serve the Dalits—the untouchables—and other minorities who had limited access to social justice and economic opportunity. Unsoeld accompanied Campbell to the Punjab and was impressed by his efforts there—especially by how Campbell and other development workers engaged with the local cultures and were trusted and respected by them.

Unsoeld's buddy moved on, but Unsoeld stayed for two months in the Campbells' home—a colonial vestige of the British Raj, located near the ancient Grand Trunk Road. A procession of guests of all nationalities—Indian activists, village workers, officials, and religious figures of all faiths—congregated around an oversized table in the high-ceilinged dining room.

Unsoeld eventually worked his way back to the United States and arrived in Los Angeles. He had been away for nineteen months. Arguably, he was an antecedent of the "world traveler" backpackers: living among villagers, eating their food, and jumping aboard local forms of transportation.

An important objective of Unsoeld's pilgrimage had been fulfilled: He had glimpsed the sacred peak of Nanda Devi. He was so taken by its beauty that he vowed he would name his first daughter after the mountain. At the time, he wasn't married. Therefore, he told a friend, he needed to head home to find a wife so that he could have a daughter.

Unsoeld's Asia odyssey also inspired him to enter the Oberlin Theological Seminary, and go on to receive a divinity degree, followed by a PhD in philosophy. Twenty years later, he would continue to speak of how meeting Ernie Campbell had drawn him toward a life of service and informed his work with the Peace Corps in Nepal.

Unsoeld and his wife, Jolene, would eventually have a daughter: Nanda Devi Unsoeld.

Chapter 6

Beyond the Tetons

*When men climb mountains together, the rope
between them is more than a physical aid to the ascent,
it is a symbol of the spirit of the enterprise. It is a
symbol of men banded together in a common effort
of will and strength against their own true enemies:
inertia, cowardice, greed, ignorance, and all weakness
of spirit.*

—CHARLES HOUSTON

THE CASCADE RANGE OF WASHINGTON AND OREGON WAS CREATED, tectonically speaking, when a piece of the Pacific plate slid beneath the North American plate, burping up a string of volcanoes. The most iconic of these not-quite-extinct domes is 14,410-foot Mount Rainier. Solid and singular, Rainier dominates Seattle's southeastern horizon, sitting like a gilded Buddha at the end of a hallway of butter lamps and chanting monks.

At close range, Rainier can be brutish and unstable. The volcanic duff that climbers plod through, when not pacing themselves up a glacier, steals one step back for every two forward. Freeze-thaw cycles eject ragged chunks of igneous rock from the bulging cliffs that cordon the glaciers, and marine storm cycles drop tons of wet snow that become forceful avalanches. Winter and summer, as it has for millennia, the mountain is falling apart.

The Pacific Northwest climbers of the 1950s displayed a Yankee sort of persistence, like New Englanders without the crankiness, sharing a fortitude (or resignation) borne from slogging through the living muck and persistent drizzle of temperate rain forests. They waded through frigid streams and whacked away at obstinate undergrowth just to arrive at the launch points of their climbs.

Willi Unsoeld was a native Northwesterner; he had grown up near soggy Coos Bay, Oregon. Identical twins Jim and Lou Whittaker hailed from similarly sodden Seattle, more than three hundred miles to Coos Bay's north. (Washingtonians refer to their rain as "the Oregon mist"—because it missed Oregon.)

Jim and Lou, both a muscular, towering six foot five, were the kind of twins who could finish each other's sentences. Their greatest sources of inspiration—and competition—were each other. "We used to wrestle in the house like bear cubs. Our mother would tell us to 'go outside and play,'" Jim said. "That's how we came by our love of the outdoors. We soaked it all in—the beach, the forest, the hillsides and the clouds." Before 1963, they were well known in northwest climbing circles, and between them had climbed Mount Rainier ninety-six times.

In 1952, after a summer of guiding, the Whittaker twins were drafted for the Korean War. They entered basic training at Fort Lewis, Washington, forty miles from Mount Rainier. "The physical side of it was easy for us," Jim wrote in his autobiography, *A Life on the Edge*. So easy that it led them on a search for tougher challenges. They learned of a unit called the Mountain and Cold Weather Training Command, a successor to the Tenth Mountain Division—the ski troops—based at Camp Hale in the Colorado Rockies. The unit was custom designed for them, it seemed, and they wanted to be a part of it.

The Whittakers had worked part-time at a sporting goods store in downtown Seattle and Jim enlisted the help of their boss—a Tenth Mountain veteran. It worked. Both Jim and Lou were assigned to train Special Forces soldiers in skiing, climbing, and other mountain maneuvers. Like the Tenth Mountaineers who preceded them, they donned white oversuits for camouflage and strapped on white rucksacks, skis, and ski poles. They played war games, "chasing and being chased by 'enemy patrols,' dynamiting (with wooden blocks) the railroad tracks that ran over the pass, being 'captured' and 'escaping' into the woods for a week at a time, building shelters out of fir trees and aspens. It was a lot more like fun than work."

The Whittaker twins were never pressed into service in Korea. Instead, "Big Jim," as he was known, was hired in 1955 as the first employee of an innovative mountain gear cooperative called Recreational Equipment, Inc. (best known today as REI). He excelled in all manner of outdoor activities and was assigned to go hiking and climbing as a means of field-testing new gear. The equipment he tried ranged from moderately functional to useless and dangerous. The backpack was evolving: The WWII-issue "kidney buster" knapsack was being replaced by the Trapper Nelson pack, which introduced a frame and waist strap. This was followed by the lightweight Kelty frame pack, crafted from hollow aluminum tubing and waterproof fabric formed into compartments and zippered pockets. The Kelty soon revolutionized backcountry travel and almost made load carrying seem like fun. New designs of tents, sleeping bags, boots, and clothing were also hitting the market, and REI introduced these outdoor products into the mainstream retail world.

In the spring of 1962, Norman Dyhrenfurth phoned the Whittaker twins. They accepted his invitation to join the Everest team without hesitation. But Lou had recently opened a ski shop near Tacoma, and one of his business partners died soon after. Lou felt obliged to withdraw from the expedition. Dyhrenfurth was disappointed, as the twins would have made an indomitable pair. "Big Jim," however, would carry on, and Dyhrenfurth named him the point man for the expedition's tents, clothing, and climbing gear.

Dyhrenfurth saw that to build visibility and lure donors, the expedition would need sponsors. White House staff urged him to contact the National Geographic Society. In Washington, Dyhrenfurth met with its chairman, Melville Bell Grosvenor, who indicated that they might be able to offer support. Grosvenor proposed that a broad-chested man named Barry Bishop join the expedition. Bishop was their director of the Committee for Research and Exploration, and a skilled climber and Asia hand.

Dyhrenfurth knew Bishop well and was delighted by the arrangement. Bishop had a wry smile and firm handshake, and his Himalayan experience conferred ready respect. So did his wide girth, which had earned him the nickname "Barrel."

After graduating from the University of Cincinnati in 1954 (he had transferred there from Dartmouth), Bishop teamed up with a colleague named Roger Ewy and flew to Europe. In Nuremberg, they picked up two Zündapp motorcycles (competitors to BMW at the time, with a drive shaft in place of a chain), and rode through the Dolomites and Alps. They climbed everything they could, and made a traverse from the Matterhorn in Switzerland to Monte Rosa in Italy. Climbers in the Alps were still wearing boots with hobnails, or Tricouni nails, pounded into the sole. "The scratches on the rock made by the Tricounies were convenient," Ewy recalled, "because they allowed us to easily follow the route." To maximize their purchase, climbers used soft nails for hard rock, and hard nails for soft rock. (Shortly after, most climbers would transition to Vibram soles, named after Vitale Bramani, their Italian inventor.)

Bishop studied glaciology during his master's degree research in Greenland. An officer on Rear Admiral Richard Byrd's staff saw a paper he'd written, and in 1957 recruited him to serve as scientific adviser to the navy's research project in Antarctica. After Antarctica, Bishop took his photographs to *National Geographic*, where he was offered a job as picture editor, and later a directorship. Giving out money for research, Bishop discovered, was even more rewarding than receiving it.

Barry Bishop had already spent time near Everest. In the winter of 1960–61 he had joined Sir Edmund Hillary's Silver Hut Expedition as a geographer, glaciologist, and meteorologist. Hillary, Bishop, and a small team set up a prefab aluminum research station high on the flanks of Ama Dablam, a statuesque, double-humped peak that presides over Everest's upper approach route. Bishop was also recruited—in the spirit of far-flung, multidisciplinary field research—as a guinea pig for human physiology studies. By exposing humans to physical stress under hypoxic conditions, Bishop's colleagues hoped to understand how people acclimatize, and possibly determine the altitude at which adaptation no longer takes place. The rigor of the tests toughened him, Bishop felt, and he was keen to evaluate his performance at even higher altitudes. That spring, with three other "researchers," Bishop pulled off a first ascent of Ama Dablam.

Throughout the climb, Bishop looked up at the thick-shouldered peak to the northeast—Mount Everest—the way a deep-sea diver peers into the depths: with a combination of dread and longing. Everest would offer an even higher physiological ceiling to push against. Bishop couldn't have guessed that he would be there within two years—and would learn firsthand the very limits of the human body's ability to survive.

Hillary's Silver Hut team had brought along a cryptozoologist, who directed a quest to find a yeti—the Himalaya's legendary bipedal primate. They weren't able to track a living specimen, but they did examine what the local Sherpas believed to be the *scalp* of a yeti. This hairy, somewhat conical object—like a rigid ski hat with thin, bristly fur—was secured in a wooden box kept in the recesses of a nearby Buddhist monastery. The quixotic search was documented, naturally, in a TV program that aired on *Mutual of Omaha's Wild Kingdom*.

National Geographic wouldn't mind getting film footage, as well as still images, from high on Everest—preferably the top. Dyhrenfurth planned to produce and direct the film, but at age forty-five, didn't intend to make an attempt on the summit himself. He did know a cinematographer who was a skilled rock climber, a lanky youth named Dan Doody, who could work as second cameraman. Dyhrenfurth had climbed with Doody in the late 1950s on Breakneck Ridge, which overlooks the Hudson River, an easy drive from New York City. They intersected again in Santa Monica, where Doody was associate producer of a TV series called *True Adventure*. Dyhrenfurth invited him on board.

Doody was also experienced with accidents and rescues in remote areas. On a geology internship with the University of Wyoming, his group was rigging a dynamite charge when the radio-triggered explosion went off prematurely. Doody lost some of his hearing and most of the sight in one eye. His instructor was killed. Doody's friends said that the experience gave him an unusual calmness and equanimity in the face of danger. And on a winter break from college, he had rescued some skiers caught in an avalanche at Alta, a ski area in the Wasatch Range near Salt Lake City. The roads out of the canyon were closed, and Doody selflessly carried a young woman with a broken leg for sixteen miles—on skis.

Gaunt and good-natured, Doody could seem socially awkward—an impression enhanced by his tendency to wear leather sandals and live something of a "beat" lifestyle. Like many climbers, he'd sidestepped the trappings of the commercial world. His apartment was located in a mixed-race neighborhood—far different than that of his childhood in Connecticut. He regarded his location on the planet, however, as more in the realm of philosophical concepts.

In 1960, Doody attempted the ominous four-thousand-foot North Face of Mount Edith Cavell in Jasper National Park in Alberta, Canada, with Fred Beckey (who was featured in the classic "Will Belay for Food!!!" poster in the 2004 Patagonia catalog) and Patagonia founder Yvon Chouinard. Role models for those who would later be honorifically termed "dirtbag climbers," they wore shaggy hair and ragged clothes and collected and sold cast-off bottles from the roadside to buy food. They summited Edith Cavell after a hair-raising climb punctuated by rock falls, rotten ice, lightning, and near-steady rain. The following year, Doody was commissioned to make a film for the Canadian National Railway. He ended that season with enough spare change in his pocket to cover the tuition for a master's degree in cinema at the University of Southern California.

Doody had grown up on a four-hundred-acre Connecticut farm called Rolling Acres, which had been in his family since 1698. His sister milked the cows and drove the tractor. When she heard that her brother had been invited to climb Everest, she knew just what to do. She knitted him a pair of gloves with a trigger finger—the better to operate his movie camera in cold weather.

Chapter 7

Scientists and Shrinks

*Attempting to climb Everest affects people strongly, and
seems to initiate fundamental changes that set them on
unexpected paths.*

—ASSESSMENT BY A RESEARCHER AT THE
INSTITUTE OF PERSONALITY ASSESSMENT
AND RESEARCH

NATIONAL GEOGRAPHIC HAD COMMITTED $144,000 TO THE EXPEDI-
tion, the largest sum from a single source, up to that point. But for the
climbing and media coverage to work in service of each other, Chuck
Huestis and Dyhrenfurth recalculated that they would need to raise a
total of $400,000.

Science might be able to help. At least a modest degree of academic research, Dyhrenfurth knew, could build legitimacy and bring
more funding to the expedition. The team needed scientists who were
strong climbers.

One of these was Maynard Miller, a tall man with a forceful
personality. Miller was the ideal scientist, in Dyhrenfurth's mind, to
extend the glacier research started by his own father. Günter Oskar
Dyhrenfurth had begun studying and cataloguing the rocks and glaciers of the Himalaya even prior to the 1921 British reconnaissance to
Everest's north side.

Miller had grown up in Tacoma, Washington, gazing from his
window at the melting-ice-cream slopes of nearby Mount Rainier. He
was fascinated by what might be going on *inside* all of that ancient

snow and ice. Years of studying mountains led him to become a dedicated academic; students referred to Professor Maynard M. Miller, when writing, as "M^3." In 1962, at age thirty-eight, Miller was already a veteran in glacial studies circles, having directed the Juneau Icefield Research Project for sixteen years. In 2012 he was still its emeritus director.

Even in the early 1960s, Miller and his colleagues were finding that Alaska's glaciers were receding at an accelerating rate. What about Himalayan glaciers, which occupy more surface area than the glaciers in any region outside of the North and South Poles? Glaciologists such as Miller start out by assessing a glacier's "health." In their physical checkup, they measure a glacier's total mass, annual accumulation of snow, movement, and the melting and evaporation of snow at its terminal moraine (the plowed-up ridge of rubble and ice where the glacier ends). Miller's task could be visualized as mapping the anatomy and physiology of a living being in motion—*slow* motion.

An extensive survey of Everest's glacier systems was more than the expedition could take on. But the team could carry out studies on the Khumbu Icefall—the treacherous frozen waterfall of ice blocks that the Everest team would have to travel through to reach the mountain's higher slopes. Of greatest appeal to Dyhrenfurth, the National Science Foundation would provide funds to cover all the glacier research expenses, plus some.

Miller nominated Barry Prather, his capable Juneau Icefield assistant, to join the team. A dozen years younger than his boss, Prather was a physical workhorse, six feet tall and 190 pounds, with the good looks and the aw-shucks manner of a strapping farm boy—which he was. Prather had grown up in a rural wooded area at the foot of the Cascades on a self-sufficient pioneer homestead, years before it became a lifestyle choice.

Honoring what seemed to be a growing tradition among Dartmouth students who climbed, Prather dropped out after his first year. He went on to get a master's degree in geophysics from Michigan State University—under Maynard Miller himself, who was a professor there. During Alaska summers, Maynard had counted on Prather to carry loads of research equipment, retrieve samples, and undertake experiments, often in freezing and miserable conditions. With enough baling wire and electrician's tape, Prather could fix anything. His skills and his optimism would transfer readily to the Himalaya.

But Dyhrenfurth had decided not to consider candidates younger than twenty-six. Barry Prather was twenty-four years old, and he received a letter from Dyhrenfurth saying that he was unlikely to be selected. "Men in their early twenties, no matter how mature and physically strong climbers they may be in the Alps or Rockies, once they have been exposed to the physical and psychological stresses of a major Himalayan campaign, are the first to crack."

Miller convinced Dyhrenfurth that, although Prather was a bit shy of experience, he had performed exceptionally in Alaska. And as part of Project Crater, Prather had lived happily on the summit of Mount Rainier for nearly eight weeks continuously—not exactly the sort of person to "crack." Soon afterward, other candidates had dropped from Dyhrenfurth's list, and Prather was signed up.

Psychology was one scientific discipline that hadn't yet found application in the mountains. But the navy wondered if the study of climbers on long expeditions might help them develop selection standards for stressful assignments, such as extended submarine missions.

Jim Lester, a UCLA-trained research psychologist, was working in a clinic in Santa Monica when he met Norman Dyhrenfurth at a cocktail party. They discovered that they lived within a half mile of each other. As Norman spoke expansively about the Everest expedition, Lester suddenly asked him—encouraged by a second martini—if a psychologist might be considered for the team. Normally reserved and thoughtful, he surprised himself with his own boldness. His first marriage had broken up a year earlier, and he had been struggling with a sense of failure and loss of self-confidence.

"Here I was," Lester wrote, "proposing a study I had only conceived of half an hour earlier." He knew that it would have been presumptuous to suggest he could enhance the team's mental health. But he was thinking on a different track—one that might bring funding *to* the enterprise, rather than require support *from* it.

In addition to trying to understand his own stressful circumstances, Lester had been researching it professionally. So far, studies of stress had been done mainly on animals, and it was defined largely in terms of physiology. Increasingly, stress as a *psychological* state was appearing in the press and in casual conversation.

Lester knew that human performance in isolated, stressful environments is determined largely by how people handle themselves: by their ability to control and express their emotions, their reactions to prolonged frustrations, and their manner of dealing with the behavior of others. He saw the expedition as an opportunity to study these dynamics in real life. A setting as harsh as Everest, in fact, might be optimal.

To Lester's surprise, Dyhrenfurth was intrigued. Then Dyhrenfurth confirmed that, as suspected, outside funding for the research would be welcome—indeed, a requirement.

Lester found a bold administrator at the Office of Naval Research who was willing to give it a try. In October 1962, the ONR approved a grant of $35,190 for Lester to study the Everest team in situ.

"While Norman screened applications from climbers who wanted to be on the team," Lester recalled, "I scoured the psychological literature for previous work on which I might build my project." He was accustomed to devising innovative studies, having worked with Dr. Timothy Leary at the Langley Porter Institute in San Francisco. (In early 1963, Leary would be dismissed from Harvard for not attending his own lectures, at the same time that his experimentation with psychedelic drugs—which were legal at the time—had begun to overflow to the faculty and student body.)

Lester wrote a letter of introduction to each member, outlining his research plan and warming them to the idea of having a "shrink" tag along. He also reassured them that he wouldn't interfere with the climbing itself. Formal, baseline testing of the team members would be done before the expedition departed, he explained, over a three-day weekend at the Institute of Personality Assessment and Research in Berkeley.

Like Alice through her looking glass, Lester was about to tumble into a world populated with larger-than-life characters. He worried that Dyhrenfurth knew little about him, and that his own personality might not mesh well with the rest of the team. Outside of his career, his most notable skills were playing the piano and trombone, arranging jazz numbers, and singing in a quartet. He was gifted at these. Dyhrenfurth liked Lester's easygoing manner, and knew that he would enhance the expedition's academic profile—which would further help in general fund-raising.

Dyhrenfurth also wanted Tetons climbing legend Dick Emerson, who had made the pact with Hornbein and Unsoeld that it was all of them or none on Everest. As a bonus, Emerson had a doctorate in sociology. One of his long-term professional interests was to examine *communication feedback*: how information is shared within a group dedicated to a task. The National Science Foundation came through with a research grant for him, too.

One of Emerson's key assumptions (which would later be measured in other, nonmountaineering contexts) is that our motivational investment in a task varies directly with our degree of uncertainty about the outcome. This means that either prolonged optimism (a form of certainty) or prolonged pessimism (*also* a form of certainty) tend to reduce one's motivational investment in the task. If the climbers felt *certain* they would reach Everest's summit, for instance, then they would have little motivation to expend energy toward that goal. Likewise, if they felt certain that they would *not* reach the summit, they would experience a similar lack of motivation. If you knew the outcome, one way or the other, why bother trying?

The second part of Emerson's theory was that *information exchanged tends to maximize uncertainty*. When things begin to look easy and a member of a group expresses optimism ("This is a piece of cake—no problem"), other people tend to counter with pessimism, in the form of negative or tempering feedback ("Well, storms can roll in pretty quickly here, you know"). The reverse is equally true: In the face of pessimism, there's a tendency to bring up reasons for hope.

Thereby, as Willi Unsoeld expressed with his usual ironic touch, "We make highly objective statements from purely subjective grounds." Thus far in the expedition—with funds not fully raised and many logistical questions unanswered—Emerson's key hypothesis was already being validated: *Uncertainty begets motivation.* They were desperately short of money, and the group wanted Everest more than ever.

In addition to exploring this dynamic between the expedition members, Emerson was curious to see how shared information would affect decision making and, ultimately, the outcome of the climb. His data collection began with a survey in which he asked each member his views about life, the future, and the expedition's objectives. ("In case you are wondering," Emerson added, "Norman and I are also taking these questionnaires.")

As part of his experiment, Emerson handed each member a sturdy blue 5 1/2 x 7-inch hardbound diary with a closing flap and a snap. In it, the climbers were asked to engage in a daily self-assessment by ranking their feelings and impressions on a scale from −5 to +5: *Weak–strong___, Tired–rested___, Weather (today)___ and (at this moment)___, Terrain (dangerous–safe)___ and (difficult–easy)___.*

Once a week, the questioning shifted slightly, and a new diary page asked each member to assess the *mountain's* personality: *oppressive, masculine, impersonal, beckoning, calm, dormant, foreboding, malicious, challenging, invigorating, menacing, exalted.* There was also an area for assessing the act of filling in the diary itself *(annoying–pleasant).*

Before the expedition departed, Lester and Emerson began a lively correspondence and agreed on one thing: Little was known about human behavior in isolated situations. The durations of space travel had been too short to draw meaningful conclusions about the effects on humans of long missions, which were on the NASA drawing boards. Everest would offer a couple of months of stressful isolation, and they wondered if that would interest the space program: *If I were launched next year, after all the preparation that NASA could provide, on a two-year journey to Mars, what would I miss? What "needs" would deprivation uncover? What behavior, normally sustained, would deteriorate? What demands would I make on my five fellow travelers in search of replenishment?*

Emerson had his hands full. In addition to his research, he volunteered to work out the logistics for getting climbing gear, oxygen, and supplies from Everest's Base Camp to the higher camps. This assignment would come in handy when it came to allocating limited supplies between the two routes they wanted to attempt. Emerson and two other team members were about to become "fanatically" attached to one route in particular, and would have to struggle to ensure that their route was adequately supported and stocked.

Chapter 8

A Trial Run . . . or Hike

*Ours has been called the Age of Anxiety, the Age
of the Bomb, the age of this and that, most of it
highly depressing. . . . It has also been an age of
Mountaineering.*

—Norman Dyhrenfurth's expedition
proposal

Five months before the team's departure, 350 individuals and companies had contributed to the 1963 American Mount Everest Expedition, although most of the donations were small. King Leopold III of Belgium donated $50. The ledger sheet also tallied a $20 contribution from actor Ronald Reagan, who Dyhrenfurth had once hired to narrate the film of one of his students.

The expedition's hefty price tag drew ridicule from some mountaineering purists. European newspapers ran a cartoon depicting Americans dismantling Everest piece by piece and packing it into a moving van. Within the small American climbing community, Charles Houston, a veteran of Nanda Devi and K2 expeditions in the 1930s, wrote a letter to Dyhrenfurth stressing that they would do fine with more modest quantities of supplies.

"What you are engaged in is a vicious and self-perpetuating cycle," Houston said. "A big expedition necessitates big money, which in turn necessitates contacts with radio, television, and the press. This requires the publicity, the development of the expedition personnel, the 'make work' scientific programs, and all the rest."

As a doctor and high-altitude research physiologist, Houston wasn't convinced it was possible to combine first-rate scientific work with a major mountaineering objective.

"One may do one thing or the other," he wrote, "but trying to do both is certain to lead to failure in one." The expedition's organizational footprint, however, had already been surpassed by the Italians on K2 in 1954, by a Chinese extravaganza on Everest in 1960, and by John Hunt's military-style British expedition to Everest in 1953. All were staged with colossal casts of climbers and support staff.

Dyhrenfurth had another reason for wanting to field a big, well-equipped team. He had been contemplating something too audacious to propose openly during the fund-raising campaign, because it could entail tremendous risk: the possibility of climbing a variation of the mountain's standard route. He hopped into his roadster and drove south to San Diego to spring the idea on a climber who had recently accepted his invitation to join the expedition: Tom Hornbein, the cerebral medical doc and Masherbrum veteran who had intersected with Willi Unsoeld on a trail high in the Tetons.

"Photos were unfurled and laid end to end across our living-room floor to make a vast panorama, held in place by children's blocks," Hornbein later wrote. "While I looked at our goal, Norm asked, with a matter-of-factness that seemed irreverent to the highest mountain on earth, 'What do you think of trying the West Ridge?'"

Dyhrenfurth was suggesting that they climb via the "standard" South Col route, then *descend* via a new route: Everest's untouched West Ridge. It was an elegant, if daredevil, enterprise that even the Europeans might envy. Feasible or not, Dyhrenfurth had brought to life some of the wilder dreams from Hornbein's youth.

How had a kid from the Midwest with strong grades and a future in medicine found himself attracted to mountains? In 1946, at age sixteen, Hornbein had written an English essay titled "Ambition," inspired by James Ramsey Ullman's 1942 historical take on mountaineering, *High Conquest*. He described squinting across the plains of Missouri at distant clouds—imagining them as snow and mountains—admitting to "feelings that are at last bursting forth after being pent up for so long a time." He seemed to be trying on his dreams of a destiny outside of St. Louis.

> It was as if a huge mass was about to engulf me, to hypnotize me with its massive grandeur. . . . I dream of the day when I shall first gaze upon such peaks as Everest. . . . Perhaps, these are just idle dreams, dreams of the unreal. No. . . . It is more real than the man-made life in this country. But people who merely look on have no understanding of the magic influence of mountains.

The prairie landscapes of Hornbein's youth may have nurtured psychologist Jim Lester's dreams, as well. They would discover, years later, that they'd attended the same St. Louis grade school but had never met because they were a few years apart in age.

When Dyhrenfurth invited Hornbein to join the expedition, he was married with five children and working as an anesthesiologist in San Diego's Naval Hospital. But the navy wouldn't let him go. Willi Unsoeld jumped into lobbying for Hornbein by contacting his boss, Sargent Shriver—the president's brother-in-law. An order would eventually loop down the chain from JFK, through Secretary of State McNamara to the secretary of the navy. Hornbein was discharged only at the last moment, in February 1963.

Before joining the navy, Hornbein had completed a residency in anesthesiology and was doing physiological research. He'd be ideal for taking charge of the expedition's supplemental oxygen. On Masherbrum in 1960, he, Unsoeld, and Emerson had used a four-valve oxygen mask designed by the Swiss for use on Everest in 1956 and had been dissatisfied with its performance. Hornbein decided to design a mask with a single valve that would supplant the Swiss system.

When presenting a lecture to the medical staff at a hospital in St. Louis, Hornbein was introduced to a colon cancer patient named Fred Maytag, the president of the Maytag Corporation. Hornbein spoke with him about the mask and oxygen delivery system that he envisioned for Everest, and Maytag connected him with his R & D department. The resulting "Maytag mask" was rugged yet simple, and testing confirmed that it offered lower resistance to breathing than the earlier masks. Plus, it circumvented the Swiss mask's chronic icing problem by being made of pliable rubber, which allowed it to be deiced by merely squeezing and flexing it.

From Los Angeles, Dyhrenfurth also drove his roadster north to Berkeley to invite a perfect candidate for the role of general-purpose expedition doc: Gil Roberts, an emergency room physician and air force flight surgeon. Roberts had a solid climbing record, too. As a teen in Claremont, he had discovered that the Sierra Nevada was an ideal playground for bouldering and climbing.

With a bushy beard and weighing a bearlike 190 pounds, Roberts was "large in body and large in heart," as one friend described him. The expedition would need plenty of both—along with his medical skills, his maturity, and rock-hard mental stability.

"Gil didn't let emotions tangle him up," said Nick Clinch, who had climbed with Roberts in the 1950s. "He would take care of situations promptly and decisively." Climbing in Yosemite, Roberts had once caught a falling partner with a body belay. His hands were worn down to the sinews from the rope friction. In his customary understated way, Roberts remarked, "I don't think I could do two belays like that in the same day."

The team was nearly complete. On September 4, 1962, seventeen members of the expedition gathered near Seattle at Jim Whittaker's home on Lake Sammamish. Willi Unsoeld was missing, and missed—already in Nepal on assignment with the Peace Corps. The rest of them swam, water-skied, wrestled on the lawn, ate sandwiches, drank beer, told stories of narrow escapes and favorite climbs, and slept in the basement or on the lawn in borrowed sleeping bags. Most were meeting one another for the first time.

In between television appearances and press conferences, they converged for a brunch in their honor at the Seattle World's Fair. The cutting-edge exhibits showcased a prechip technological utopia of aerodynamic cars and video-image telephones, all centered around the futuristic Space Needle. The hourglass-shaped tower, resembling a flying saucer perched on chopsticks, had opened only five months earlier.

Jim Lester, the expedition psychologist, was the most silent and studious of the group—an objective outside observer, though a personable one. He noted a quiet throb of tension beneath the excitement and conviviality. "Each man was looking the others over carefully. *Am I good enough to be on this team? Is there anyone here who thinks like I do? Is there anyone who wants to climb Mount Everest more than I do?*"

Some answers might arise while testing the expedition gear on a practice climb of Mount Rainier. The mountain's changeable weather, abundance of crevasses, and sheer size were said to best simulate, within the United States, what climbers would encounter in the Himalaya.

For the eighty-mile drive to Paradise, a lofty overlook at 5,400 feet on the mountain's south side, Lester hopped into an old pickup truck with Lute Jerstad, a veteran Rainier guide. With boyish enthusiasm and a Jerry Lewis grin, Jerstad spiritedly described the beauty of glacier travel and the dangerous parts of Rainier. His crew cut hair rose like a cliff above his forehead, and it amplified his perpetual look of astonishment. During the drive, he gently probed Lester, whom team members had already nicknamed "Sigmund" for his Freud-like beard and demeanor. Lute and the others were quietly curious about what a headshrinker might be seeking within the minds of restless, impassioned mountaineers. Most climbers already knew that they were misfits with obsessive tendencies; had Lester been called in to make it a formal diagnosis?

Lute Jerstad grew up a Lutheran in Minnesota. He saw mountains for the first time at thirteen, when his family moved to Washington State. *Some day I'm going to climb that,* he vowed when he beheld the volcanic form of Mount Rainier. Before long he adopted Rainier as his mountain home. Chronically cheerful, Jerstad once opened his backpack on Rainier's summit and pulled out a watermelon to share with his companions. Head fund-raiser Chuck Huestis had climbed Rainier with Jerstad and had been impressed enough by his mountaineering skills and wacky good spirit to recommend him to Dyhrenfurth.

The official activities at Paradise began when Barry Bishop emerged from the lodge. "Hey, guys," he announced. "The bar's open!" In the auditorium of the rustic log Guide House they drank Rainier beer, threaded reels of 16 mm film through a projector, and watched movies that Dyhrenfurth had shot in the Himalaya. The flickering images transported them to the pastoral beauty of Nepal, its sixty-foot rhododendron bushes and terraced hillsides set off against the white glare of gargantuan peaks.

The men spoke of mountains and equipment and food, and of levels of "tolerable risk." Jim Lester, a flatlander, began to wonder about his own role on the expedition. "These men were so at home—they belonged up here more than they did on a street in town, in city clothes."

September was late in the year to climb Rainier. The team plodded up a near-endless snowfield to Camp Muir, at ten thousand feet, where they pitched a tiny village of tents on the edge of the Ingraham Glacier. They tested a portable winch with a half-horsepower gasoline engine. It worked—haltingly—and was able to pull loads short but useful distances up the mountain. And they tried out battery-powered shavers, which would be needed for their faces to make a good seal with the snug oxygen masks.

A dream—phrased mostly in the form of a question—circulated quietly through the group. Should they concentrate on a military-style ascent of Everest via the South Col, like the British and Swiss before them—and try for a "Grand Slam" by throwing in the neighboring, interconnected peaks of Lhotse and Nuptse? Or, might it be possible, against tremendous odds and obstacles, to make a summit attempt by the unclimbed West Ridge?

The notion of ascending the "standard" route via the South Col, then doing a "first descent" via the West Ridge, sounded risky. Such a traverse would commit the climbers to down climbing, and possibly rappelling, into unknown terrain. On the other hand, a traverse that began with a climb *up* the West Ridge—a new route—was an exquisite prospect.

An open discussion of a West Ridge traverse, however, would have to be postponed. Dyhrenfurth was concerned that the climbers would get carried away by the idea—that it would be love without first sight. Once they were safely on the approach march, he said, they could talk more freely and consider it.

A heavy weather pattern set in on the day of their Mount Rainier summit climb, and they were forced to cancel the climax of their shakedown trip. The men refused to take it as a portent of bad luck and nasty weather patterns to come ("Don't take it cirrus," one of them quipped).

The team wasn't quite ready. They still had to pack.

Dick Pownall had thrown cans of mismatched soups into a single pot while guiding on the Grand Teton, but he'd never planned the meals for a major Himalayan expedition. Approaching the task methodically, he studied the menus of other expeditions and the logistics that went with them. In a questionnaire, he informed the team members of their options and asked their preferences. For months, he prodded food distributors and manufacturers. He managed to get all of the provisions donated, from ninety-five different suppliers.

Boxes, crates, and bulk shipments arrived at a warehouse next to the REI store in Seattle. Pownall recruited cinematographer Dan Doody, glaciologist Barry Prather, and a group of friends who dubbed themselves the "Ellensburg Sherpas"—a loosely bound club of American climbers from the eastern slopes of the Cascades who had adopted Sherpa names. They slept on the floor of the warehouse, and every day for six weeks painstakingly sorted and packaged the food into individual meals. Those who prepared rations destined for the *real* Sherpas scribbled notes and sneaked them into their food packets—along with pennies, *Playboy* magazines, and other American souvenirs.

Pownall sent the expedition menu to a dietician, who saw nothing to improve—although each dinner serving included cigarettes. Dyhrenfurth reminded the packers that nothing on the food labels could refer to "beef" or show a picture of a cow (aside from condensed milk cans). Most Nepalese are devout Hindus, and the killing of a cow—even inadvertently—was viewed by the authorities (and sometimes dealt with) more harshly than negligent homicide.

Meal portions consisted of everything from butterscotch pudding to Vienna sausages, from canned tuna to pineapple slices. Special treats included dill pickles, liver paste, dried vegetables, Wheat Chex, Ovaltine—and Rainier beer. They would also field-test a new category of product: freeze-dried foods. These lightweight, high-tech delicacies included banana slices, peaches, crab, shrimp, fish cakes, spinach, corn, meats, chicken tetrazzini, and even martinis.

The meals were nested into sturdy, waxed cardboard boxes, each weighed out to a porter load of sixty-five pounds. They ended up with 416 boxes of food, each one numbered and color-coded for the chronological stages of the expedition.

The crew turned to packing the expedition gear. "We were paid something in cash for this," recalled Fred Dunham, an Ellensburg Sherpa, "though it wasn't enough to buy any of the Eddie Bauer gear we were packing." At the end of November, twenty-three tons of food and equipment were shipped by sea to Calcutta.

Sponsorships continued to trickle in. The Head company, founded by aeronautical engineer Howard Head, had recently developed the first widely available metal and wood-laminate skis; they donated thirty pairs. Pan American Airways offered $1,500 in exchange for thirty seconds of film coverage.

By December 1962, most of the expedition budget had been raised; the team was short by only $13,000. Still, some members dawdled in delivering their required personal contributions of $500. One invitee called Dyhrenfurth to ask if his share was still needed. Another pleaded to be released from this duty, as he was utterly broke.

"Most of you who profess to be destitute," Dyhrenfurth wrote in his July 1961 newsletter to the team, "seem to be able to squeeze in family trips and climbing expeditions without starving to death. I know from personal experience what problems you are facing. Ever since my first Everest trip in 1952, my family has moved from one crisis to another."

In a subsequent newsletter Dyhrenfurth admitted that he spent every waking hour (and many sleepless nights) "planning, scheming and praying." He apologized that some of his letters must have sounded "frightfully stern, schoolmasterish and exasperating." Dyhrenfurth wanted to climb more than Everest; the budget would need to cover the proposed climbs of Lhotse and Nuptse, too, to complete the "Grand Slam." And the West Ridge? Not at the expense of the other objectives, and not until more was known about it.

Jim Lester's grant from the Office of Naval Research was about to be activated, and he began by collecting baseline psychological data. In January 1963, one month before the team's departure, he summoned the Everest team to Berkeley for three days of testing at the Institute of Personality Assessment and Research (IPAR). Each member took tests and filled out questionnaires, and a battery of psychologists interviewed and observed them. Each of them was confidentially rated and ranked.

Lester—"Sigmund"—wanted to compile data about individual differences in attitude, values, personality, and life history, then examine those differences again under the stress of the expedition. The findings, once interpreted, would yield information about how the men responded to stress and how they differed from people in other reference groups.

Dave Dingman and Gil Roberts found the IPAR testing tedious. "MD's often have a dismissive view of such nonobjective research," said Dingman, "and I think Gil and I were sort of wiseasses about that. But we were that way about some other things, too."

The team members were curious if Lester could predict who would reach the top of Everest first. The answer would have to wait until after the expedition. One assessment that *did* leak out concerned the group as a whole. In the somber tones of an astrological reading, one IPAR researcher wrote: "Attempting to climb Everest affects people strongly, and seems to initiate fundamental changes that set them on unexpected paths." This vague but prophetic observation, neither ominous nor propitious, seemed to pulse through the group. If only in a small way, they just might be changed forever.

In the short term, Everest was bound to change them physically, too. At the nearby Lawrence Lab, not far from Berkeley's IPAR, nine of the climbers were recruited for a set of physiological tests conducted by team member Will Siri.

Siri had a nineteenth-century, Sherlock Holmesian air about him; his smoking pipe was his muse, and it accented his sober manner. In 1954, he'd led an expedition, of which Willi Unsoeld was a member, to Makalu, the world's fifth highest mountain. Siri's strength and Himalayan experience intrigued Dyhrenfurth sufficiently to name him deputy leader of the expedition.

Siri was a biophysiology researcher studying human responses to altitude. High-flying bomber aircraft were unpressurized at the time, and the air force wanted to understand and predict the effects on flight crews of spending long hours at high altitudes and of sudden elevation changes. The "bends"—the formation of nitrogen gas bubbles in tissues and joints occurring when air pressure drops rapidly—commonly incapacitated flight crews at altitudes above twenty thousand feet.

To show good faith in his research protocol (or because he was unable to find willing subjects), Siri himself had climbed into the Lawrence Lab's decompression chamber. The pressure was rapidly reduced to a simulated altitude of seventeen thousand feet. He spent four days battling headaches, nausea, and dizziness—symptoms of high-altitude sickness—and a battery of scientists took measurements while he made attempts at physical exertion.

Drawing the Everest team into his physiology research, as captive subjects in a realistic setting, was a delectable prospect. From each member, Siri extracted blood samples to establish baselines for levels of plasma iron, red cell volume, and erythropoietin, a hormone that controls red blood cell production.

While Siri was sealed in the decompression chamber, the United States was teetering on the brink of war. U.S. intelligence had discovered that the Soviet Union had provided Cuba with nuclear missiles capable of striking the Eastern Seaboard of the United States within minutes. The Cuban Missile Crisis had begun. Perhaps it was just as well, some climbers felt, that they were leaving the United States for a few months. What better place to seek refuge and safety than high in the Himalaya?

Chapter 9

To the Other Side of the Earth

*The first pitch was the absolute limit of human
possibility. The second pitch was even harder. But,
overcoming all, we attained to the place where the
hand of man has never set foot.*

—DICK IRVINE, FOUNDING MEMBER OF THE
RAG TAG PEAK BAGGERS ASSOCIATION,
QUOTED WITH UNCERTAIN MEMORY BY
BARRY CORBET

IN THE BERKELEY LABORATORY THE TEAM MEMBERS—LIKE THE
boxes of food—had been labeled and inventoried and were ready to
ship out. On the evening of February 2, 1963, they gathered at the
Hyatt House near the San Francisco International Airport. The next
morning, they lifted off in a Pan Am 707 with sky-blue stripes, bound
for Tokyo.

Like many who travel to South Asia, they were about to undergo a
transformation that begins on the airplane itself. Once airborne, a feeling arises of being in limbo between an old life—now suspended—and
a new life, charged with expectation and uncertainty. Tom Hornbein
withdrew some stationery and wrote a reflective letter to his wife, ex-
pressing a restless desire to come to grips with Everest, while compar-
ing the venture to his time in Pakistan in 1960, climbing Masherbrum.

After three years of civilized living I need proof even of my ability to tolerate such an environment once again. . . . I wonder

what lies ahead—not material, not objectives so much, but what is it I seek? And where on the mountain does it lie? Everywhere? Anywhere? There is something luring, no, *pushing* maybe, me on.

If Hornbein was tentative when departing the United States, his medical colleague, 1938 K2 veteran Charles Houston, was downright anxious. A few months earlier Houston had placed his private practice in Colorado on hold and set out for a two-year commitment to live and work in India. The Peace Corps' Sargent Shriver insisted that Houston was their man for India, and he had relentlessly cultivated and coerced him—just as he had zeroed in on climbing legends Bob Bates and Willi Unsoeld for Nepal.

"It suddenly occurred to me that I was going into God knows what," Houston wrote. "It washed over me afresh that I had abandoned my medical practice, my medical research. I wept. I despised my weeping. Which made me weep more. Which made me despise my weeping even more. God, what a trip."

The Pan Am jet refueled in Hawaii, and again on Wake Island. In Tokyo the team visited the Nikon camera factory, then gathered at the Japanese Alpine Club, where the members screened the film of China's disputed 1960 climb of Everest. The footage shed no light on China's claim of reaching the summit.

In Hong Kong, Gil Roberts and Dave Dingman hired rickshaws, placed their drivers in the passenger seats, and raced each other around the city. The team flew onward to Thailand, then India. Landing at Calcutta's Dum Dum Airport, they stepped from the plane into withering heat and humidity.

Dan Doody, Barry Bishop, and Barry's wife, Lila, had arrived in Calcutta ahead of the team, and were absorbed in clearing the expedition's sea freight consignment through Indian customs, in order to send it on to Nepal. Doody was transfixed by the dizzying kaleidoscope of urban India. He lost himself in streets thronged with cars, rickshaws, bicycles, donkeys, ox carts—"the whole history of transportation," he wrote in typed, carbon-copied dispatches to his relatives. "And on the sidewalks, totally disinterested in all that passed, lay hundreds of people sleeping beneath blankets, all their worldly possessions on them or under their arms. Someday, they will fall asleep in a doorway or on a sidewalk and not wake up. Their bodies will be collected and taken off to be cremated, their only hope that their next reincarnation might be better." Doody was ashamed to be spending $15 a day on room and board in a land where a family of four survived on less than that each month. Like many visitors, he felt a sudden urge to help, to offer something from his own meager belongings.

On the morning of February 8, 1963, Doody and the Bishops checked out of their hotel and drove to a *godown,* a warehouse on the edge of the city. They were met by six Tata trucks with Sikh drivers, their assistants, and a variety of officials assigned to oversee the loading of the twenty-three tons of gear into the trucks.

It would be too expensive to fly all the supplies from Calcutta to Kathmandu, so Doody and Lila would escort most of the trucks to Patna, closer to Nepal's border. There, the crates would be loaded onto a Royal Nepal Airlines propeller plane that would make a dozen shuttle trips to Kathmandu.

The vehicles traveled mainly on the Grand Trunk Road, a hair-raisingly congested and unpatrolled artery. Lila Bishop, self-sufficient and comfortable even when alone in India, luxuriated in the chaos; she had spent time in India and Nepal while her husband was doing research near Everest with Sir Edmund Hillary. Doody finally relaxed, now that his initiation into the distinctly nonwestern pace and lifestyle was complete. After serial stops for tea, naps, and lengthy train crossings, they arrived in Patna—having covered four hundred miles in thirty-seven hours.

Barry Bishop and a few of the trucks continued northward. His mission was to accompany the supplies that couldn't be transported by plane—oxygen cylinders, gasoline, and cooking gas—a trip that would take at least five days on a sometimes-impassable road.

The morning of February 3, 1963, the rest of the climbing team checked out of the Calcutta hotel and grabbed taxis back to Dum Dum Airport. Dave Dingman, a pilot as well as a doctor, was concerned by Royal Nepal Airlines' spotty safety record. He was relieved to see that their plane, waiting regally on the tarmac, was a DC-3. Known as a "Dakota" in England and Asia, DC-3s are among the safest aircraft ever built. This one's engines were dripping oil—reassuring Dingman that it was alive and functioning. He sat in an aisle seat near the front, and when they reached cruising altitude he politely asked if he could visit the cockpit.

"Surely, sahib," the steward said, and ushered him in. After introductions, the copilot insisted that Dingman take his seat, then disappeared into the back of the plane. The pilot nodded to Dingman, who took over for most of the flight.

The plane headed northwest over the fertile Gangetic Plain and its sacred river. Faces pressed to the circular windows as a labyrinthine web of villages and croplands passed below. The Appalachia-sized Siwalik Range, the first of the forested waves of foothills that herald the Himalaya, appeared in the distance.

"There they are!" one of the team members announced. The passengers rushed to the right side, rolling the plane briefly to starboard. They squinted at a thin, jagged white line stretching the breadth of the horizon: the Himalaya, Abode of the Snows. The range unfolded in a panorama stretching from Kanchenjunga in the east to Annapurna in the west, a span of 250 miles. Mount Everest barely stood above the others, but its singular plume of snow flew from the summit like a pennant. The sky above faded to blue-black darkness.

The Dakota throttled back as it passed over the rim of the Kathmandu valley. The team peered down at tidy, terraced fields and whitewashed houses with thatched roofs, meticulously arranged like features in a handcrafted diorama. Golden light glinted off pagoda roofs in the late afternoon sun.

The plane bounced onto Kathmandu's dirt airstrip. Norman Dyhrenfurth—who'd arrived two weeks earlier to clear the formalities—greeted the team and shot movie film. Elizabeth Hawley, a studiously dressed, no-nonsense American woman who had lived in Kathmandu since 1960 as a Reuters correspondent, stood near the front of the reception line, grilling the members as they deplaned. The American expedition was already big news in the small country.

They adjourned to the "International Terminal," an open-air shed flanked with battered trucks and antique touring cars. Their passports were stamped loudly while handbags and checked luggage were shouldered by dutiful porters.

The team rumbled into the city in vintage jeeps, skirting cows, pedestrians, pilgrims, pushcarts, and rickshaws. They passed houses built of sun-dried bricks and roof tiles quarried from nearby fields—structures that seemed to have sprung from the earth in spontaneous blooms of earthen red, gray, and ochre. A passable road had tentatively connected the Kathmandu valley with the outside world only seven years earlier, and the city hadn't grown accustomed to cars. Most were jalopies with patches on patches and welds on top of welds, heaving and wheezing about as if devolving merrily to a handmade world. Until 1956, every car in the valley had been brought over the foothills from India on bamboo palanquins, carried by scores of porters hunched over like pyramid-building slaves. In similar fashion, the cars were carried back for repairs.

It was only in 1950, after centuries of isolation, that Nepal had opened its doors to the outside world. A slow, medieval ambience still pervaded Kathmandu, even in the vicinity of the Royal Palace, a quasi-modern edifice that looked like a primitive attempt at building a futuristic shopping center.

The team's convoy of jeeps passed the palace bastions, turned a corner, and pulled into a sprawling compound where two guards dressed in white stood at stiff attention. At the foot of the drive sat the Hotel Royal, an ornate neoclassical former palace. The vehicles clattered into a porte cochere draped in blooming pepper flowers. Attendants appeared and promptly unloaded the group's baggage.

Hand-chiseled stone steps led to an outdoor landing where guests could pause before entering a drafty and poorly lit foyer, safeguarded by two mounted rhinoceros heads. To the right of the reception desk (which was attended only twice a day, when guests arrived and departed) a staircase swept up to a verandah, and to the Yak and Yeti Bar.

The matron of the Hotel Royal, a diminutive Danish woman, greeted the guests. She wore Tibetan clothing bought from recently arrived refugees, and her blond hair was wrung tightly atop her head into a bun that erupted in a burst of curls. A pet red panda sat near her when not wandering in and out of the rooms.

The high-ceilinged Grand Ballroom was furnished with threadbare oriental rugs and crystal chandeliers. Its walls were graced with splendid life-size portraits of the building's landlords and their ancestors: royals and generals in velvet ceremonial dress and plumed helmets.

To compensate for the lack of central heating, some of the rooms' floors were covered in tiger or bear skins. The heads were still attached, looking all the more gruesome as a result of shoddy taxidermy. Once checked into a room, a guest might notice constellations of holes puncturing the repoussé tin ceiling, configured in the outlines of arrows. The hotel staff explained that these were meant to release malevolent spirits.

The antiquated plumbing, when it worked, clanked and shuddered loudly enough to interfere with conversation, and the flow of water was sporadic. Lila Bishop recalled how rumors spread through the frigid hallways about the time of day—always unpredictable—when the pipes to the shared bathrooms might fill with hot water. This required a succession of rare events: After the water flowed through the city water pipes—seldom—and electricity flowed to the pump on the roof—intermittently—it would be heated in a rooftop tank, then released to the guests on a use-it-or-lose-it basis. Even if one was lucky enough to get the timing right, there might be no cold water to mix with the hot.

The hotel staff were commanded and coddled by the already legendary Boris Lisanevich. Boris, then in his midfifties, had been a solo performer with Sergei Diaghilev's Ballets Russes until 1929. He'd opened the "300 Club" in Calcutta in 1936, and in 1944 met Nepal's King Tribhuvan—who, in 1951, invited him to create Kathmandu's first luxury hotel. By the time Tribhuvan's son Mahendra rose to the throne in 1956, Boris was languishing in jail on the charge of distilling alcohol without a license. He was released when the authorities realized that no one else could properly cater the coronation festivities.

Boris had hunted tigers, and he kept a small menagerie of Asian wildlife—including a bear, pheasants, and wild boar—conveniently caged near the kitchen. The kitchen walls were black with soot, but the meals that emerged (including Boris's signature borscht) were exquisite. And while guests might criticize the standard of general cleanliness, the Nepalese were equally horrified by the foreigners' abhorrent habit of blowing their noses into pieces of cloth, then *placing the soiled cloth in their pockets.*

Guests at the Yak and Yeti Bar gathered around an elevated hooded fireplace in the center of the room. Beer and soda water weren't made locally, so most drank Scotch with Rose's Lime Juice. Boris presided, wearing one of the many striped madras shirts he'd had tailored in Calcutta. He was portly, yet floated across the room, invoking his days as a dancer. His hair, combed straight back with a part in the middle, accentuated his naturally bulging eyes.

Evenings in the Yak and Yeti Bar were rambunctious, and the Everest team enjoyed an audience of just enough women to inspire arm wrestling and one-arm pull-ups, fueled by a round or two of beverages. U.S. ambassador Henry Stebbins dropped by, and the team met the embassy's vice consul, Ron Rosner, who was clearly enjoying his "hardship" post. Rosner had mailed tracings of the Sherpas' feet to Dyhrenfurth, who had ordered mountaineering boots for them. Thirty-five Sherpas from the Everest area would be joining the expedition.

For Lila Bishop, an impressionable twenty-eight-year-old from Cincinnati, the scene was exotic to the point of being intimidating. "These large, intently focused men had work to do," Lila said, "moving about with broad shoulders in their blue sweaters with red and white stripes—planning, organizing, and packing, their attention consumed by a place even more distant than Kathmandu."

Venturing into the city's bazaar, the Americans were surrounded by monks and monkeys, by bronze temple bells, juniper incense, and vermillion powder offerings. They shared mutual glances of wonder with ornamented, turbaned—and sometimes ragged—hill villagers who were in the city on combined pilgrimages and shopping sprees. They ducked into dimly lit stalls of silversmiths, goldsmiths, woodworkers, and cloth sellers—shops so small that a man couldn't stand upright or turn around. Thrift and ingenuity were everywhere. The shopkeepers who sold electrical items could fix a burned-out incandescent lightbulb while you waited, by carefully removing the metal base and rewiring the filaments with tweezers.

"We were drawn to one temple," Jim Lester wrote, "where by candlelight, five old men were playing instruments, making an unholy but mesmerizing sound in the warm night air." Lester felt he had stepped into a fairy tale—an endless stage play set in an unfamiliar, but extraordinary, new world. Kathmandu, he saw, was a place where belief and imagination took form in art and architecture, a sacred valley where people led lives defined by ritual. It was a city where anything could happen—and just might, in the very next instant.

Chapter 10

Convergences and Close Calls

*In the long run, mountains have more effect on human
life than politics, and no government has been so
majestic or so long-lasting as the Himalayas. It is they
that made the Gurkhas brave and upright, while the
Ranas and the others came and went, not melting a
single glacier as they passed across the scene. No one
can say what lies ahead for the Nepalese in the
immediate future, as they find themselves tossed about
in the push and pull of political forces. So let us just
count them as the people of the Himalayas, now and
forever, and may they prosper.*

—CHRISTOPHER RAND IN A *NEW YORKER*
ARTICLE, "LETTER FROM KATHMANDU,"
1954

LEGEND SAYS THAT THE BUDDHIST DEITY MANJUSHRI SAW A JEWEL-
like, crystal clear lake in the middle of the Himalaya. He drained
it with a pass of his sword, creating the Kathmandu valley. Geologi-
cally speaking, the lake emptied recently: a mere twenty-five thousand
years ago.

One of Asia's richest cultures sprung from this fertile lakebed.
Terraced hillsides now encircle a basin where rice and mustard grow
in loamy soil one hundred feet deep. The Newar—the valley's native
ethnic group—forbade the use of beasts of burden, so farmers tilled
the land with plows pulled by barefoot humans. These were the first

urban farmers: They crafted their three-story townhouses from clay and wood, harmonizing their physical world with the ancient channels of spiritual energy that flowed along the natural features of the valley.

The Newar weren't just builders. They were also superior artisans, excelling in painting, bronze work, wood carving, and stone sculpture—religious art that articulates a unique blend of Hinduism and Buddhism. The love of ornamentation apparent on their temples, shrines, and stupas extended to their bodies. Women wore much of their family wealth in layers of necklaces, earrings, and nose pins, a more secure means of safekeeping than locking it up.

A family oligarchy—the Ranas—ruled the country for a century, from the mid-1800s to the mid-1900s. They arrived in the valley much later than the devout and artistic Newar, and forcible occupation was more on their minds than art or religion. The Ranas made Nepal's king their puppet and established an unusual line of succession that would assure the future of their lineage. The role of prime minister passed from brother to brother—or to the oldest male relative on the father's side. That meant power would never fall to a minor heir, a means of succession that has hastened the downfall of other dynasties.

When the Ranas abdicated in 1950, they left behind a populace that was proud and self-sufficient, but also isolated, poor, and illiterate. The people desired to see and to learn; to cease living like "frogs in the bottom of a deep well," as one former prime minister described his people. They wanted to catch up with wise and worldly India.

This would require money. But with no industries and nothing to export, Nepal faced a fiscal crisis. In 1958, the kingdom's foreign minister traveled to Seattle to meet with Secretary of State John Foster Dulles to ask for help. The United States was facing a budget deficit of $12 billion, and Dulles suggested that funds would be more readily available from the World Bank. The United States could, however, offer humanitarian aid.

A year later, King Mahendra made a state visit to the Soviet Union. He accepted an assistance package that included a printing press, which began producing books highlighting the warm friendship between the Soviet Union and Nepal. Not to be outdone, the U.S. State Department promptly invited the king to visit the United States, and in 1960 Mahendra met with President Eisenhower. Soon afterward, on Kathmandu's New Road—the capital's grandest boulevard—the U.S. Information Service opened an American library and stocked it with titles extolling American democracy and modernization.

A pattern was developing: The United States and the Soviet Union were more concerned with Nepal's strategic geography—as a buffer state between India and China—than with the needs of the country's people. To its neighbors, Nepal didn't account for much. Very few Chinese even knew where Nepal was, and most Indians assumed that it was a state of India.

Nepal's new prime minister, B. P. Koirala, also met with President Eisenhower and Secretary of State Christian Herter. Herter was aware that, in early 1960, Koirala had visited with Chairman Mao Tsetung in Beijing. Herter asked the prime minister whether the Chinese Communists had laid claim to Mount Everest. In reply, Koirala relayed details of his meeting with the chairman.

Mao, wearing his customary baggy suit, had impressed Koirala as a gentle and sensitive man. While discussing recent border disputes, the subject of Mount Everest arose.

"You have a name for the mountain?" the chairman asked.

"We have a name: Sagarmatha," Koirala responded. In truth, the government had not recorded a local name for the peak until the 1930s, when they concocted a Nepali moniker out of Sanskrit words that mean "head in the sky."

"No, it is Chomolingam, and it's in the territory of China," Mao said, offering a version of the Tibetan name. "But let us not call it Chomolingam," he continued. "Let us call it *Friendship Peak*."

Neither leader was willing to relinquish a claim to the peak, nor their names for it. This led Koirala to express concern over Nepal's tiny size and vulnerable position relative to China. Mao insisted that the reverse was true: that a small country, an underdog, could quickly rally international support and create trouble for China. In this way, the chairman said, Nepal had an advantage over China.

"I think this was said partly in joke, and partly in seriousness," Koirala later remarked.

Others, too, had tried to claim Everest, or at least a piece of it.

One memorable grab at the peak was made in 1962 by a small band of nervy, self-funded Americans seeking notoriety—or perhaps just a wild and reckless adventure.

Few of the '63 Everest team were aware of how close their attempt had come to being postponed—or scuttled—by an incident that had occurred only nine months earlier. In the spring of 1962, Dyhrenfurth had traveled to Kathmandu to finalize arrangements for the '63 expedition's Sherpas and porters. While there, the U.S. Embassy informed him that a climber named Woodrow Wilson Sayre—grandson of President Woodrow Wilson—and three of his colleagues had not returned from their attempt on Gyachung Kang, a peak close to Everest on the Nepal-Tibet border.

The embassy tried to organize an air search for the missing men. An embassy officer had collected passport photos from Sayre and his team, should they be needed to match names with bodies.

Dyhrenfurth, a veteran of three expeditions to the Everest area in the early 1950s, was the obvious choice to guide the search; most pilots wouldn't have known where to begin. The problem was that Nepal's three Pilatus Porters—high-performance single-engine Swiss airplanes—were languishing on the tarmac in Kathmandu, their Swiss pilots at home on leave.

As alternate plans were being made, the U.S. Embassy received another message. This one was relayed from the police post in Namche Bazaar, a village on the approach route to Everest. Sayre and his men had managed to crawl on hands and knees to the nearby Sherpa village of Khumjung, and were requesting evacuation.

Dyhrenfurth squeezed into a Bell helicopter with a Swedish pilot. Despite turbulence and heavy cloud cover, they were able to land in Namche. Woodrow Wilson Sayre, disheveled and emaciated, was loaded into the backseat. On the flight out, Sayre admitted to the very ruse that Dyhrenfurth had suspected: He'd secured permission to climb Gyachung Kang for the sole purpose of making a sneak attempt on Mount Everest.

Operating on a tiny budget and without oxygen or porters, Sayre's expedition had ferried their meager supplies to the Nup La, a twenty-thousand-foot pass on the Nepal-Tibet border. There, they'd diverted from their proposed route and made their way onto the rugged terrain of Tibet. From the West Rongbuk Glacier—in the shadow of Everest's West Ridge—they traversed to the East Rongbuk Glacier, arriving at the North Col. Sayre's party likely reached twenty-four 24,000 thousand feet before bad weather, a miserable bivouac, and a string of bad falls forced their retreat. Sayre was barely able to make it back into Nepal.

The team had gone undetected by the Chinese during their forty-five-day sojourn in Tibet, and subsisted on only twenty days' rations. When they returned to their base camp near Gyachung Kang, they found that their Sherpas had descended to the lower valley to report the four climbers missing. The Sherpas had taken all of the food with them.

Dyhrenfurth feared that if news of Sayre's outlaw attempt on Everest reached the press, a grave international incident would ensue—and permission for the '63 American climb would be in jeopardy. The Chinese were sensitized to any activity in the border region between Nepal and Tibet following China's occupation of the country and the Dalai Lama's escape to India, in 1959. Plus, the CIA had already begun supporting a clandestine Tibetan resistance movement against China, an operation that would continue until Nixon visited Beijing in 1972.

In the hospital, Sayre's unruly hair and piercing eyes gave him a feral look. With animated sincerity, he vowed to Dyhrenfurth that he wouldn't talk about his junket—at least until the official American Everest team reached Base Camp, nine months later. Ambassador Stebbins was livid. "The grandson of President Wilson lied to me," he fumed. (It was especially galling because Sayre's wife had been a classmate of his at Milton Academy.)

Within the month, however, Dyhrenfurth was contacted by Ralph Graves, an editor at *Life* magazine—who had persuaded Sayre to sell the story of his adventure. Dyhrenfurth promptly drafted a letter to President Kennedy, suggesting that a published account might even precipitate "a possible take-over of Nepal by the Chinese Communists, who have been looking for some pretext for quite some time."

A takeover of Nepal by China was unlikely. Nonetheless, later that same year the Chinese army would show frightening military strength along its border with India, escalating into the Sino-Indian War. *Life* finally agreed to delay publication of the Sayre story until late March 1963—when Dyhrenfurth and his team would be "safely" on the mountain.

For the 1964 release of Sayre's book, *Four Against Everest,* the publisher exaggerated the implausible—yet basically true—tale with a dramatic full-page display ad in *Publishers Weekly*:

> In 1962, four men made a secret dash into Chinese Communist Tibet. They were in constant danger of being shot or captured by the Reds, of starving, or of being crushed by the mountain itself. Their equipment: only the few articles carried on their backs!

The American Everest team fairly took over the cavernous Hotel Royal. With the addition of Colonel Jimmy Roberts, selected to be their transport officer, they were all finally gathered in one place. A balding, confirmed bachelor, Colonel Roberts had retired in Nepal after decades of service with the British army in South and Southeast Asia. Helpful and affable, he was also rather particular about things, in a British sort of way. In fluent Nepali he directed the Sherpas in organizing the nine hundred loads of supplies spread across the hotel grounds—and barked orders to the hotel staff, too, if they ventured near.

Gil Roberts (no relation to the colonel), as the expedition's medical officer, had compiled drugs and medical supplies in the States. He and fellow doc Dave Dingman concentrated on dividing it all into accessible units while puzzling out "what if" strategies for inevitable medical crises.

Dan Doody spent his days sorting through filming equipment. He met a young American woman who worked at the embassy, and the two of them began to spend time together. The group cheered him on; Doody, lanky and easily embarrassed, wasn't regarded as the team member most likely to attract women.

For the previous three months, Willi Unsoeld had been working in Kathmandu as deputy director of the Peace Corps. (Finally, after years of studying religion and philosophy, he could put into action the ethics he had ruminated on and had taught to college students.) He was swept up in training, and then overseeing, the first group of volunteers—a ragtag but enthusiastic bunch of schoolteachers and agriculture specialists who had been dispatched to remote villages on two-year assignments. The Nepalese had come to regard education as a stepping-stone to opportunity, and the rural hinterlands were beginning to awaken to the outside world. For many village children, Peace Corps volunteers—and climbers—were their first contact points with the strange and exciting universe that existed beyond their villages.

To his dismay, Unsoeld hadn't been formally released to join the expedition. His request for leave was still being processed, while paperwork from Washington, DC, and from field volunteers continued to pile up on his desk.

Dyhrenfurth and Bishop, the most experienced Himalayan hands, were well aware that the expedition wouldn't be possible without the Sherpas. Their skills included managing the lowland porters, carrying mail, buying local food, cooking meals, and route finding. When needed, the Sherpas also carried loads, and they would be the primary load carriers on the mountain, above Base Camp.

Thirty-five of the Sherpas selected for the expedition had hiked out to Kathmandu from their homeland of Khumbu, a community of villages at the foot of Everest. In the 1960s, the Nepal government required that negotiations for expedition Sherpas be conducted through an employment agency known as the Himalayan Society, which set the wages for various levels of labor. The expedition foreman received sixteen rupees per day (just more than a dollar in 1963), and a high-altitude porter less than half that—though they could earn substantial bonuses. The Sherpas were fed and clothed.

The society also functioned as a labor union, protecting the Nepalese Sherpas from the more experienced Darjeeling Sherpas, who might otherwise corner the best expedition jobs. The upwardly mobile

Darjeeling Sherpas had immigrated to India from Nepal a generation or more before, leaving their subsistence, pastoralist Khumbu relatives behind. The Nepal-based Sherpas treated their Darjeeling Sherpa brethren courteously, but warily.

Sherpas in one group tended to be related to Sherpas in the other, anyway. In Khumbu as in Darjeeling, Sherpa internal hierarchy was based on family ties. Kin were proffered for jobs before strangers, because a kickback or reciprocity likely would be involved. And veteran Sherpas tended to recommend their peers over younger blood, though the young Sherpas often showed superior strength and drive when climbing high.

Kancha, a Sherpa from Namche Bazaar, had been hired as a mail runner. It hadn't been easy securing the job. He and the other candidates had to submit to a physical at the Himalaya Society health post, and for every twenty Sherpas examined, they were told, only seven would be selected. "We were more frightened by this checkup than we were by the crevasses and avalanches," Kancha said. "We weren't worried about accidents or death—we were worried about not having work."

Few Sherpas had homes in the city. When they trekked to the Kathmandu valley, as many as twenty would rent the floor of a Newar home. They pooled their coins to buy food, which the women cooked over an earthen wood-stoked hearth. After eating (cross-legged on straw mats on the floor), they unfurled their blankets to sleep in an orderly line. In the morning they drank tea, stashed their bedrolls, and went to town.

"The problem," said Sange Dorjee, a Sherpa who traveled with such groups as a boy and now lives in Wyoming, "is that they drank a fair amount of *chang,* our local barley beer. *Chang* has a sweet smell when it's freshly brewed, but an altogether different smell in a roomful of healthy drinkers who seldom bathed, and had removed their boots. In Khumbu, the houses are cold and drafty, and we leave our shoes on. But when twenty Sherpas in the heart of a subtropical city remove their buffalo-hide boots in a musty apartment, the smell is *overpowering.*"

Three days before the team was scheduled to depart, Foreign Ministry officials were still demanding U.S. dollars (or pounds sterling) for payment of the permit fee and the wages for the expedition's liaison officer. Funds from *National Geographic* and the U.S. government had been provided in Indian rupees—the U.S. was awash in them—but Nepal's government wouldn't accept them. (Never mind that merchants in the bazaar preferred Indian over Nepalese rupees.) Dyhrenfurth shuttled between the cavernous ministry and the U.S. Embassy, breezing in and out of offices, desperate to find a way through the impasse.

Modern embassies wouldn't dream of functioning at the 1963 level of security of Kathmandu's U.S. Embassy. A single marine guard was posted on duty, and the windows of the rented two-story embassy building opened out onto a city alley. Many of the doors remained unlocked, and a private vehicle could drive, unimpeded, into the inner compound. This was remarkable considering that Russia and China were the U.S. Embassy's main diplomatic concerns, and the three embassies were largely absorbed in monitoring one another's activities. The CIA case officers in Kathmandu ended up spending most of their duty time recovering from hangovers—sustained from boisterous drinking bouts with their Russian counterparts. The relationship with the Chinese was different. "Our staff weren't on speaking terms with the Chinese," said Vice Consul Ron Rosner. "If we were introduced to their officials, we would not acknowledge them."

America's monitoring went beyond ground-level spying. Rosner recalls seeing the contrails of a high-flying jet, traveling west to east, far above Kathmandu—at an altitude that only America's U-2 spy plane could reach. The U-2's images of road construction in China would be especially useful to India. Rosner wondered if the Nepalese were aware of these flights. During World War II, one story goes, an American plane came spy-hopping over Kathmandu; the indignant prime minister, Juddha Shumsher, blasted away at it with his rifle.

After the 1960 incident in which a U-2 was shot down over Soviet airspace, South Asian countries wondered what surveillance tactics and subterfuge the Americans might try next. The easiest way to improve its profile in South Asia, diplomats figured, would be to offer humanitarian aid. In Nepal, early projects funded by the U.S. Agency for International Development (USAID) focused on education and health care delivery.

It wouldn't hurt America's image if they could reach the summit of Everest, too—and take some Nepalese Sherpas with them; none had yet reached the top. At the last moment, Nepal's Foreign Ministry—recognizing America as a faithful ally and (hopefully generous) future friend—allowed the expedition fees to be paid in Indian rupees. The team could embark for the mountain.

On February 20, 1963, nineteen team members finished their omelets and departed the Hotel Royal in a caravan of jeeps, trucks, and Land Rovers. They were heading to Banepa, a hamlet near the easternmost rim of the Kathmandu valley, twenty miles from the capital. Early morning light filtered through the poplar trees, with millet and wheat fields greening up on either side of the dirt road. A crowd had gathered at the end of the road—the beginning of the 180-mile trail to Everest. Farmers, merchants, schoolkids, local functionaries, Liz Hawley of Reuters, the embassy's Ron Rosner, Peace Corps volunteers, and hundreds of onlookers had come to see them off—or to simply behold the spectacle. It resembled the set for a movie with a biblical theme.

Jimmy Roberts had arrived in Banepa the previous day with the Sherpas and a fleet of trucks. When the team arrived, the expedition's twenty-three tons of gear were arrayed on a parade ground–sized field. The Sherpas were dividing the loads and transforming the chaos into a line of human beings a thousand strong. More than nine hundred of them were porters, and each wore a numbered tag that corresponded to a load. Colonel Roberts carefully jotted porter and load numbers in his ledger book. Nine *naikes*, or group leaders—generally men from the porters' village area who knew how to read—were assigned to manage the porters: roughly one *naike* per hundred, with a Sherpa overseer for each group.

Some of the loads would be consumed during the trek toward base camp. Colonel Roberts had gone so far as to match up porters with specific food loads that he expected would be used up at camps that were close to those porters' villages, so they could be paid off and dismissed near their homes. Shortly after 11 a.m., the porters moved out in single file, each load supported by a tumpline across a forehead.

Jake Breitenbach scribbled the closing words of a letter to his wife. He described life in Kathmandu, said that he loved and missed her, and glossed over the dysentery he'd been suffering since the day they arrived in Nepal. He handed the Wyoming-bound aerogram to an embassy official to send out in the diplomatic pouch.

Barry Bishop said good-bye to his wife, Lila. They spoke a few brief words.

"You know, I may not come back," Bishop said. His tone was matter-of-fact.

"It was unsettling," Lila said later, "because when he said that, I felt that something wasn't entirely right. I had a premonition that something might go wrong—and not necessarily for Barry. But I didn't get much more out of him. Back then, people didn't routinely share their emotions and deep inner feelings the way we do now."

Chapter 11

Treading a Path Between India and China

The reason that solitude seems so beneficial is that moving off into this remote mountain range you are able to simplify your life. You reduce stimuli until finally you are faced only with your own ego, and then it is a relatively simple step to jettison that awareness of self, fading out under the overpowering awe of this greatest of mountain ranges, and then you are not in the picture. What is left? The answer is ananda, *or* bliss, *the peace that surpasses all understanding and cannot be reduced to words.*

—WILLI UNSOELD, FROM A LECTURE
AT THE EVERGREEN STATE COLLEGE,
FEBRUARY 13, 1979

LIKE A MILLIPEDE WITH NEITHER HEAD NOR TAIL, THE LINE OF POR-ters rippled its way from Banepa toward the rim of the Kathmandu valley, passing over flagstones worn concave from a millennium of passing feet. The trail climbed gently past villages and descended through pastures and brushy drainages to the subtropical hamlet of Panchkhal.

The three-mile procession took two hours to pass, snaking into the terraced and forested hills to the east. The front of the line might arrive at the next camp, one climber suggested, before the last of the line left the previous camp. One climber quipped that it might work just as well if the porters simply lined up along the trail and *passed* the loads to the front of the line, hand to hand. "And when we reach Base Camp," he added, "we can pile up all the supplies, and climb that pile. The summit will be just a step across."

Food had been brought for the thirty-nine Sherpas. But how would the nine hundred–plus porters, who were responsible for their own meals, feed themselves? Many brought grains and potatoes grown in their villages, and cached additional rations in homes along the trail. Also, farmers from nearby drainages would appear at points along the trail, bearing grains and vegetables for sale. Word of the expedition sped mightily along the approach route (as it tended to in the absence of modern communication).

In addition to sixty-five-pound loads, the porters carried their personal belongings—typically a felted wool jacket, a blanket, and a bowl made of burl wood turned on a lathe, polished smooth from years of use. Every third or fourth porter carried pots and pans for their subgroup. Several women porters balanced babies atop their loads.

Few locals would turn down the opportunity for work; Barry Prather, the young Washington State climber and assistant to glaciologist Maynard Miller, guessed that a few of the porters were children. "I felt funny with my 30 pounds and their 65 pounds," he wrote in his diary. "But these people treat their jobs like our truck drivers back home—they really roll."

The porters' feet were protected by sole-length calluses as thick as buffalo hides. Few complained of sore feet or muscles, but cracked calluses were persistently annoying and painful. Along the trail the porters hummed, sang, whistled, chatted, chanted prayers, and let loose with salvos of laughter, everyone pulled along by the swell of their collective momentum. Compared to the sahibs, they owned little. Compared to other villagers they enjoyed decent wages, and they relished the break from farmstead chores.

Tom Hornbein described the site of their first camp as lovely and luxurious, surrounded by rolling, fantastically terraced hills. The beauty of the walk, he felt, exceeded that of Pakistan's enchanting Karakoram Range, which he'd traversed en route to Masherbrum.

Sargent Shriver, the director of the Peace Corps, released Willi Unsoeld from duty at the last possible moment. Unsoeld had spent the morning of February 20, 1963, clearing up his desk in Kathmandu. He caught up with the expedition on the trail at the edge of the valley.

Unsoeld favored his own Kelty pack over the expedition-issue brand, and the team noted his endearing nonconformity with a smile. Dyhrenfurth had appointed Unsoeld as the climbing leader, and some wondered if Dyhrenfurth might feel his leadership challenged by Unsoeld's dynamic presence. But Unsoeld had pinned Everest onto the wagging tail of a demanding life and had no notions of a leadership struggle. A heavy load of administrative tasks and the training of incoming Peace Corps volunteers had challenged even *his* substantial leadership skills, and struggles with balancing his work with family life had burdened him with about as much as a man could bear. He wanted a break from that role, and a retreat to the mountains. With the expedition's onerous organizational work in other hands, he could contemplate and sort through his own problems and find direction and focus for his life and career. Yet, challenges should be welcomed, he felt. They offered real-life opportunities, however uncomfortable, to explore the great philosophical teachings and to tap into his study of Eastern religions. En route to Everest, though, he knew one thing for certain: He was there on the trail, first off, for Hornbein and for Emerson, with whom he had made a pact. All for Everest, or none for Everest.

The expedition historian and scribe, James Ramsey Ullman, had also made a promise—to his doctors—that he wouldn't do anything overly athletic. Ullman, with his easy manner and quiet dignity (accentuated by his ready notebook and salt-and-pepper beard), quickly gained the friendship and respect of the climbers. He had written the novels *Banner in the Sky,* which became the 1959 Disney movie *Third Man on the Mountain,* and *The White Tower,* which was adapted as a film starring Glenn Ford and Lloyd Bridges. His history of mountaineering, *High Conquest,* served as Tom Hornbein's literary escape hatch during his youth in the Midwest; it affirmed that a climber's real reward comes in the form of self-knowledge and inner strength. "It is not the summit that matters," Ullman writes in conclusion, "but the fight for the summit; not the victory, but the game itself."

Jim Ullman had climbed with Norman Dyhrenfurth in the Tetons during the 1940s, and in the 1950s they had scrambled up Breakneck Ridge, overlooking the Hudson River. Now they were headed to Everest. Finally. In the late summer of 1960—long before permission for '63 had been granted—an editor at *Sports Illustrated* had phoned Ullman at his Manhattan apartment to ask if he would like to tag along, as correspondent, with an American group that was hoping to climb Everest. Ullman had guessed that Dyhrenfurth was its leader, and jumped at the chance. Dyhrenfurth was an unstoppable force, Ullman knew, and this was no idle invitation.

Ullman was regarded as a full-fledged team member, but he was recovering from two recent operations for peripheral vascular disease. The team was only a few miles along the trail, and now they were abruptly forced to bid him farewell.

"Jim Ullman had been a smoker, and the blood supply to his feet and legs was terrible," said Dave Dingman, who'd been selected to tell him that it would be best to stay behind and write about the expedition from Kathmandu. "Even if we *carried* him to Base Camp he wouldn't have survived there. I pictured having to amputate his leg in some remote, mountainous location. Gil Roberts and I laid down the law."

Ullman's departure was painful for all, but the climbers promised to write and to update him over the radio. The mail runners could deliver expedition updates to him, and the team allowed him to glance at their letters home—missives that might contain observations even more candid than their diaries.

From Kathmandu, Ullman flew to New Delhi, where the *Times of India* found him in the hospital, undergoing treatment. Under the headline MOUNTAIN BECKONS—BUT FLESH IS WEAK, the paper reported that Ullman was "55 and, according to his wife, old enough to stay away from mountains." It would be a month before he and his wife could return to the Hotel Royal to live in tattered luxury while awaiting the radio calls from Base Camp at five o'clock each evening.

Aside from sunburned legs, blisters, and diarrhea, the approach march wasn't exactly hardship. The Sherpas unfolded tables and chairs—lawn party style—and erected tents, blew up air mattresses, and laid out sleeping bags with the sahib's pajamas set upon them. Throughout, it remained a mystery how the cooks could wrap up a meal, rush ahead on the trail, and have the next meal ready in time for the team's arrival.

"So many extras," Unsoeld remarked, "yet we're in considerable danger of running out of toilet paper." A runner was dispatched to bring more from Kathmandu. They did, however, have purified drinking water. Drawing from medical technology, Hornbein had developed a high-capacity water filter powered by gravity that delivered ten gallons in less than two hours.

The expedition meandered through villages, skirted millet and corn fields, and ascended through pine forests. From the tops of passes they gazed southward across layers of ridges, each a paler shade of bluish purple, until the whole collage melted into the haze of the Gangetic Plain. To the north, the peaks drew them like a magnetic force. The summits, when visible above the clouds, were so startlingly white that camera film couldn't handle their contrast against the rocky ridges and forests below.

Raised umbrellas helped deflect the sun's rays, but the team members sweated heavily—an American habit, it seemed. The loaded porters barely perspired and seldom drank water. When they congregated with their loads at wayside tea stalls they drank mainly tea or *chang*: unfiltered barley beer. Though the food boxes contained plenty of instant coffee, the team came to prefer tea, which is less dehydrating.

The camp shuffled to life before sunrise with the crackle of wood fires, clatter of pots and pans, and coughing and throat clearing (hacking up deeply lodged phlegm was an essential part of the lowland porters' morning ablution). Some chanted prayers and mantras. As the tents were pulled down—sometimes prematurely, with the climbers still in them—the first vanguard of porters merged onto the trail, pushed along by the pressure of those behind them. Songs and banter filled the mornings, and after *chang* stops, arguments sometimes broke out over hierarchy, infidelity, or unpaid debts. Some porters were enmeshed in clan feuds that would erupt on the trail, and end with men brandishing their T-shaped walking sticks at each other in a tense standoff.

At the riverside village of Dolalghat, Unsoeld, Emerson, and Hornbein floated a short stretch of the Indravati River on their backs as the sun dropped behind the ridge. Above the far bank, they saw a group of identically dressed Chinese surveyors lounged next to a cluster of white canvas tents. It was the local base of operations for a road that Red China (as Americans referred to it) was building from Lhasa—the Tibetan capital—to Kathmandu.

Back at camp, the expedition's liaison officer passed along a note that a Chinese engineer had handed him. In English, it said that taking photographs of the work site—especially the bridge that was under construction several hundred yards downstream—was strictly prohibited.

Dan Doody deduced that the road would offer a convenient route for China to invade Nepal—or secure a byway to India. On the far shore, a small drill rig—a jarringly foreign object in this pastoral environment—was positioned for digging the foundation of a bridge abutment. "The footing dug on this side would make a nice latrine," one climber mused in his diary. "I might go down in a short while and utilize this facility."

The Sino-Indian War had tentatively concluded only three months earlier, but China's border with India remained unclear. All that existed was an outdated agreement between India (drawn up when it was a British colonial state) and the Dalai Lama's government—neither of which China recognized. China still regarded India as having obstructed the "peaceful liberation" of Tibet by supporting the uprising of Tibetans and harboring the Dalai Lama.

In November 1962, Chinese troops had surged over the nebulous border. India panicked and called upon Britain and America for help. The United States, which wanted to secure India as an ally, promptly flew C-130s and C-119s ("flying boxcars") into Calcutta and other airports.

U.S. vice consul Ron Rosner feared that the Chinese could have stormed down one of the river valleys that transect the Himalaya near Everest. Or they could have invaded by air. "We urged the Nepalese to take defensive measures," Rosner said, "such as parking vehicles on the runway of the Kathmandu airport at night." Within a month, India and China made concessions, but tension between the two countries congealed into a cold war that has lasted to the present day.

The American climbers at the riverside camp—also engineers of a sort—were driven by goals surely as obscure to the Chinese bridge workers as the Chinese objectives were to the Americans.

A vague suspicion was brewing among some of the climbers, especially those who distrusted Red China's geopolitical intentions. Could the Chinese have indeed summited Everest before the Americans?

China conducted its first reconnaissance of Everest in 1958 and proposed a joint Chinese-Soviet expedition for the following year—possibly propelled by rumors that India planned to dispatch a team to Everest in the spring of 1960. They wanted to get there before the Indians did.

A road had been constructed across Tibet to the remote Rong-buk monastery, at 16,000 feet on the north side of Everest. Trucks and jeeps could now drive all the way to Base Camp, a few miles beyond the Buddhist lamasery. But in 1959 a popular revolt among Tibetans—known as the Lhasa uprising—led the Soviets to cancel their participation. That March, while the Dalai Lama escaped into exile in India, the Chinese mountaineers redirected their efforts to 24,750-foot Mustagh Ata, in distant Xinjiang Province. Everest would have to wait until the following year.

In an account published in the *Alpine Journal,* Shih Chan-chun wrote that the 1960 Chinese expedition consisted of 214 climbers (a third of them Tibetan) and included peasants, People's Liberation Army soldiers, farmers who had just been freed from serfdom in Tibet, teachers, scientific researchers, and government functionaries. The supporting cast numbered well over one thousand.

Shih's account said that when the first scouting group set out from base camp, hurricane winds were raging around Everest's upper slopes. "The North Col was shrouded in dense fog. Tornados tore past the slopes and churned up huge columns of snow." When the weather cleared they made gradual progress over a period of weeks. Then at 4:20 a.m. on May 25, 1960, "with great excitement Konbu drew from his rucksack the five-star national flag and a small plaster bust of Chairman Mao Tse-tung, placed them on a boulder and secured them with small stones."

Beijing announced that a party of three—two Chinese and one Tibetan—had climbed the mountain. Shih attributed their success to "the fidelity of our mountaineers to the Communist Party and the people, [and] their confidence in victory of the revolutionary cause." Their team also claimed to have found the bodies of Maurice Wilson, the solo British climber who was lost on the mountain in 1934, and possibly Andrew Irvine, who disappeared with George Mallory in 1924, headed toward Everest's summit.

The international climbing community was skeptical of these Chinese claims. They had arrived on the summit in pitch darkness, so no photos existed. T. S. Blakeney, editor of the *Alpine Journal*, cited inconsistencies in their highest-elevation photograph, and in the vagueness of topographic detail.

Presumably if the Americans were to reach the summit and find the bust of Mao, the issue would be settled. But the primary motive of the Chinese expedition may not have been to *leave* an object on the summit at all. They may have wanted to *remove* one.

The convoluted story behind this theory did not emerge until twenty years later, in the form of a book titled *Spy on the Roof of the World*, by Sydney Wignall. In 1955, two self-funded British explorers—John Harrop and Wignall—sneaked into an isolated region of western Tibet. Wignall had volunteered to serve as an informant for an Indian Army general who was keen to gather intelligence about a possible Chinese military buildup in western Tibet.

After trekking for weeks through northwestern Nepal, Wignall, Harrop, and their young Nepalese liaison officer arrived on the Tibetan Plateau. They had reached the base of the seldom-glimpsed Gurla Mandhata, a spectacular peak they hoped to survey and possibly even climb. Within two weeks, though, they were captured by soldiers of the People's Liberation Army and held in crude, frigid prison cells for more than a month. Wignall was accused of spying—not for Britain or India, but for the American CIA.

Their captors were relentless in extracting confessions about their assignment and motives. At one point Wignall was brought before Chinese general Chang Kuo-hua, the "Butcher of Tibet," who had commanded Tibet's occupation. Hoping to attain their release from the primitive prison, Wignall made up a story about a UK-based spy ring operating on behalf of the American CIA. He told them that the CIA's mission was to plant high-tech surveillance devices on remote Himalayan peaks as a means of locating Chinese military bases and tracking their activities. To some extent, he said, this mission had already succeeded.

In a fanciful elaboration, Wignall told his captors that two years earlier—in 1953—Edmund Hillary and Tenzing Norgay had succeeded in placing a spy apparatus on the summit of Mount Everest. The device was aimed at Lop Nur, a known Chinese military base in northern Tibet. The power to operate the device, he explained, would last a lifetime: It was fueled by a small amount of uranium 235.

Wignall was surprised by how readily his Chinese captors believed him. Indeed, he had only confirmed their suspicions. He went on to elaborate that, just as the Chinese had suspected, the metal cylinders that Hillary and Tenzing carried to the summit were not oxygen bottles, but uranium canisters.

Wignall was convinced that he had "placed in their minds the seeds for what was to become the largest, most expensive and most incompetent attempt on Mount Everest ever made." Two decades later, he recounted, he met a Chinese Nationalist Party agent who admitted to him that the 1960 assault on Everest was cover for a huge military exercise designed to locate and destroy American surveillance equipment. "It failed on all accounts," the agent told Wignall. "They didn't even get to the top of the mountain."

Prior to their 1960 Everest extravaganza, the Chinese didn't exhibit much interest in mountaineering. Wignall was later intrigued to learn that the two other peaks the Chinese climbed between 1955 and 1960—the five years following his "confession"—were precisely the peaks where he said the CIA had placed surveillance devices.

By 1960, the Chinese were convinced that the Indians were planning a siege-style assault on Everest, led by Brigadier Gyan Singh of the Indian Army, with climbers from the military-sponsored Himalayan Mountaineering Institute. Were the Indians staging the climb to refuel or repair the spy device that Hillary and Tenzing had left on the summit? One account said that the Chinese climbers packed pistols as they headed toward Everest's summit—presumably in the event that they encountered the Indians on top.

The Indians, climbing from the Nepal side of Everest, may have been blissfully unaware that the Chinese were on the other side of the mountain at exactly the same time. But the Indian climbers were turned back by weather only seven hundred vertical feet short of the summit—the same storm that may have hobbled the Chinese team.

Understandably, the Chinese didn't want to return from Everest empty handed. The 1960 expedition had been launched during the frenzy of the Great Leap Forward, and the team could expect that a false report wouldn't be questioned by Beijing.

Chapter 12

Goals and Roles

*If the patient, persistent efforts of a few men, striving
in unity to attain such a goal as Everest, fortified in the
attainment of their ideal by many others, can result in
victory, can we not equally apply this power to solving
other problems, less lofty but more pressing, in this
sorely troubled world?*

—Sir John Hunt, leader of the 1953
British Everest Expedition

EXPEDITION PSYCHOLOGIST JIM LESTER WAS ENTRANCED BY THE
rugged yet delicate beauty of the landscape, as if it sounded chords
that aroused his sense of musical arrangement. He began "to find pleasure in the color of a wall, to notice how the angles fit together as
you look down a path through a village, or to notice how your mood
changes depending on how far you can see—all this is intensely *re-
freshing* in a strange way. Some people call it seeing again as a child
sees, as if for the first time."

Lester's dreams had turned astonishingly vivid. He noted that several members of the team reported dreaming of their childhoods, and
of long lost places and people. A few reported the appearance of a
red-haired woman in their dreams, a coincidence that Lester was at
a loss to explain. More of their dreams were in brilliant color, too, as
if they were storing up a mental palette in preparation for the chromatic monotony of the mountain. They were headed to a place of

stark contrasts, of supreme darkness and intense light, largely devoid of indigenous life.

It was February 21, 1963, and the expedition was two days into the approach march. Above the hamlet of Dolalghat, the trail steepened into an uphill grind of five thousand vertical feet. They crossed a pass, then descended to a river where Unsoeld and Hornbein stopped for "a freezingly delightful swim motivated by an initial overall soaping to insure against faintness of heart," Hornbein wrote. "Most skin-tingling invigorating, hurting the feet at first and the testicles next, but supplying a wonderful mood to the last hour of walking."

At first, Dan Doody felt uneasy about being referred to as "sahib" and being served by the Sherpas. The Sherpas were supportive and attentive, yet supremely self-assured. To decline their help would suggest that their services were below par or not needed. Doody was fascinated by the much poorer lowland porters, and was tormented to see women carrying such heavy loads. They were tragically underpaid, he felt, and privately he wouldn't have minded if the porters had gone on strike. This might or might not have worked. Porters were subject to free market forces. If one didn't like the pay (and most did, at least in 1963), an eager replacement would jump in to fill the vacant spot.

The Sherpas, on the other hand, were familiar with labor strikes and were skilled at making it work for them. Situations of urgency, when their help was most needed, presented the best opportunities to strategically withdraw their services—a useful bargaining tool.

Dyhrenfurth had given Doody free rein in the filming, with no script or shooting schedule, but he did want Doody to get shots documenting the expedition's progress. Doody tended to turn his camera, though, more on the local people and village scenes. Dyhrenfurth grew increasingly dissatisfied with Doody's errant creative ideas, and tensions between them grew.

One afternoon, the two filmmakers witnessed a horrifying event. At the bottom of a steep hill they were obliged to cross an ancient hanging bridge made from hand-forged iron chain links. Doody set up his camera to film the porters as they crossed. Dyhrenfurth pointed out a link of the chain that had separated into a C. It had been that way for some years, the porters assured them. Dyhrenfurth suggested they build some cinematic suspense around the link. He scrambled down the bank to the riverbed while Doody filmed from above. The first dozen porters, wary of the bridge's fragility, moved across slowly. But this caused those behind them to pile up and begin to push.

Doody was changing lenses when he heard noises and shouts. The weak link had failed. Planks from the bridge were strewn everywhere, and one of the bridge's suspending chains hung down uselessly. Eleven men, each carrying a full load, had fallen into the river or onto the bank—a drop, fortunately, of only ten feet. Three men were swept downstream as they struggled to get free of their loads. All three eventually made it safely onto the bank.

The three doctors—Dave Dingman, Gil Roberts, and Tom Hornbein—had trekked on ahead, but were alerted. They ran back two miles to attend to the injured. Eight porters required medical attention, with bruises, cracked ribs, and a couple of badly cut heads. "After thorough cleansing and bandaging," Hornbein wrote, "all were able to hobble stoically under their own steam. Truly a miracle of good fortune." Those who could not carry loads would still receive their six rupees per day. "No complaints, no lawsuits, no insurance," Doody commented.

Several porters suggested that the bridge collapse was an ominous event, and spoke quietly of what might befall the expedition next. That evening, Jake Breitenbach wrote to his wife, "The phenomenal luck we've been experiencing has lessened, at least to some degree."

In the village of Kirantichhap (pronounced like "karate chop"), a crowd gathered to watch the men do practice climbs—bouldering—on the spreading banyan tree in the center of the village. In the evening, the team convened at their nearby campsite to discuss expedition objectives—the first of several democratic team meetings.

Willi Unsoeld felt that the expedition, with its space-age budget and exceptionally strong party, needed a worthy challenge. He was referring to the West Ridge. After only two successful expeditions to the summit via the South Col, by the British and the Swiss, that route had been nicknamed "the Milk Run." It offered a relatively certain, though weather-dependent, path to the summit and a reliable ticket to at least modest prestige and recognition. To the climbers who were intrigued by the West Ridge, however, that kind of secondhand victory was less fulfilling than a quest into the unknown. Dave Dingman framed the issue bluntly: "Would you rather fail while exploring the West Ridge, or reach the summit by the South Col?"

"His question was oversimplified," Emerson said later, "for success was far from assured even by the South Col—and we did not *know* we would fail by the West Ridge. I'm sure psychologist Jim Lester had a field day watching people wrestle or rationalize their way through Dingman's question." Dyhrenfurth, as expedition leader, didn't mind the discourse. But he feared that if the West Ridge prospect leaked to the public or the press, it would raise questions among the sponsors who were banking on them delivering the summit by whatever route possible.

"Early in the discussion, Tom Hornbein made an impassioned plea for abandoning all other objectives in order to throw our full force onto the West Ridge," Willi Unsoeld later recalled. "In a mood of considerable horror at such extremism, the expedition quickly: (1) voted down Tom's suggestion, (2) decided on the summit via the South Col route as the primary aim, with the West Ridge as a strong secondary goal, and (3) labeled Tom a 'pathological fanatic' for his single-minded dedication."

As climbing leader, Unsoeld couldn't betray his strong favoritism for the West Ridge. Hornbein became his proxy voice, and together they lobbied, one diplomatically and the other boisterously, to keep the West Ridge option alive.

Adding an attempt via the West Ridge would entail more than simply shifting gears once (and if) the South Col was climbed. A serious reconnaissance—and the tiresome effort of establishing a route and ferrying supplies—would have to be engaged from the outset, concurrent with the South Col push. The expedition's limited resources, however, might not be sufficient for two climbing objectives. Some feared that adding the West Ridge would weaken the chances of reaching Everest's summit by *any* route.

But risk and uncertainty can be managed. Dick Emerson—in charge of logistics—was building enough flexibility into his elaborate load-delivery scheme to support both routes. In long evening sessions, he and Hornbein refined the logistics even further, allowing for different-sized parties on each route and inevitable changes in plans. For both routes, they would need to build a pyramid of supplies, from the lower camps on up, so that the highest camps would have food and fuel—and especially oxygen—when the time came for a summit push: "Okay, four men for three days at Camp 5 (allowing for bad weather to stand-fast); two bottles each for assault; one bottle per two-man night for sleeping; four bottles 'emergency.' That gives $8 + 6 + 4 = 18$ bottles at about 13 pounds each. . . ."

Colonel Jimmy Roberts, an old hand at this sort of planning, grinned as he looked on. "We could almost read his thoughts," Emerson wrote. *"Bloody ambitious, these young Americans."*

Climbing the West Ridge would demand skill on both snow and rock at high altitude. But the rocky ridges up high seemed configured in a huge question mark. Oxygen, load deliveries, weather, personal dynamics, the climbers' health, and the Sherpas' level of dedication—all were unpredictable. These weren't big enough questions, though, to deter seven of the team. Hornbein, Unsoeld, and Emerson were already committed to the West Ridge route; Dingman, Corbet, Bishop, and Breitenbach signed on as well. For Breitenbach, the West Ridge was the only way he would have it—his road less traveled, a supreme challenge to aspire to and work away on, whether he made it or not.

Hornbein noted a curious distinction between the personalities and backgrounds of the West Ridgers compared to the South Colers. Five of the seven self-selected West Ridge crew were veteran Tetons climbers. All tended to be more adept at climbing on rock than on snow. Not surprisingly, the upper reaches of the West Ridge presented more bare rocky pitches than the South Col, which is traveled almost entirely on snow. Also, the West Ridgers were more attracted in general to the untried and the untraveled. Risk takers. And they tended to excel at individual sports: skiing, small boat sailing, kayaking, flying. The "South Colers" gravitated toward team sports. Hornbein and Jim Lester were intrigued by this coincidence and wondered if any conclusions could be drawn from it.

In mountaineering, goals are palpable: a summit of snow or rock, or a new route to that summit. Motivations, on the other hand, are less clear—even to the climbers themselves. Spiritual quest. Escape. Self-understanding. Triumph. For some, it might be penance. For others, it's recreation—a gaming challenge, an artificial pursuit in which the rules are configured to present the *ideal* level of uncertainty.

On one level, the West Ridgers may have been drawn by glory—the historical high note that would be played should they knock off a new route to the top of the world's highest peak. But Hornbein, like Jake Breitenbach, felt that a desire for recognition or prestige might interfere with the purity of the mountaineering challenge. In his introspective, philosophical way, Hornbein puzzled over the extent to which a vainglorious motive might have crept into his own pure love of the mountains. The motive that most appealed to him was clear: companionship among friends, working together in a shared struggle. The Brotherhood of the Rope.

Chapter 13

Intersecting Worlds

*We had been for some forty days in a part of the world
seldom visited by Europeans. We had marched
150 miles or more over rough mountain trails to the foot
of the highest mountain in the world, there to find a
small community, centered in religion, self-sufficient,
self-respecting, healthy, and happy. In all our travels we
had met nothing but friendliness and courtesy. Our
eyes had been opened to a different way of life, a
different religion, and our minds to different thoughts
and motives.*

—CHARLES HOUSTON, ON VISITING THE
SOUTH SIDE OF MOUNT EVEREST IN 1950,
WITH THE FIRST PARTY OF FOREIGNERS

SWEAT DRIPPED FROM EYEBROWS INTO DARK GLASSES AS THE TEAM
climbed to Chyangma, a pass at nine thousand feet. The small patch
of level ground was crowded with mani walls: rows of flat stones incised with Buddhist prayers and arrayed as offerings to deities that
are believed to frequent breezy passes and high places. From there,
they could see Lamjura—*another* pass, twelve thousand feet high. But
to reach it they would first have to drop several thousand feet to the
river below.

Pownall and Bishop took a side trail to a small Swiss-built cheese
factory. They bought a wheel evocative of a flavorful Gruyère, made
from the milk of *naks,* yak cows. The brother of one of the 1956 Swiss

Everesters oversaw the factory, which had been conceived as a means to help subsistence herders and farmers generate income. It worked, though some of the local Nepalese wouldn't consume this "scientific" cheese: It was made with rennet, extracted from the fourth stomach of an unweaned calf—the sacred cow of the Hindus. Diplomats in the capital, however, coveted "yak" cheese, and the factory had it carried by porter to Kathmandu for sale. U.S. Embassy staff traveling to India sometimes carried a wheel of it for Ambassador John Kenneth Galbraith in New Delhi.

At the campsite beyond Chyangma, smoke from the porters' evening campfires settled into a ground-level haze, wreathing the dusk in softness. When night fell the porters huddled, squatting, absorbing warmth from a constellation of a hundred fires. A few amber lights twinkled near the hamlet where they would camp the next day. To the north, the tops of snowcapped peaks loomed over the hillsides like giant magnolia blossoms.

At the apex of the eight-thousand-foot vertical climb to Lamjura pass, ice-encrusted prayer flags flapped gently from rhododendron trees just emerging into bloom. Hornbein and Unsoeld padded through a strange and unusually silent mist, into "a shrouded forest of gnarled, chaotically arranged, moss-draped and snow-buried trees, along a thin winding track made icy brown by many feet, some barefoot and impervious to the cold. The mood was one of indescribable aloneness."

At every overnight stop, Gil Roberts and Dave Dingman held evening medical call for villagers. By the time they erected and stocked the makeshift clinic tent, fifty or more people had lined up to present bruises, abscessed teeth, parasites, broken bones, double pneumonia, infections, and tuberculosis. "Witnessing the scope and severity of the medical problems of rural Nepal," Dingman would say, "largely inspired my later surgery work in the Third World." The doctors offered what little they could, knowing it would never be enough. Follow-up visits would be needed but were not likely to occur. To bring lasting change to Nepal's public health, historian Jim Ullman pointed out, "would require not the ministrations of transients, but social change, measured in generations."

In the village of Junbesi, in the lowland Sherpa territory known as Solu, a badly injured woman appeared at the clinic just before sunset. A few days earlier, a kerosene pressure lantern had erupted into flames in front of her, and her face and arms were charred with third-degree burns. She was lucky to be alive but would likely die of infection—and certainly would not survive being carried all the way to Kathmandu. At the age of forty-nine, one climber noted, she had already lived longer than most Nepalese.

Norman Dyhrenfurth's soft heart prevailed. An evacuation helicopter should be summoned, he felt, and the $500 cost paid by the expedition. Gil Roberts agreed. "As an MD, one sees and treats diseases like TB every day, but something dramatic like this snaps one back to a sense of Western idealism." They asked their radio operator, Al Auten—the last member to be selected for the expedition—if he could send a message to Kathmandu.

"It would normally have been impossible to find the radio set among the nine-hundred-plus boxes," Auten said, "but in anticipation of something like this I had spray-painted fluorescent triangles on opposite corners of the three radio boxes before we departed Kathmandu. I found the boxes, extracted the radio, threw up thirty-odd feet of the sectional wire antenna, and worked on firing it up."

Auten, of average height and build, was introverted and self-deprecating to a fault. But his professional background had bordered on the intrepid. During his last year of high school in Springfield, Illinois—Al was another Midwesterner—World War II broke out. He joined the navy, which gave him an opportunity to play with the technical side of radios.

Auten had found his passion. After the war, he mastered Morse code and ham radio operation. He saw a job opening for a technician with a commercial radio operator's license, and was hired by the Denver Research Institute. With a small crew, he drove around in a Jeep station wagon setting up recording stations as explosives crews posted miles away would trigger large explosions. Auten and his team measured the shock waves that bounced off the atmosphere. "We knew of no hard objective to this testing," he said, "but I *was* aware that various countries were experimenting with nuclear bombs."

In the early 1950s, Auten spent three months near the town of Darwin, Australia, recording atmospheric waves from atomic bomb tests in the South Pacific. "Our sensors were so sensitive that we could place the unit on a table and then on the floor, and measure the difference in barometric pressure. The thunderstorms that came through swung the meters from one end of the gauge to the other."

The blasts were triggered several thousand miles away, near Bikini Atoll. Standing outside the station, Auten could feel the distant blasts—which again sent the needles skittering off the paper. "We learned that if anyone were to set off a nuclear explosion anywhere in the world, America would know about it. There was no place on the planet where even a small atomic bomb test could go undetected."

In 1961, Norman Dyhrenfurth came to Denver to present a program about his planned Everest expedition. Auten asked Dyhrenfurth what he planned to do about two-way communications.

"Well . . ." A pained look crept onto Dyhrenfurth's face.

Three weeks later, Auten received a special delivery letter from Dyhrenfurth, inviting him to join the expedition.

The woman with the burn was in luck: Auten's radio set worked. "Most of the stations we contacted," Auten said, "were in Australia or New Zealand. I reached one guy who had just set up his ham radio set and wanted to know how *his* system was working. I asked him to send a message to Kathmandu through the U.S. Embassy in Australia, requesting that a helicopter be sent." Someone in the embassy message chain suspected that it was a fraudulent notice, but it was eventually believed. The helicopter arrived and the burn victim was evacuated to Kathmandu.

By whipping up the complicated radio rig on such short notice, Auten's stock shot up among the group—though he wasn't entirely comfortable with the unexpected attention. "I don't always like to talk to people," Auten admitted to Dave Dingman. "I enjoy doing Morse code."

Radios were the expedition's sole means of connection to the outside world. Auten was concerned that, once under way, the team would have no access to replacement parts, and electrical power would be unreliable. He'd selected equipment with a low power demand, and included a generator that could charge twelve-volt automotive batteries. For the mountain, he'd selected robust walkie-talkies—"idiot-simple models, with an on-off switch and volume control."

Modern communications had only recently begun to connect Nepal's far-flung districts to the Kathmandu valley. The ruling Ranas and the Hindu caste aristocracy regarded the outlying areas as primitive backwaters, and lorded over them in the manner of a family estate. The rulers were famously inattentive to the people's needs, and their appointed staff rarely visited their posts. Development—education, especially—might lead villagers to become politically active, so the government thought it best to leave them be. The Rana oligarchy was overthrown in 1950, but thirteen years is recent history in remote hill time.

The expedition also used the traditional medium of rural communication: word of mouth. Mysteriously, this seemed to outrun the mail runners who carried news and letters to and from Kathmandu.

On March 4, 1963, the team descended to the Dudh Kosi ("Milk River"), and crossed a rickety, Dr. Seussian bridge made of logs cantilevered high over a raging slot canyon. Spooked by their earlier experience, the team strung ropes for use as a handrail and safety line. As at previous bridges, the porters to the rear piled up, pushing forward like a flock of sheep. The Sherpas stood by with bamboo switches to maintain an orderly procession.

The opaque, glacial waters of the Dudh Kosi tumble from the south side of Everest and its neighboring peaks. The valley walls are so steep that the trail switchbacks far above the river, to ten thousand feet—touching the snow line before dropping again to riverside villages and their invariably tottery bridges. Dyhrenfurth knew that, upon their return, the bridges might be swept away by surging monsoon flows. They'd decide later how to make their retreat.

The expedition was beginning to enter the cooler, more sparsely settled high country. Fields were planted less with rice and corn, and more with barley, buckwheat, and potatoes. The two-story stone houses here were plastered in white lime that contrasted aesthetically with their solid, hand-hewn door and window frames, some decorated with ornamental carving. Glazed paper windowpanes were more common than glass, which was a rare luxury reserved for the wealthy. The roofs of thick wooden shingles were held down with rocks—and with ravens, it seemed, which squawked away on every roof crest. The women wore woolen skirts, or *angi*, to their ankles, and multicolored aprons hung from their waists. The men's earrings dangled from quarter-inch holes, their weight often supported by loops of leather cord hooked over the tops of their ears.

The expedition had finally merged with the path traveled by Charles Houston and the first party of foreigners to trek into the Dudh Kosi valley, just over a dozen years earlier. The Houston party witnessed a country just awakening from a charmed, medieval slumber. His group had entered southern Nepal from India and hiked through subtropical jungle and foothills, then trekked for five days up the Arun River valley, southeast of Everest. Climbing out of the Arun drainage, they crossed a high pass, where a chorten—a small stone reliquary—marked their entry into the Buddhist territory of the Dudh Kosi valley. In 1950, Western influence had hardly touched the Sherpa villages; Houston's team didn't even see axes or saws. The villagers used traditional curved knives to fell and hew their timbers, and all but the tips of the blades of their single plows were made of wood.

Even Houston's roundabout approach to Everest was easier than through Tibet. During the first half of the twentieth century, British climbers and explorers had to set out from Darjeeling, in a far northern corner of India. They trudged through Sikkim and surmounted two high passes before entering Tibet. It took two more weeks of trekking before they arrived at the north side of the mountain.

In 1950, access to Mount Everest changed dramatically. In a coincidence of geopolitical history, China closed Tibet to foreigners at virtually the same time Nepal opened its doors to the outside world. The British were fine with that: They jumped into planning expeditions from the southern side. The approach through subtropical Nepal was shorter and more pleasant, anyway, than the route across the wind-blasted, desertlike Tibetan plateau. They also knew that Everest's rocks offered better purchase on the south side. When the Indian subcontinent collided with Siberia, the sedimentary strata of the ancient Tethys Sea tilted as the sea floor uplifted, creating the Himalaya.

This tectonic activity caused the layers of Everest rock to slope, like roof shingles, toward the north—offering up nicely frayed edges to climbers from the south. Most appealingly, though, the southern route would keep climbers in sunlight for most of the day.

On the trail near the village of Ghat, a boy was escorted up to Gil Roberts and Dave Dingman. He was a porter who had been with them since Kathmandu, and a rag now covered much of his head. When the doctors withdrew the cloth, they saw that pustules, with dimples in their centers, had spread across his entire face. They realized to their shock—though neither had seen it before—that they were beholding smallpox.

"It immediately raised the question of how we would get vaccine up there," Dingman recalled. Al Auten again set up the radio, and the porters were instructed to not run away—at least until the vaccine arrived. "They were aware that smallpox is highly contagious—but some ran off, anyway," Dingman said. The boy with smallpox was accompanied to the missionary hospital in Kathmandu, but he died the day after he arrived.

Several days later, a batch of Russian-made vaccine arrived by runner, and the doctors were able to vaccinate the Sherpas, porters, and themselves. Dingman suspected that they were seeing only the tip of the iceberg. Smallpox was apparently spreading to Nepal from the Indian state of Bihar, carried by traders and by Gurkha soldiers visiting their mountain homes while on leave from the Indian Army. The epidemic would have been more deadly had the country been more urban—and if development workers from America and other countries hadn't been there to respond.

West of Kathmandu, two young Peace Corps volunteers who had enlisted under Willi Unsoeld were horrified to see the disfiguring disease radiate through their own hilly region. "Rumors spread wildly that smallpox was propagating uncontrollably," recalled volunteer Don Messerschmidt, "and it caused panic even in the remotest places." They hiked down from their village to ask the USAID mission in Kathmandu for help. The vaccine, they were told, had already been requested from Pakistan.

"We were able to carry about two thousand doses out to our village," Messerschmidt said, "then more was choppered in by the first helicopter to ever land there. We tried to inoculate children on the forearm, but some kids' sleeves were bound so tightly to their arms that this wasn't possible—they had quite literally grown into their clothes." The volunteers found an open area of each arm to clean with soap and water, then sterilized it with distilled alcoholic spirits. This startled some of the abstinent, high-caste Hindus who regarded the use of alcohol as sacrilegious. Some villagers were also concerned that the vaccination, if it succeeded, might anger Sitala, a Hindu goddess—by interfering with her jealous control over each person's destiny.

It was the more worldly Gurkha pensioners and soldiers, with one foot in the village and one in foreign service, who helped persuade villagers to be vaccinated. Once the village leaders agreed, the citizens complied. Messerschmidt and his colleague were able to inoculate some twenty-five thousand children under the age of twelve, across three districts. America had earned another humanitarian merit badge.

The expedition was approaching the region known as Khumbu. This is the geographic headwaters of Sherpa country, formed by the watershed of the Dudh Kosi and Bhote Kosi rivers, which drain some of the world's highest peaks. From this point on, the expedition's Sherpas were related to many of the families living in the hamlets along the trail. Routinely, they were dragged into wayside tea shops for force-feeding sessions of potent *chang*—a continuous flow that could be cut off only by their departure.

One evening, traditional line dancing broke out among the Sherpas and their extended clan. The men formed a fluid semicircle, arms linked across shoulders, and were joined by the women. "Like a light breeze coming up on a summer evening, a spirit of gaiety—not boisterous, but gentle and effortless—was moving through the group," Jim Lester noted. The dancers swung and shuffled and stamped their legs in hypnotic rhythm with the songs: ballads of adventure and love, sung in a melodic chant that gathered in intensity before again falling away. Two or three dancers, then as many as fifteen, linked and unlinked into and out of the line, "as a flock of birds will change its composition as it goes," Jim Lester wrote, "honoring agreements of which we know nothing."

It was no surprise that Lester, with his interest in group dynamics, was captivated by Konjok Chumbi—the elder headman of Khumjung, one of the main Sherpa villages. When Chumbi linked in with the line of dancers, "he instantly communicated a sense of command. It wasn't pride—at least not as we know it—that made him so beautiful. It was simply grace and experience and the sharing of these things. He made me think of a surfer who both rides on the crest of the wave *and* guides that wave to shore. His even and subdued movements, and above all the quiet joy in his eyes, spoke of a people who have somehow come upon a quality of living that is hard to find in the world."

Tom Hornbein and Jim Lester were the first team members to arrive in Namche Bazaar, at 11,400 feet. They were greeted by two Sherpa women who offered them cups of *chang*. "Tom is a task-oriented guy," Lester recounted, "and I'll never forget the look on his face as he realized how much one cup of *chang* was undermining whatever determination he felt." Expedition Sherpas invited them to their homes for meals of flavorful meaty stew and fried dumplings—and more *chang*. "We were almost invariably sick within hours," Lester said. "Never had throwing up seemed so exotic."

"It's dangerous to go through Namche Bazaar when you have friends there," Willi Unsoeld explained. "They will feed you to death, cramming into you the last potato pancake they have in the house because you are their guest and they want to honor you."

Signs of the region's most famous foreign visitor—Sir Edmund Hillary—were in evidence. Hillary had not only been the first to reach Everest's summit—with Tenzing Norgay—he was virtually the only foreign climber to return afterward and dedicate his life to the people and environment of Khumbu. In the early 1960s he founded the Himalayan Trust, one of the country's first humanitarian aid agencies, as a vehicle for bringing assistance to the region.

Like many visitors before and since, Hillary was impressed by the Sherpas' dedication and hard work, and profoundly aware of their desire for health care and education. In a festive gathering in 1960, a young man from the village of Khumjung read aloud to Hillary from a scroll-like petition that asked him to construct a schoolhouse. "Our children have eyes, yet they are blind," the youth pronounced, reading from the long preamble.

Hillary knew that it would be difficult to attract trained teachers from the lowlands to chilly and remote Khumbu, so he recruited the school's first headmaster from Darjeeling. To get the children to enroll, the headmaster went door-to-door, cajoling parents to send their kids to school on a trial basis. Some of the elders understood, from their experience as traders, that math skills and an ability to read contracts would be useful. The headmaster rounded up forty students, mostly barefoot and clad in rags. On June 11, 1961, the Khumjung school opened. The single class—Grade 1—was attended by children of all ages, because none had ever been exposed to schooling. All were starting at precisely the same level.

Chapter 14

Words from on High

For the stone from the top for geologists, the knowledge
of the limits of endurance for the doctors, but above all
for the spirit of adventure to keep alive the soul of man.

—GEORGE MALLORY

IN NAMCHE BAZAAR, THE LOWLAND PORTERS WERE PAID OFF. MOST
had come from villages below eight thousand feet; porters seldom visited the northern border areas, and few had sufficient clothing for the
high valleys. Colonel Roberts hired on a new group, Sherpas mostly, to
shuttle the loads to Everest Base Camp.

The team meandered up a glacial moraine overgrown with rhododendron, fir, and juniper, and arrived at the monastery of Tengboche,
just below thirteen thousand feet. Snow had begun to fall. It continued throughout the next day, eventually depositing fifteen inches.
Several members were granted an audience with the high lama, the
abbot of the monastery.

An attendant monk guided them through a dark, low-ceilinged
corridor to the abbot's private chambers. The young abbot was seated
on a decorated dais and appeared demure and beneficent, "learned
yet lonely," Jim Lester observed. A gold-trimmed brocade breastplate
peered from within his maroon monk's robes. The members bowed,
and extended white *kata* blessing scarves. He touched each man on
the head, then chanted a prayer for the safety of the expedition. The
team drank brothlike butter tea and studied the contents of the high
lama's room. Stacks of clothbound folios filled the shelves, and gilded

bronze statues graced a small altar. A framed *kata*-draped photo of the Dalai Lama in simple robes and flip-flops was positioned next to a photo of the king of Nepal in royal regalia.

The abbot was suffering from a nagging toothache. Perhaps the doctors could take a look. Roberts and Dingman asked if he could adjourn to the sanctuary's courtyard, and the abbot promptly swept up his robes and led the way outside. The doctors dosed him up with some pain medicine, then pulled his tooth. The high lama reciprocated by inviting the entire expedition to dinner.

In the evening, the team gathered around several low tables lit with candles. A monk ushered in the high lama, who took a seat in the corner. Through his interpreter, the abbot apologized for the simplicity of the meal, then the team dug into yak meat stew, potatoes, and rice as if it were home cooking. Their glasses were endlessly refilled with *arak,* the stronger, distilled version of *chang.*

The abbot recounted details of the destruction, three years earlier, of the famed Tibetan lamasery at Rongbuk, on the windswept northern hem of Everest—more than a week's walk away. Many Sherpas had taken Buddhist teachings and monastic training at Rongbuk, and sent their sons there. The older ones could remember the British expeditions of the 1920s stopping at the monastery en route to the mountain.

Dan Doody, who was becoming more anti-Chinese with each story he heard, scribbled the high lama's account in his diary. "Most of the monks at Rongbuk were killed, and those who escaped had tales of horror to tell of crucifixions, mass murder with a machine gun, and bodies dumped to rot. The *gompa* (monastery) was sacked of all the gold, silver, and anything else of value, then it was shelled to the ground. The lama and monks fled to Nepal, over the 19,000' pass that Sherpas used for trade with Tibet, and took refuge in monasteries of Khumbu and elsewhere."

As they listened to the abbot, Doody realized that the date was March 10, 1963: the fourth anniversary of the Lhasa uprising. That was the evening when, in 1959, the Dalai Lama—disguised in peasant's clothing to avoid detection by the Chinese—was spirited from the Potala Palace in Lhasa to begin a long journey into refuge in India.

The abbot spoke about the subsequent sacking of the Potala's vast and priceless collection of treasures, and of the pyre of Buddhist texts that burned for seven days. "Much of the history and information about Tibet and our form of Buddhism was lost forever." The lama scratched his head at the senselessness of it all, but showed no visible anger.

For the past few years, the abbot continued, bands of Tibetan refugees—and their livestock—had surged over the nineteen-thousand-foot Nangpa La, the only pass that can be easily traveled between Khumbu and Tibet. The refugees began to settle in Khumbu. But the Sherpas couldn't easily accommodate them, and most of the Tibetans moved on to India, to live in refugee camps closer to the Dalai Lama. A handful lingered in Khumbu, herding livestock, practicing Tibetan medicine, and taking odd jobs.

It was late when dinner at the monastery ended. By the light of a single candle nursed by an ancient monk, the team fumbled their way down a dark stairway and stumbled out into the mountain air. Moonlight rimmed the clouds in halos of silver and cast a ghostly sheen to the snow and rock that towered above them in nearly every direction.

The next morning dawned clear. Jake Breitenbach, Dick Emerson, and Al Auten set out for a short warm-up climb on a modest peak overlooking the monastery. They bushwhacked through thickets of rhododendron and undergrowth, then broke out onto a rocky slope that demanded tricky scrambling. "I was greatly impressed with Jake's combination of skill and caution," Emerson wrote that evening in a letter to his wife. He reassured her of "the careful attitude with which all of us approach this task."

On the twelfth, the team left Tengboche. Sunlight reflected from the surrounding peaks so brilliantly that their eyes hurt. For some members, the approach had come to feel like a pilgrimage. They passed dome-shaped chorten reliquaries, cliff faces incised with Buddhist mantras, and prayer flags strung in tangled lengths across rivers and between boulder tops.

This was no ordinary remote mountain valley. The team was entering one of several sacred valleys of refuge designated by a ninth-century saint revered by the Sherpas as Guru Rinpoche. During periods of adversity or persecution, when Buddhist religion was at risk of being lost, devout people could retreat to these sacred valleys to reclaim their faith. Such valleys, Khumbu included, are blessed with spiritual energy, and must not be defiled; the Sherpas say that even impure thoughts should be avoided when passing through their sacred landscape.

At the yak pasture of Pheriche, at fourteen thousand feet, the team camped near a cluster of vacant stone huts that were blanketed in snow and silence. Herders would bring their yaks to the area to graze when the pastures greened up in late spring. Lying in his tent, pitched next to a low stone wall, glaciologist Maynard Miller tuned his Zenith radio to a station in northern India. In a letter to his wife and daughter, he described "a frightening program called *India and the Dragon,* the gist of which was that China is bent on devouring all of Asia." Miller then spun the dial to hear Radio Peking spewing propaganda about protecting the fatherland. "It is all too familiar to us who heard similar cries from Europe in the 1930s." He again rotated the dial and found Radio Nederland "broadcasting some lovely Handel— a pleasant aftermath to a rugged day."

The next day they moved up to another summer pasture, at 16,200 feet. Snow still covered the ground, and at night the team climbed into their down parkas. Miller again lay in his sleeping bag, this time in mild distress. During the day he had paused several times each hour to gasp, hyperventilating in a series of deep, rapid breaths—an involuntary response to high altitude known as Cheyne-Stokes breathing. "Man has rather narrow ranges within which he must live," he continued in his letter from the night before. "We are subject to controls in our lives, regardless of how 'tough' and 'self-sustaining' we may think we are. We must have humility and faith to give us the strength we need."

Three climbers walked a few hundred feet up a nearby hill. From there, they were able to view Everest and much of the West Ridge— their first unobstructed view of the mountain.

"The sight of Everest, now looming almost directly above us, looked so *attainable* to my unpracticed eye," Lester wrote. "It was too compelling for anyone to be distracted from it."

"The West Ridge looks horrendous," Barry Corbet said. "Five

thousand feet of rock, almost no snow, and very steep. I've downgraded our chances of success by quite a bit—but it's an alluring objective." He was more prepared than previously to fail, he said, and also more prepared to enjoy the struggle. "Everest from here is a huge, fantastic, soaring peak, and not at all the ash heap it appears to be in many of the photos."

Their next stop was Base Camp. As if dressing formally for the last leg of the approach, the Sherpas donned their newly issued uniforms: black boots, burnt orange gaiters, green pants, international orange anoraks, scarlet hats, and glacier goggles. Laughing hysterically at their strange yet identical dress, they shared the convivial cheer of a glee club chorus. A team as unified, disciplined, and good-spirited as this one, they seemed to say, will make short work of Mount Everest.

The gradual uphill climb led first along the edge of the glacier and then through Phantom Alley, a maze of ice towers known as *nieves penitentes*. Then there it was: the site for Everest Base Camp, at 17,800 feet on the margin of the Khumbu Glacier. High peaks and ridges encircled them at neck-twisting angles: Pumori, Lingtren, Khumbutse, Nuptse, and Everest's West Ridge. On a sweep to the north and east, the lowest point on the horizon was the 20,000-foot Lho La, a snowy pass on the border with Tibet.

Immediately to the southeast rose Base Camp's most undeniable feature: the Khumbu Icefall, a tortured vortex of glacial ice more than two thousand feet tall. It hung over them like a monstrous, frozen waterfall of deranged clutter—emitting a sinister allure, daring climbers to find a path through its weak spots.

Squeals and grunts emanated from the Icefall's inner workings, as if it were emoting in an unfathomable marine mammal dialect. Climbers said it expressed a personality that shifted daily; sometimes peaceful, often malevolent. Jim Whittaker and Norman Dyhrenfurth quietly surveyed it. Dyhrenfurth said that the Icefall appeared even more treacherous than on his previous expeditions.

Most of the remaining sahibs and Sherpas pulled into Base Camp and began erecting tents on every flat spot of snow or rubble they could find. They pitched several four-man tents to store the climbing gear and research equipment. Nearby, two twelve-by-twelve-foot tents were arrayed facing each other to form a dining, medical, and radio center. Two wires arced upward to a forty-foot mast—the antenna for their daily radio contact with Kathmandu. Maynard Miller's tent site doubled as a meteorology station, with a dancing wind direction indicator, spinning anemometer cups to measure wind speed, and a box containing a hygrometer to measure humidity—lending a purposeful, scientific air to the scene.

Porters ferried in loads from the previous night's camp and piled up boxes of gear, forming alleyways and cargo depots within the caravansary-like setting. The Sherpas fashioned a kitchen by draping a large tarp over a ridgepole and anchoring it with stones on either side. Danu, the head cook, employed the expedition food boxes as both kitchen walls and supermarket-style shelves to hold the food. As many as a dozen Sherpas could gather inside, squatting around the fire to eat potato pancakes or *tsampa*—roasted barley flour and sugar, kneaded with butter tea into a tenacious paste. In the evenings they drank *chang* or *arak,* delivered to camp in wooden bottles or jerricans by family members.

Dan Doody arrived at Base Camp in rough shape, suffering from nausea and near-continuous headaches. His filming came to a virtual halt. Even Barry Corbet was distracted by diarrhea and vomiting— sometimes simultaneously. "Now I know how the guided clients in the Tetons must have been feeling all those years," Corbet remarked.

Deputy leader Will Siri emerged from the tent he used as a human physiology laboratory and drafted an update on the team's condition for expedition scribe Jim Ullman in Kathmandu: "No expedition has had the variety of fascinating medical problems we have enjoyed (or endured). The team left Kathmandu in the poorest of health, which proceeded in the next three weeks to deteriorate. At the moment, the wheezing, coughing, blowing, sniffling and squatting are astonishing and chronic. Despite this," Siri said in closure, "everyone is in the best of spirits."

Mostly good spirits—except when they had to satisfy Siri's unquenchable thirst for blood and urine for his physiological studies. Siri tracked down every climber who came within range of his laboratory tent and held them hostage until they produced. He combined and swirled the urine specimens in large tubs and allowed it to freeze into giant urine-sicles. "Every Saturday," Willi Unsoeld explained, "he chopped up the frozen specimens with his ice ax and boiled it up in a big, foaming vat—what we called the 'Saturday Night Special.'"

Even when on the mountain, the climbers were required to pee into their bottles—at specified altitudes and at specific times of day— and carry it all back to Base Camp. This custom delighted and puzzled the Sherpas. One of them helpfully suggested that it might be easier to simply pee into the snow and leave it there—the way the Sherpas do.

The spirits were further dampened when a runner arrived at Base Camp with a letter from Sir Edmund Hillary's Himalayan School-house Expedition. Hillary's team was preparing to build primary schools down valley, and three Sherpas in the villages there had developed symptoms of smallpox. Hillary feared the epidemic was growing. Gil Roberts sent a number of doses of vaccine back with the runner. Several days later a Swiss-piloted Pilatus Porter made an airdrop of vaccine over Khumjung, the home village of many of the expedition Sherpas.

At Himalayan altitudes, solar radiation can be as fiercely intense as the cold. At 4 p.m. one afternoon, Unsoeld's thermometer registered 106 degrees Fahrenheit inside his sunny tent. An hour later, when the sun dipped over the ridge to the west, he measured again: 6 degrees above 0. Mornings were even colder. The team burrowed into their down sleeping bags, to be roused at sunrise by two delectable words: "Sahib—tea." When the tent flap was unzipped, a Sherpa's hand delivered a steaming cup of sugary milk tea. They quickly grew accustomed to the taste and the tradition.

At five each afternoon, the climbers at Base Camp assembled in the dining tent and pulled their folding chairs around the radio set for the call to Kathmandu. They shared their progress on the mountain and devoured news from the outside world. Al Auten was usually able to reach the embassy's military attaché, a polite southern gentleman who transmitted from his "radio shack" on the top floor of his rented home in the city. A reliable backup was Father Moran, the amiable ham radio–operating Jesuit priest and headmaster of St. Xavier's, Nepal's premier private school. If the connection became garbled, Father Moran would resort to Morse code by making clacking sounds with his mouth. Auten clacked back, delighted to put his arcane skills to work.

At night, viewed from the moraine next to camp, only the dim interior lights of the tents in the foreground betrayed the presence of life—imparting a feeling of having reached the end, or perhaps the beginning, of the earth. Humans were minuscule and fragile here, like grains of rice offered to the towering, moonlit peaks.

Daily avalanches rumbled off the steep valley walls, sending clouds of white spindrift through Base Camp. By midafternoon, warm air from down valley drew clouds and light snowfall into camp, and wind strafed the high ridges, emitting a terrifying howl. The world around them constantly reminded them to remain humble.

No wonder the Sherpas regarded this place as sacred and viewed themselves and the climbers as mere guests at Base Camp. Without invitation, they had stepped into the palace and playground of Miyolangsangma, the Tibetan goddess regarded as one of the five "Long Life Sisters" who reside on Everest and its neighboring peaks. Radiating stern benevolence, this "Goddess of Inexhaustible Giving" provides spiritual nourishment to the residents who dwell on her flanks. Only when the Sherpas had made offerings to her at a makeshift shrine at Base Camp would they feel comfortable entering the Icefall.

Barry Prather, Maynard Miller's young colleague, had already ventured onto the glacier below the Icefall with a gravimeter, which he used to measure the differences in density between rock and ice at various places on the glacier. The figures would help graph the glacier's depth and mass—adding a chapter to the story of glacial growth and decay. But Prather noted that as they gained elevation, and especially at Base Camp, he felt he was gaining as much spiritual as scientific understanding. He had been brought up in a churchgoing family, but admitted that he found an even more profound sense of peace in the mountains than he did in church.

On March 22, 1963, Whittaker, Unsoeld, Jerstad, and three Sherpas saddled up with loads of rope and climbing hardware. As they threaded their way through the Khumbu Icefall's crevasses and seracs (overhanging spires of ice), Norman Dyhrenfurth and Will Siri relayed route-finding suggestions by radio from a high vantage point across the valley.

The Icefall was complex and unnerving, fraught with "objective dangers," or hazards beyond the climbers' control. Fixing a route through the heart of the beast might take several days. At its top, at nineteen thousand feet, they could pitch Camp 1, then enjoy a relatively flat walk through the glacial valley of the Western Cwm to Camp 2—Advance Base Camp—at its far end. Just beyond Camp 2, the South Col and West Ridge routes would diverge.

On the first day of route finding and rope fixing, they pushed to within eight hundred feet of the top of the Icefall—until their upward movement was thwarted by a thirty-foot-high solid barrier of ice. The ice wall appeared to stretch the entire width of the glacier, with no route through it or around it. To Whittaker, this bulwark looked eerily fragile—as if it might be a thin, freestanding slab with another crevasse immediately on its far side. Finding no other route, they tediously worked their way up the wall using ice screws, then fixed a rope. They set anchors at its top and fixed a rope, then retreated to Base Camp as the day grew late.

Whittaker was impressed by Nawang Gombu, who exuded good humor and a natural climbing sense. Gombu had been the strongest Sherpa on Will Siri's 1954 expedition to Makalu, the world's fifth highest peak, and he had reached twenty-eight thousand feet on Everest in 1960, the Indian team's high point that year. He had started his career in the mountains as a seventeen-year-old porter on the British expedition of 1953, when his uncle, Tenzing Norgay, reached the summit with Edmund Hillary. Gombu was keen to climb out of Tenzing's shadow and was a logical candidate to be a full-fledged member of the climbing team—as he had been with the Indians in 1960.

Like Tenzing, Gombu was born in a remote valley in Tibet. At a young age his parents trundled him off to the Rongbuk monastery, on Everest's north side. After two years of rigidly enforced study, he escaped by wrapping his clothes in a bundle and sneaking out through the latrine hole of the monastery's outhouse. He hid out in a friend's home for several days before trekking over the nineteen-thousand-foot pass to Namche Bazaar, in Nepal. From there he walked to Darjeeling.

Gombu, barely more than five feet two inches tall, was perpetually cheerful and helpful. "He told me that he had switched from Buddhism to climbing for the money," Jim Whittaker wrote in *A Life on the Edge,* "but I could see something else in his eyes: that same burning desire to summit that I had."

Part II

The Vast Unknown

We felt the lonely beauty of the evening,
the immense roaring silence of the wind,
the tenuousness of our tie to all below.
There was a hint of fear, not for our lives,
but of a vast unknown, which pressed
in on us.

—THOMAS F. HORNBEIN, FROM
EVEREST: THE WEST RIDGE

Chapter 15

Long Live the Crow

So casual. Ice gives wiggle. Then silent.

—Willi Unsoeld, written in the
bottom margin of a letter to his
wife, Jolene

The following morning, March 23, 1963, a fresh climbing party took over, intending to push the route farther through the Icefall. Dick Pownall and Jake Breitenbach tied into the first rope and placed a strong Sherpa, Ang Pema, in the middle. Expedition doc Gil Roberts led a second rope, followed by another Sherpa. As they left camp, Jim Lester overheard talk that, judging by the strong progress of their first day in the Icefall, the team might climb the mountain by the first of May—well before the start of the summer monsoon. "You could practically see optimism rising like a balloon above Base Camp," he wrote.

The two rope teams navigated their way through a torn-up section of the glacier, clearing chunks of ice and fixing rope. "Then we stopped for a break," Pownall recalled, "and were relishing the moment. Here we were, finally, on the mountain. Jake had a smoke, and I said, 'Put that out, and let's go.'"

Pownall led, with Breitenbach at the rear, though they were only several yards apart, with most of the rope coiled loosely in their free hands. Mesmerized by the warmth of the sun and the translucent, bluish-white features of the Icefall, Pownall had the sensation of going into a peaceful dream state. "I'm sure Jake had the same feeling," he said.

They arrived at the ice wall that had challenged Whittaker and the others the day before. It appeared unstable, and Pownall paused to study it. "Look around the corner at this, Jake," he said. "It's pretty spooky up here." He turned to Gil Roberts, who was below Breitenbach on the second rope, and asked him if he could see a more solid-looking route. Roberts could see no better way.

They resumed climbing. "I was a step or two behind Jake," Roberts said, "and my goggles had fogged up because it was actually kind of hot in the middle of the day. I stopped to clean them."

Suddenly, almost silently, a house-sized block of ice broke from the wall and collapsed around them, breaking and shattering in chaos and confusion. Roberts was thrown a few yards down the hill by debris ejected from the collapse. He and the Sherpa on his rope were enveloped in a blinding, white fog of snow.

Stunned, Roberts checked himself over to confirm that he was alive and ambulatory, then scrambled back to where he had stood. Dick Pownall was pinned by a block of ice; only his head and one hand were showing. His rope snaked into a depression, where the Sherpa tied into the middle of his rope, Ang Pema, was jammed upside down—but still conscious. They traced the rope farther along. It disappeared under a multiton mass of ice—precisely where Breitenbach had been a moment before.

Pownall was barely able to breathe and was beginning to turn blue. Working quickly, Roberts and the Sherpa on his rope chopped away at the ice block that immobilized his chest, and pulled him out. Then they quickly disentangled Ang Pema.

Roberts turned to make a desperate search for Breitenbach. After a half hour, ready to drop from exhaustion, he finally gave up. He stood for several minutes feeling helpless and disembodied—as if pinned, himself, in a surreal nightmare. Then he slowly bent down. Time seemed to slow as he cut the rope that led from Dick Pownall to Breitenbach's glacial grave.

Carefully, Roberts and the other Sherpa helped Pownall and Ang Pema back toward Base Camp. Then Roberts stopped. "We had descended maybe a hundred vertical feet when I heard a noise," Roberts recalled. "A strangled cry. I thought, '*Oh, my God*—Jake's *alive* under there.' Then a *gorak,* a Himalayan raven, flew up and out of the Icefall debris where Jake was."

The Sherpas believe that human souls, after death, can take flight in the form of *goraks* before they find a new incarnation. Their throaty calls and intentional movements also bear messages and predictions that can be interpreted.

Maybe the *gorak's* message was more prosaic. Barry Corbet's wife, Muffy, would recall that Old Crow bourbon was Breitenbach's beverage of choice; when a bottle was emptied, Breitenbach would pronounce, "The Crow is dead—long live the Crow!" and fetch another one to be shared by all.

Through binoculars, the climbers at Base Camp could see four climbers descending toward them, walking erratically. One man was missing. They feared it might be Breitenbach; he had been carrying the two-way radio, and they'd lost contact. Dyhrenfurth immediately dispatched a rescue party.

The seven rescue climbers met the descending party in the middle of the Icefall. They radioed to Base Camp the distressing news about Breitenbach and requested a stretcher: Ang Pema could no longer walk. Whittaker loaded him onto his back and carried him through the steep section of the Icefall, blood dripping on his clothing, until three Sherpas arrived to relieve him.

Four of the rescuers continued up to the site of the Icefall collapse. "We had a nagging fear that Breitenbach was still alive, imprisoned in the ice," Willi Unsoeld said. "Whittaker and Gombu lowered me into the crevasse and I yodeled, waiting for the possibility of Jake's answer."

They dug a full four feet through hard-packed snow before giving up, and returned to Base Camp in the dark—silent, exhausted, despondent—as clouds rolled in to shroud the mountains. Dick Pownall, who credited Gil Roberts and the Sherpa on his rope with saving his life, had a cracked collarbone. Ang Pema suffered a skull fracture, a shoulder injury, and a deep gash on the side of his face. He was initially convinced he wouldn't survive. But Dave Dingman stitched and bandaged him, and the Sherpa recovered quickly.

———

Why Jake, and not me? the Icefall climbers asked themselves. It could have just as easily been any of them—or all of them. "I mean, I didn't do anything special to not get killed," Gil Roberts said. Jim Whittaker was rattled by the thought that his twin brother would have been on Breitenbach's rope, had he joined the expedition. The Sherpa assigned to work with Breitenbach had known him only five weeks. The morning after the accident, Dan Doody found him in Breitenbach's sleeping bag, crying and heartbroken. The Sherpa had remained at Base Camp to prepare loads for the high camps, and was ashamed that he hadn't been with Breitenbach at the time of the accident.

The next afternoon, Al Auten raised Kathmandu on the radio and relayed the news, and a message was sent with a runner to the five climbers still at Gorak Shep, the last camp before Base Camp.

The Gorak Shep camp fell silent. They hadn't even arrived at Base Camp, and now a team member had died. Feeling orphaned by distance, and now by loss, they asked themselves what Jim Lester described as "silent, stupid questions." *Is it true? How could it happen? What's the meaning of it? What can we do now?* A few bites of dinner was all they could eat.

Breitenbach's closest friend, Barry Corbet, was hit hard. His head spun with emotions, regrets, and questions. "How the hell can 11 years of living in one another's pockets end so insanely?" he wrote. "Pretty stupid goddamned gentleman's sport that gets people killed in their prime of happiness. How about Ang Pema, who only wanted to make a day's wages?"

"The mountain hadn't played according to the rules," Dick Emerson wrote. "Surely, it should have allowed us to bury our own, in our own way, but it left only absence for us to mourn."

The sullen crew at Gorak Shep departed for Base Camp early the next morning. For two days, they grieved. Gil Roberts, Dick Pownall, and Barry Corbet got drunk. Others retreated to their diaries and their thoughts. Some wrote letters.

Jim Lester tried to distill some sense from it. "It seems that in ordinary life, death always comes as something unnatural. For one or two days it seemed terribly wrong, a miscalculation on someone's part.

And then the accident took its place among the natural things of the world. It just *was,* and there was no hidden meaning to be found in it. Life is an unending stream of events and no one is sure of the meaning of any of them, really. It was easier to reach this way of feeling because we were living close to the earth, close to simple, important things."

In a note to his wife, Jolene, Unsoeld wrote, "As deaths go, this was a clean-cut, kindly one. If Jake could have chosen his final resting place, no improvement could be imagined."

But something had changed. Everest was no longer a lark. One member suggested—after the promising first day on the mountain— that they had become overconfident. The Sherpas spoke quietly of it being a possible omen.

Gil Roberts didn't want to walk again over Breitenbach's grave. Dick Pownall, too, was profoundly shaken; he had witnessed a trauma that only a climber can comprehend. The image of Roberts cutting the rope that had joined Ang Pema to Breitenbach, with its frayed end trailing away into the depths of the glacier, was seared into their memories. Pownall and Roberts decided they would go through the Icefall only two more times: once up, and once down.

Cutting that rope had also severed Jake's umbilical link to Wyoming, its peaks, and its people. Pete Sinclair, Breitenbach's climbing buddy from Dartmouth and a fellow Tetons guide, was in Laramie when he heard that Jake had been killed. He knew that Jake's people— the dispersed yet persistently clan-loyal climbing community—would convene for a memorial in Jackson Hole.

"I borrowed a car and drove the 400 miles from Laramie in 5½ hours on snow-covered roads," Sinclair wrote. "It was high country, flat and barren, with mountains on the horizon in every direction. The sun blazed on the snow and the snow lifted and rolled after me. I wanted to be detached from the ordinary world—and driving at 100 miles an hour was a way of doing that."

Friends instinctively congregated at Breitenbach's house and stood about, speaking softly. "I did what I could in the way of talking to Jake's widow," Sinclair recalled, "but the isolation at such times is almost complete. The situation was made worse because we all felt inadequate to the situation. We felt culpable. We lacked a proper procedure, the empty boots backwards in the stirrups of the rider-less horse."

"One may love mountains," another guide concluded, "but it doesn't mean that mountains love you. Jake had done nothing wrong. He was a player in a Greek tragedy, and the gods had picked him out for their own sport."

The grieving comrades were quietly aware that other members of their clan were still on Everest—especially Breitenbach's neighbor and friend Barry Corbet. A faint uneasiness filtered through the gathering, an acknowledgment that the fate of their colleagues on the other side of the world pivoted on forces that they could not know and did not entirely trust.

That night at Base Camp, Barry Corbet wrote in his diary. "Three days of grey surviving, just learning all over again how to feel. Time and a bottle of bourbon, Jake's drink, had the appropriate healing effects."

As the team lay in their tents, listening to the peculiar grinding of glacial ice under tension, some wondered whether it was worth it to continue. To accept death is not the same as to invite it.

"Should we quit?" Barry Corbet asked. He concluded that, logically, there need not be a reason for everything. "Does Detroit quit making cars because of the accidents? Sure, it hurts to know a good friend lies beneath thirty feet of ice, but what kind of friends would we be to give up the thing he died for?"

There was more reason than ever to climb the mountain, Corbet decided. Most of the others felt the same way. Breitenbach had wanted to attempt the West Ridge. Now, the West Ridge effort would need every man it could muster. Could they climb the route without him? "We won't be climbing the West Ridge without Jake," Willi Unsoeld pointed out. "We'll be climbing it for Jake."

Chapter 16

Taming the Beast

I cannot hide the truth—I love them. And at times they drive me stark, staring mad.

—COLONEL JIMMY ROBERTS, REFERRING TO THE SHERPAS IN HIS EMPLOY

BARRY BISHOP, DAVE DINGMAN, AL AUTEN, AND BARRY CORBET ventured back into the Icefall on March 26, 1963, with twelve Sherpas and mixed emotions. Jake Breitenbach's death was the first ever to occur in the Icefall, and the loss pressed heavily on them—even physically so, constricting their stomachs and chests. They had been lulled into believing that the Icefall wouldn't collapse—on them, at least. That happened only to other people. Sure, continue with the expedition, some expressed, but get it over with, by whichever route. Then get the hell out of there before more lives were lost.

Barry Bishop's wife, Lila, had worried daily about her husband—ever since her momentary premonition when the team departed the trailhead that something would go wrong. "Oddly," she said, "when I heard that Jake had been killed—as horrible as it was—I felt that whatever wasn't quite right with the expedition had been resolved. And I knew that Barry would be all right."

Two of the climbers worked on pushing the route farther through the Icefall, while the other two cut steps and fixed ropes through tricky passages where a fall could be fatal. The Sherpas followed, carrying pine logs for spanning crevasses and bamboo wands to flag the route in case of a whiteout. They all returned to Base Camp following a slow but productive day.

Another team set out the next morning, hoping to push the route through to the top of the Icefall. Unsoeld, Whittaker, Jerstad, and Gombu reached the middle of the Icefall in less than two hours and stopped for coffee. Pushing onward, they silently passed the train wreck of ice blocks where Jake Breitenbach lay buried. Then around noon, a daunting obstacle appeared just below the top of the Icefall: a seventy-foot wall of ice.

The climbers were separated from the wall by a seemingly bottomless crevasse, several feet wide. Whittaker paused to consider it. He clipped some long ice screws onto a carabiner hanging from his waist, then gulped and took a flying leap. "I cleared the crevasse, and rammed the ice ax and the front points of my crampons into the face of the wall," he said. "I stuck like a fly on flypaper." He screwed a hollow aluminum ice screw into the wall, then clipped a carabiner through its metal eye and slipped the rope into the carabiner. Setting one screw after the other—each as high as his arm could reach—he worked his way up. After two hours, Unsoeld spelled him and finished off the ice wall.

Four other climbers followed, joined by Sherpas carrying aluminum ladder sections in six-foot lengths. They lashed together the ladder sections, then tilted up the contrivance as if laying siege to a medieval castle. The barrier was surmounted: Climbers and Sherpas with loads could advance into the Western Cwm. Finally, their gaze could dwell on a horizon more distant than the features of the diabolical Icefall. And much of the "traditional" route to the summit was now revealed: the Lhotse Face, Geneva Spur, Yellow Band, South Col, and Everest's South Summit. The West Ridge—known only from grainy photos taken by the Indian Air Force in 1953—remained a mystery, hidden from view by the sheer proximity of the West Shoulder, four thousand feet above them to the north.

The hike from Camp 1 to Camp 2 was like strolling up the aisle of a mountainous cathedral—gothic arches and stained glass replaced by monumental ridges, wind-sculpted ice flutings, alabaster clouds, and brilliant blue sky. Lhotse, the world's fourth highest peak, formed the altar at the head of the valley, while Everest presided majestically from the wings. Evoking the valley's churchlike sanctity, the Swiss had referred to the Western Cwm as the "Valley of Silence": a place where light avalanches of powder snow noiselessly drift like windblown veils from the north face of Nuptse, opposite Everest.

"We slogged on, over little snow bump after little snow bump, for what seemed like an eternity," Lute Jerstad said, "until I began to feel like a Mount Rainier client on a bad day." Tired and dazed.

In a shallow trough halfway up the Western Cwm, below Everest's Southwest Face, a hamlet of tents sprang up. This was Camp 2—Advance Base Camp—at 21,200 feet. It would soon be adorned with mountaineering gear, boxes of food, and stacks of oxygen bottles, most of it bound for the higher camps.

More than a hundred loads would need to be delivered to Camp 2 on a timely schedule. A team of twelve specialist Icefall Sherpas had been assigned to carry loads through the Icefall to the load dump at Camp 1. For the duration of the expedition, they would also make adjustments to the route as the glacier shrugged and shifted.

Transport officer Colonel Roberts oversaw the Icefall Sherpas, who approached their job with levity and cheer. But Roberts could coax only one of them into speaking over the radio—an intimidating device possessed by an alien spirit. (Some Nepalese didn't trust that a voice heard over the radio was "live," and suspected it was a hoaxlike recording.)

"I'm told by the climbers that the lead Icefall Sherpa would stand a yard away and shout at the radio handset," Colonel Roberts recalled with a smile. "He came through loud and clear, though I don't think he listened to my replies. You couldn't give him orders over the radio, but he could relay the news—saying who was sick, what they needed, and so on."

On April 2, 1963, a group of the Icefall Sherpas approached Colonel Roberts at Base Camp to negotiate the weight of loads they would carry. An argument erupted. The Sherpas stressed the danger in the Icefall. They were being asked to make multiple trips through the beast while the sahibs sat safely above or below. Loads of thirty-five pounds, instead of fifty, would allow them to scoot through it more quickly.

The expedition was a team effort, Colonel Roberts reminded the Sherpas. He pointed to Dave Dingman and Barry Corbet's feat, the previous day, of carrying Sherpa-sized loads to Camp 1—and arriving before the Sherpas. ("I'm afraid the Sherpas weren't impressed with my ability to do this every day," Corbet admitted, "as I have barfed solidly for two days following this memorable carry.") Throughout the approach, the Sherpas were perplexed and amused by how the Americans behaved compared to the Indians and the British. Rather oddly, the Americans wanted to carry loads along with everyone else—they even seemed to compete for the honor. And the Americans were solicitous of the Sherpas' well-being—intent on making sure they were comfortable and taken care of. The Sherpas had assumed that offering personal attention and care was *their* job.

The Sherpas gave in with good humor, and agreed to carry fifty pounds through the Icefall. This concession, however, gave them traction for a follow-on argument—and threat of a strike—over the issue of goose-down sleeping bag liners. The sahibs had inner bags, and the Sherpas didn't. Colonel Roberts relented, agreeing to rent them from the Sherpas themselves: Most had inner bags from previous expeditions stored in their houses. Roberts sent a runner to fetch them.

During the arguments, Gombu and the three other Darjeeling Sherpas were caught uncomfortably between the sahibs and the Khumbu Sherpas, and hesitated to speak out. The experience, climbing skills, and passable English of the Darjeeling Sherpas made them indispensable, and the Khumbu Sherpas felt that the expedition had placed the Darjeeling Sherpas on a higher tier. Norman Dyhrenfurth knew from earlier Himalayan expeditions that the expedition would face bitterness if a Darjeeling Sherpa—and none of the thirty-five local, Khumbu Sherpas—reached the summit.

The self-selected West Ridge climbers were itching to launch their reconnaissance. Beneath the brilliant sun of April 3, 1963, Willi Unsoeld and Barry Bishop set out from Camp 2 to search for a route to the West Shoulder, which would connect them to the West Ridge.

Ascending steeply out of camp, they skirted a small icefall above Camp 2 and turned to the left, then traversed back to the northwest.

Over the following days, Tom Hornbein and Dave Dingman joined them in pushing the route well up the steep slope below the West Shoulder. At 23,800 feet, they carved out a platform for Camp 3 West, or 3W. They hadn't been sure the West Shoulder would be accessible at all from the Cwm, and were encouraged by the tentative progress. The Sherpas' morale picked up, too, especially when Dingman removed Ang Pema's head bandages, revealing a jagged line of fancy stitches.

Camp 3W was soon stocked with enough food, fuel, and oxygen for a few days of reconnoitering. The climbers used oxygen for sleeping, pairing up on a single bottle's hose with a T splitter, in order to preserve as many full tanks as possible. The plastic sleeping masks tended to become clammy with moisture, though this annoyance was overcome by the welcome sleep that oxygen provided.

The next morning—April 10, 1963—the four climbers worked their way up the remaining three hundred vertical feet to the West Shoulder. "Drifting clouds obscured the route ahead," Bishop said, "or gave tantalizing glimpses of rocks and snowfields, couloirs and buttresses—but in such disjointed order as to make a valid route assessment almost impossible." They returned to camp.

After two dreary days blanketed by clouds, they again repeated the short climb to the shoulder. This time, the skies parted to reveal a range of snow-capped peaks a hundred miles to the north, in Tibet, and the immense Rongbuk Glacier spilled away into the valley below them. To the northeast they could peer straight across to the North Col and Northeast Ridge, the route of the first British climbers. Somewhere up there, they speculated—not far from where they stood—must lie the icy graves of George Mallory and Andrew Irvine, last seen in 1924 as they headed into the mist, toward the summit.

Twenty miles to the north, at sixteen thousand feet on Everest's approach route from the Tibet side, they thought they could make out the sprawling ruins of the great monastery of Rongbuk, from which the Sherpas had drawn much of their religious tradition. Its chapels, assembly halls, and monks' quarters lay in jagged shambles, just as the Tengboche Lama had described. A cluster of gray structures (believed to include Chinese army barracks and a weather station) sat imperiously to one side.

Their gaze rose steeply to the West Ridge. What little they could see through the mist was not promising: The ridge itself was rocky, ragged, and formidable, presenting no obvious route. It might be climbable for a skilled party, but safeguarding loaded Sherpas over such terrain would be technically difficult and time consuming. They returned to Camp 3W. By the time the evening meal was prepared, they were beginning to think that—with their limited resources—the West Ridge option should be abandoned.

Digestion gave them time to reflect. They spoke about the next day, which had also been allotted for reconnaissance. All of them were feeling good—strong and well acclimatized—and were keen to have another look. Besides, they hadn't even reached the base of the summit pyramid.

On April 12, 1963, Unsoeld, Hornbein, and Bishop slogged up the West Shoulder to the rocky base of the West Ridge, at 25,100 feet. "At last, we had our fingers on steep, Everest West Ridge rock," Unsoeld wrote, "and it was purely rotten crud." Hornbein had surmised from the 1953 aerial images that veering to the north side of the mountain (in Tibet, technically) would offer easier climbing. He noticed one straight, steep couloir (gully) on the North Face that appeared to offer a snow route to a point about 1,000 feet below the summit.

"This was also one of the cons, as far as Willi was concerned," Hornbein said. "Who wants to climb an easy snow slope all the way to the top of the mountain?" Hornbein also feared that the couloir could act as a funnel for falling snow and rock.

On their way back from their tour, Hornbein and Unsoeld spotted a snowy shelf at the base of the final four thousand feet of the West Ridge: an ideal site for Camp 4W. Reaching the shelf, they looked across to Everest's Southwest Face, with Lhotse to its right. Then they leaned over the edge and spied Camp 2, four thousand vertical feet directly below them in the Western Cwm. As they plunge stepped back to 3W, peaks appeared and vanished, and an unearthly light illuminated the wreaths of mist swirling about them. Amid all the grandeur, it was easy to overlook their lack of solid information about the route.

No matter, Unsoeld and Hornbein figured. "By the time we

reached Camp 3W, we were firmly convinced that such a fine camp-site as 4W *deserved* to have a route extended above it," Unsoeld said. "Needless to say, poor Dave Dingman, who had spent the day in the tent at 3W, was sorely puzzled by our confident assertion." Despite changeable weather, spotty visibility, rotten rock, and a ridge that "loomed larger than our wildest dreams and nightmares," the couloir on the north side appeared to offer good snow at a reasonable angle.

Unsoeld radioed Base Camp. "We found it! We found it!" he exclaimed to Dyhrenfurth. ("Base Camp thought we had found the route," he later remarked, "but we meant we had found the *campsite*. Very often decisions get made in the Himalaya on grounds such as these.") Mainly, he had wanted to lodge in Dyhrenfurth's mind that the reconnaissance was successful. The next morning, they descended from 3W and arrived at Camp 2, tired and happy.

In their absence, however, the sentiment of the other team members had shifted. Loads were piling up at Camp 2, and the expedition was facing the decision of where on the mountain to send them: the South Col or the West Ridge. In the West Ridgers' absence, Dyhrenfurth had gathered the team for a vote. The outcome: They would direct most of the expedition's supplies and manpower, for now, to the standard South Col route.

"They held the vote while we were up on reconnaissance," Unsoeld noted, "so for *some reason* the West Ridge was outvoted. You gotta watch the democratic process." Unsoeld and Hornbein were also dubious about Dyhrenfurth's new decision that the South Col summit attempt should be made by two four-man parties, instead of two two-man parties.

Several climbers were viable candidates for the first South Col summit party, but for sheer strength Jim Whittaker and Nawang Gombu were the obvious choice. They had worked hard in the Icefall and in carrying loads to Camp 3 (the camp above Advance Base)—earning them positions as the expedition's "Sir Ed and Tenzing."

Dyhrenfurth was desperate to get footage from the mountain's upper reaches, hopefully from the summit. But cameraman Dan Doody was hit with thrombophlebitis, a vein inflammation in his leg that placed him at risk of a blood clot that could break off and lodge in his lungs. Doody had made his way to Camp 2, but Gil Roberts confined him to his tent with an intravenous anticoagulant. He wouldn't be climbing any higher that season.

Dyhrenfurth was the only other member with cinematography experience. Unsoeld, in his role as climbing leader, suggested that Dyhrenfurth and a Sherpa join Whittaker and Gombu on the first summit team. Dyhrenfurth deserved a shot at the top, and if his strength held up, he just might make it. Some were concerned—as he was, himself—about his advanced age of forty-five, but his obsession with the mountain (built over four previous expeditions, on top of a family legacy) had birthed the confluence of events that brought them all together.

It was agreed that a *second* party, composed of *another* four climbers, would follow a day later.

Tom Hornbein wasn't happy. He felt that Dyhrenfurth's configuration for the South Col was hardly logical; four-man teams would require more supplies and oxygen at the high camps than two-man teams, which would be faster and more flexible. And one good storm could wipe out their strongest summit chance. After they climbed the South Col route, would sufficient resources remain for a West Ridge attempt?

The logistics that Emerson and Hornbein had carefully worked out weeks before were now in disarray—lopsided in favor of the South Col. They sat down and carefully recalculated the available time, oxygen, food, fuel, and Sherpa manpower. Unless the South Col assault went flawlessly and on schedule, they concluded, the West Ridge effort would never achieve liftoff. Fortunately for the West Ridgers, the idea of a "Grand Slam" —ascents of Lhotse and Nuptse, along with Everest—had been abandoned. The available oxygen and supplies wouldn't likely support a triple assault. At the same time, even those who were dedicated to the South Col route shared a curiosity about the West Ridge.

Hornbein admitted that focusing on a South Col blitz was not an irrational decision, considering the interests of the financial backers. "But to sit still for two weeks while the others finished their job seemed to knell the death of our route," he wrote to his wife. "Of course, we were invited to join the South Col route as a third party of four, and then go to work on the West Ridge afterwards if we still felt like it—which is selling man long and mountain short." Hornbein felt that the agreement forged on the approach march had been nudged aside. He wondered if Dyhrenfurth had been hoping to delay the West Ridge effort all along.

Dyhrenfurth had stressed that everyone should have an equal shot at the summit—depending on the circumstances, their physical condition, and their own desires. Hornbein's unremitting passion for the West Ridge had caught him by surprise, and he revived his earlier moniker for Hornbein—"pathological fanatic." The West Ridge threatened to morph from a peripheral enterprise into an independent empire, and Dyhrenfurth hadn't envisioned being the leader of two separate, competing expeditions. Irritation grew between the two groups as each staked claims to their favored routes.

"One of my major functions," Unsoeld would say later with a smile, "was to keep Hornbein under control." With the added gravitas of being the climbing leader, Unsoeld could mediate and pass wise judgment, while displaying tolerance for Hornbein (and quietly favoring him). "We would be in full congress and my job was to just sit there, with one clutching claw on Tom's shoulder, to keep him from tearing the place apart." Hornbein pointed out that his single-mindedness might be regarded as "stubbornness" by some and "tenacity" by others. Dyhrenfurth, too, could be as fanatical and obsessive about Everest, the mountain, as Hornbein was about the West Ridge.

Chapter 17

Uncertainty

The only thing that makes life possible is permanent,
intolerable uncertainty; not knowing what comes next.
—URSULA K. LE GUIN

FOR THE WEST RIDGERS, MATTERS WERE GETTING MORE COMPLI-
cated. Where there were originally seven West Ridge climbers, and
then five, now there might be even fewer. Dave Dingman—who'd
climbed admirably during the first few days of the reconnaissance—
began to feel uneasy about the feasibility and safety of the West Ridge.
He shifted his allegiance to the South Col route.

"The West Ridge looked dangerous," he said, admitting that he
might not have been ready to tackle its ominous-looking features. "I
had been sitting at sea level for four years without doing any climbing,
so I thought it might be above my ability." Dingman had initially offered to help the West Ridge reconnaissance because Dick Emerson
had been flagging: He simply hadn't acclimatized, and wasn't able to
overcome sickness and a lack of strength that had plagued him ever
since they arrived at Base Camp.

Then Barry Bishop approached Hornbein and Unsoeld. He told
them that *National Geographic,* his employer and the expedition's
main sponsor, had sent him a letter saying that they were counting
on him to reach the summit—by any route possible—and return with
photographs. Hornbein sensed that Bishop was relieved that the society had gotten him off the hook from what promised to be a difficult
undertaking. On the South Col, Bishop would be a strong contender

for the second summit team. He promised Hornbein and Unsoeld that he would return and offer support on the West Ridge once he'd finished with the attempt via the South Col.

"We knew that nobody came back from the summit of Everest worth anything," Unsoeld said. "You descend straight to Base Camp and never return." The seven original West Ridgers had represented a sizable share of expedition strength. Now, Jake Breitenbach's death had cost them one dedicated member, two were lost through defection, and one was out because of sickness. Meanwhile, virtually all of the Sherpas had been redirected to the South Col.

Unsoeld, like Hornbein, steeled himself for disappointment. "We were awfully close to tossing in our chips and joining the stampede to the South Col." Hornbein wasn't immune to second thoughts himself. "Why do the four of us sequester ourselves away from the chance to stand on the highest point on the Earth?" he wrote to his wife, as if using a distant confidante to explore his own resolve. "Why jeopardize this goal by tackling some other route, the hard way, an unknown way, with a barely sufficient party, lagging the main effort? I wish I knew all, or even some of the answers."

To climb the West Ridge properly, Hornbein suspected, a whole expedition might be needed, not just an offshoot. He prepared his wife for the possibility that his name might be missing from the roll call of summiters hailed in the press. But this wasn't something to regret, he stressed, as he would not be missing *fulfillment*. "For whether or not I find it on the West Ridge, I know it does not lie in wait as the 9th, 10th, 11th—or even first—American to climb Mount Everest by the South Col. There is something about the Col route which seems too familiar, too traveled. It's only a matter of moving from camp to camp, not easily, but probably, to the top."

Hornbein and Unsoeld weren't entirely discouraged. It was the end of April, after all, and nearly a month of potential expedition time remained. They would benefit from having even *more* of the uncertainty that fascinated Emerson—the uncertainty that is essential to being motivated toward a goal. Finding out whether a small, determined group could pull off the West Ridge on a shoestring only added to its appeal. Analogous to the process of scientific inquiry, the West Ridge was perfect for posing questions, presenting hypotheses, then testing them. Hornbein, a legitimate research scientist, was captivated by the challenge—hopefully one with an adequate margin of safety. Having unlimited oxygen, support, and time would certainly provide them more security. But it would also reduce the number of unknowns—and exploring the unknown is what experiments are all about.

Ultimately, Hornbein was betting on lightness, speed, hope, and a lot of luck. It felt right. On board were two other exceptionally strong climbers: Unsoeld and Corbet. And possibly Emerson—who was with the West Ridge in spirit, while his body was trying to hold down food.

Hornbein and Unsoeld jump-started the West Ridge "experiment" by cajoling the Camp 2 cook and his assistant into carrying loads. They also launched the West Ridge's secret weapon: *the winch.*

The gas-powered winch had already been delivered to Camp 2, and supplies were piling up at a load dump below the West Ridge, waiting to be hauled the thousand vertical feet to Camp 3W. Barry Prather's experience on a farm and on remote glaciers had included fussing with small motors, and he would be perfect to run the winch—except that he'd joined the South Col effort. The West Ridgers would have to get the winch going on their own.

Radio operator Al Auten was the other mechanically minded member of the team. Hornbein and Unsoeld gleefully realized that he was the only climber who hadn't yet chosen a route.

Auten had dutifully operated the radio at Base Camp for more than a month, but his passion for radios was subsiding as the task turned into a chore. He recalled the moment when Hornbein and Unsoeld approached him. "I was so keen to escape my radio duties that *any* climbing assignment appealed to me," he said. "And since I wasn't expecting to get to the top of *anything,* the West Ridge sounded interesting." As a bonus, Auten was turning out to be a strong climber. He had completed some respectable technical climbs in the United States, yet so consistently downplayed his ability that everyone had come to believe him when he said that he wasn't very good.

"Growing up," Auten recalled, "I was always the one picked last for team sports. I wore glasses and could never catch a ball. But at Starved Rock State Park on the Illinois River—when my parents weren't looking, because they wouldn't have approved—I did one simple climb that dumbfounded people. 'How did you do that?' they wondered."

Perhaps glaciologist Maynard Miller could replace Auten on radio duty, now that the doctors had confined Miller to a small radius around Base Camp. Miller had been hammering wood stakes into the Khumbu Glacier to measure its movement. As the sun set, he meandered back toward Base Camp through the boulders and detritus littering the glacier, and placed his hand atop an unstable one-ton rock. It rolled onto his foot, pinning him in place.

Barry Prather heard Maynard's shouts. He called a Sherpa and together, with great effort, they used their legs and bodies for leverage to slowly budge the boulder. Miller's foot was freed, but five metatarsal bones were fractured. Dave Dingman ordered Miller to stay off it, and the Sherpas fashioned him a patio in front of his tent so that he could encircle himself with his scientific instruments. Miller could handle radio duty.

The expedition didn't need any more accidents, or news of accidents, but one item leaked in from the outside world during a mid-April evening radio call to Kathmandu. On April 10, 1963, Barry Prather's brother-in-law was aboard the nuclear-powered attack submarine USS *Thresher* when it sank off the coast of Massachusetts. A leak had developed, and the nuclear reactor failed. In the worst peacetime naval disaster in America's history, all 129 crew members were lost. Prather's sister—now a widow—was pregnant with their fourth child.

On April 16, Barry Corbet and Al Auten left Camp 2 to climb up and install the winch below the West Ridge. Carrying sixty-five pounds each, they kicked and chopped steps in the hard snow to Camp 3W, and pulled into camp so exhausted that they skipped cooking dinner. The next day, Auten created an upper station just below 3W to anchor the winch. Corbet and a Sherpa unspooled the winch cable as they dragged the sled (six short skis locked together with crossbars) down the slope to the load dump. It should have been a simple process: Start the engine, and the sled would creep up the slope carrying 1,500 pounds of food, fuel, and oxygen.

Messing with the device put Auten into a mechanic's heaven. The engine started and hauled the sled—with Corbet and a Sherpa aboard—a few hundred feet. Then Auten killed the motor to unspool more cable. When he fired it up again, the starter cord broke. He didn't have a screwdriver to remove the housing and make the repair.

The next day, just as the motor showed signs of sputtering back to life, the starter cord broke again. Three days of being foiled by a simple winch while being blasted by high winds was enough. Auten wondered why the team hadn't designed a gravity-powered system. Two sleds could work as counterweights at opposite ends of a long cable that passed around a pulley at the top. One sled could descend, loaded with snow or rocks—and pull up the other sled, loaded with gear.

The West Ridge winch detail descended to Base Camp. They ate, slept, listened to music, and wrote letters—seeking rejuvenation of their morale as much as their bodies. For the time being, they were happy to let the South Col climbers make their move on the summit.

The South Col of Mount Everest is one of the most windswept, oxygen-deprived, inhospitable places on earth. For Jim Whittaker and Nawang Gombu, standing on the eastern edge of the Col was like being strapped to the fuselage of an airplane flying at twenty-six thousand feet—their precise elevation. Most of the world lay beneath them now, as they took in their first view of the eastern Himalaya. Makalu, the world's fifth highest peak (only eighteen hundred feet higher than the Col) sat regally to their southeast. Kanchenjunga, the world's third highest peak, was visible on the eastern horizon at the intersection of Nepal, Tibet, and Sikkim. In Tibet, eight thousand feet beneath them, the corrugated Kangshung Glacier made a broad turn and tapered off into the lower valley.

For Whittaker, Gombu, and the six other hopeful summiters, this was the final push. The seemingly endless phase of preparation was complete, and they had transitioned to the short, intense period of *execution*: the summit climb. They had also entered the so-called death zone. The human body begins to deteriorate at altitudes as low as twenty thousand feet, and this process accelerates over twenty-five thousand feet. Their time here was temporary and precious, as was their supplemental oxygen. ("In the death zone," Willi Unsoeld would remark, "you are supposed to be dying faster than you are living. So we looked at each other for signs of death.")

Getting here had not been easy. On April 27, 1963, a few days after the West Ridgers had descended from their reconnaissance, Whittaker and Gombu prepared to leave Advance Base Camp for the summit push. An American flag, wrapped around a four-foot aluminum picket, was tied to Whittaker's pack with orange tape; larger than most summit flags, it had once flown from the spire of the U.S. Capitol.

Whittaker hoped the Sherpas might break trail through the snow that had accumulated on the Lhotse Face, and he waited for them to make the first move out of Camp 2. "They managed to outwait me waiting for them," he said. He took the lead and forged on up to Camp 3, then onward to Camp 4, which was perched on the steep, open expanse of the Lhotse Face. Norman Dyhrenfurth and Ang Dawa, the other half of the first summit team, followed behind with twelve Sherpas.

Ang Dawa's oxygen regulator began to leak and it emitted a continuous, sickening hiss. Dyhrenfurth offered to swap regulators with him, but Ang Dawa declined. Gombu and Ang Dawa—both Darjeeling Sherpas—asked the Khumbu Sherpas who were planning to descend if they would offer them a working regulator. It made sense. They wouldn't need to use oxygen while descending, or when sleeping at a lower camp.

The Khumbu Sherpas refused. The oxygen systems conferred status on them, and no one wanted to forfeit functioning equipment for something inferior. The Khumbu Sherpas were also peeved that none of their own had been selected for the first summit party. Dyhrenfurth was at a loss to intercede. Laryngitis had reduced his voice to a feeble, rasping whisper. They had no choice but to carry on.

Above Camp 4, the slope steepened into a wind- and avalanche-scoured field of ice. Whittaker and Gombu switchbacked upward and to the left, and onto a feature called the Yellow Band: a light-colored, snow-free outcrop of rock glazed over with ice. Even with crampons, climbing across it was like roller-skating on an upward-tilted ice rink. From the far side of the Yellow Band, they contoured up and over a hump of rock called the Geneva Spur, then traversed to Camp 5 on the South Col itself. Dyhrenfurth stopped frequently to set up his tripod and film; he was in his element: high on Mount Everest, operating a movie camera.

When Whittaker and Gombu returned to the tents from their hike to the eastern side of the South Col, Gombu made another entreaty to the Khumbu Sherpas. He insisted that one of them offer his regulator to Ang Dawa. A Sherpa named Ang Nyima complied. But the next morning—unbeknownst to Dyhrenfurth—the faulty regulator was passed back to Ang Dawa like a bad penny.

The first four-man summit party departed Camp 5. They crossed the flat saddle of the South Col and ascended a slope of blue ice beneath the triangular face that leads to the Southeast Ridge. On the ridge, they passed the tattered remains of the yellow tent that Sherpa Tenzing and Raymond Lambert had pitched as their high camp during the Swiss expedition of 1952. At 27,450 feet, they found a site for Camp 6 on the only level terrain on the Southeast Ridge: a patch smaller than the size of the tent.

The Sherpas completed the carry to Camp 6 and dumped their loads. But as they turned to head back to the South Col, they refused to relinquish their oxygen bottles. In an argument punctuated by gasps for air, the Sherpas insisted they be allowed to descend on oxygen, as they had in 1956 with the Swiss.

"They love to argue," Jim Ullman wrote of the Sherpas. "They are dedicated to what they conceive to be their rights. But at one and the same time they are trustworthy, loyal, helpful, and just about everything else in the *Boy Scout Handbook*—and, most of all, they are good-natured. They argued, they made their point, they won it, and in the next moment they were grinning, shaking hands, and wishing them the best of luck."

Two hundred feet below Camp 6, Dyhrenfurth trudged upward. He was horrified, as Whittaker had been, to see seven Sherpas heading down the mountain with precious oxygen tanks. As consolation, a Khumbu Sherpa—the only one not breathing oxygen—stopped and traded his regulator for Ang Dawa's faulty device.

At Camp 6 it took two hours of breathless digging to carve out narrow, sloping platforms for the tents. At midnight the wind picked up furiously, sounding like a distant, high-pitched scream. Whittaker had heard that this was the nighttime call of the yeti, the abominable snowman of the Himalaya. The wind, the altitude, and the anticipation of what was to come made sleep impossible for all—especially Gombu, who feared yetis.

Whittaker caught a moment of sleep but awoke abruptly. His tank, set on a sleeping flow of one liter per minute, had run out. "Lying in my sleeping bag, I felt the cold work its way up my extremities," he said. "My body was telling me it was slowly dying, moving my blood to my vital organs. The cold crept toward my middle, and my feet and hands grew numb. I lay there, inert, waiting for daylight." His inertia—like early onset rigor mortis—cleared up when he plugged into a fresh tank.

The first of May was bitterly cold and snowy. High winds continued to thrash the tents, and wicked tendrils of snow and ice blew off the Southeast Ridge to the east. At Base Camp, Dan Doody jotted in his diary. "Expect all above are staying put for the day." Edmund Hillary, who was climbing on nearby Tawoche, looked over at Everest and came to the same conclusion.

Gombu and Whittaker looked up at the mountain. They agreed they had climbed in worse conditions, and at this altitude they couldn't waste a single day. The already depleted oxygen supply wouldn't last through another night and still suffice for a summit attempt a day later. They forced down some tea, crabmeat, and hot, sugary Jell-O mixed in water. Then they donned every shred of clothing they had, including three pairs of socks, boots, and nylon shell overboots to which they would strap their crampons. Dyhrenfurth shouted from his tent that he and Ang Dawa would follow shortly. He hoped to at least film their ascent through a telephoto lens.

Gombu's and Whittaker's fifty-pound packs—ungodly heavy for

that altitude—were stuffed with camera gear, oxygen, and water. They dialed their oxygen flow to an austere two liters per minute, which slowed their rate of ascent to only seven hundred feet in the first two hours. The sky remained clear but the wind speed increased, sand-blasting their legs with a ground-level blizzard of crystalline snow.

Below the South Summit, Gombu paused. A small green metal can—a tin used for a typewriter ribbon—caught his eye against the reddish rock. Inside, he found a crucifix and a medallion of Pope John XXIII. The talisman, he realized, had been left by the Indian Expedition of 1962 at the highest point they had reached. Ham radio whiz Father Moran, Gombu learned later, had presented it to the Indians when they came through Kathmandu en route to the mountain. For now, Gombu pocketed the keepsake. Perhaps he would leave it on the summit, along with his own family remembrances and Buddhist offerings.

The Southeast Ridge steepens at the base of the South Summit. Whittaker and Gombu cached their two partially consumed oxygen tanks for use on their descent. Plugging into full tanks, they resumed their slow, zigzagging climb, moving between rock and snow, taking turns belaying each other. At 11:30 a.m. they reached the South Summit, and rested—beholding the grail-like summit only 287 vertical feet above.

Whittaker was as thirsty as he was exhausted, but his water bottles had frozen solid. "Stupid from lack of oxygen," he wrote, "I had put them in the outside pockets of my pack and now they were completely useless. (Even more stupid, it had not occurred to me to cache them with the spare oxygen bottle to lighten my pack.)" He harvested some precious fluid by breaking off the icicles of condensation that formed inside his oxygen mask.

After descending thirty feet on the far side of the South Summit, they worked along a knife-edge ridge to the base of "Hillary's Chimney" (now known as the Hillary Step). This thirty-foot near-vertical clutter of rock, bracketed by ice and snow on its eastern edge, was the first pitch of truly technical climbing they had encountered since the Icefall. Breathing heavily, Whittaker slowly forced his way into the cleft between snow and rock, straining to gain purchase. His pack seemed heavier and was annoyingly awkward, and his moves were slow and deliberate. Exhausted, he flopped onto the near-level platform at the top of the step. Then he belayed Gombu, who followed.

Only six people had ever climbed higher, and Whittaker and Gombu felt a deep sense of gratitude. "They knew what they owed to their own fellow climbers, American and Sherpa, now strung out down the mountain beneath them," Jim Ullman wrote, "and to the vast amount of labor, dedication and sacrifice that had put them where they now were."

Along the summit ridge, blistering winds had sculpted three massive cornices—frozen breaking waves of ice and snow. Cantilevered out over the Kangshung Face, the monster cornices were held in place by tremendous undulating drifts that had been swept into place by the jet stream. Whittaker and Gombu rose to their feet and began the final ascent over these barren spines of ice.

"Just before we reached the top," Gombu recalled, "Whittaker said, 'You go first.' It was hard to speak through the oxygen mask, but I said, 'No—*you* go first.'"

They stepped onto the summit together. The time was one o'clock.

"I slapped Gombu on the back," Whittaker recounted. "We hugged each other. I dug my ice ax in and slung my pack over it. It was very windy, very cold, and my fingers and toes were numb." To the north, Tibet was mostly layered in clouds, but for a moment Gombu thought that he could see the Rongbuk monastery—where he had studied as a boy before escaping through the hole in the outhouse. And from the same place he could also see the Tengboche monastery, three vertical miles below them in Nepal. Its gilded roof spire reflected a sparkle of golden light.

Whittaker unfurled the American flag and planted it into the summit snow, then took photos of Gombu holding flags of India, the United Nations, and Darjeeling's Himalayan Mountaineering Institute. Gombu photographed Whittaker with the *National Geographic* and Nepal flags flapping from his ice ax. At the base of the American flag Gombu gently placed a *kata* blessing scarf given him by his renowned uncle, Tenzing Norgay.

May 1, it turned out, was also International Labor Day, an important holiday in Communist China. Gombu and Whittaker—citizens of two democracies—had inadvertently solemnized the day atop a peak that China regarded as hugely symbolic, perched as it was on their southern border. They found no sign of the bust of Mao Tse-tung that the Chinese claimed they'd left on the summit three years earlier. Its absence was not, however, proof that the 1960 Chinese attempt had failed; the bust could have been buried in snow or blown away.

As Jim Whittaker stood on top of the world, he felt "not expansive, not sublime . . . [more] like a frail human being." The frailty soon hit him quite literally: His oxygen ran out while the men stood on the summit. Gombu's tank had emptied, as well. The atmospheric pressure at 29,035 feet is less than a third of that at sea level; the two climbers gasped for air that simply wasn't there.

Gombu led the descent, with Whittaker a rope's length behind. As they skirted the summit cornices, a trailer truck–sized section of ice broke away between them and fell soundlessly to the Kangshung Glacier, two miles below.

"Gee, I guess I'd better move over a foot or two," Whittaker recalled thinking. He hopped to the right, blinking at the point in space where Gombu's footprints had been a few seconds earlier.

They climbed down the Hillary Step and traversed to the base of the South Summit. Whittaker's pack became entangled in the rope, and he fell backward. After a panicked, hypoxic struggle, he found his footing, but it took him twenty minutes to retrieve his dropped camera and climb the thirty feet to the South Summit. On its far side Gombu and Whittaker crept downward; uncovering their stash of partially used oxygen tanks, they inhaled deeply and gratefully.

At five thirty that evening, they arrived at Camp 6. Whittaker could only lift his fingers into a silent victory sign. During the past eleven hours they had taken in virtually no liquids. Ang Dawa and Dyhrenfurth melted masses of snow to rehydrate them. The radio that Whittaker had taken to the summit hadn't worked all day; the world had no idea of where they were, much less that they had just made history.

Chapter 18

Retreat in Victory

*It was written I should be loyal to the nightmare of
my choice.*

—Joseph Conrad, *Heart of Darkness*

For Dyhrenfurth and Ang Dawa, the day had been arduous.
They'd left Camp 6 an hour behind Whittaker and Gombu, but the
footprints ahead had already filled with snow. When Ang Dawa's first
oxygen tank ran out, Dyhrenfurth tossed it down the Kangshung Face,
into Tibet: "A gift for the honorable comrades of Peking and Lhasa," as
James Ramsey Ullman expressed it. Dyhrenfurth hooked Ang Dawa
up to another tank.

They never reached the South Summit. Ang Dawa had been anxious to forge onward, but Dyhrenfurth calculated that—at their lan-
guid pace and current rate of oxygen consumption—their tanks would
run dry between the South Summit and the top. They wouldn't even
be *dead* heroes on the summit of Everest, he said to Ang Dawa, em-
phasizing the risk of continuing.

The second, follow-up party of four—Lute Jerstad, Dick Pownall,
Barry Bishop, and a Khumbu Sherpa—had dragged themselves into
Camp 5 on the South Col a day behind the first group. That night,
winds funneled across the Col at even higher speeds than at Camp 6.
"Our tent floor rose off the ground twice," Lute Jerstad wrote. "I had
no doubts about our survival, but I did wonder how much frostbite
we'd have if the tent ripped away and we had to evacuate. Barry

Bishop went outside to defecate this morning, and feared he had frozen his testicles. It was minus 18 degrees F., with the wind at 40 miles per hour."

Neither party had working radios. The second party concluded that the first party must have stayed put, so they decided to spend another night on the moonscape-like Col. This resulted in even greater oxygen consumption. Jerstad noted that the Sherpas and sahibs breathed from separate bottles when they slept; a more sensible strategy would have been to T the hoses and share tanks. In the morning, they were left with several half-full bottles instead of three or four full ones.

On May 2 the successful first party descended while the second party headed upward. They intersected below the Southeast Ridge, between Camps 5 and 6, and shared hugs all around. Then Whittaker told the second party that virtually no oxygen awaited them at Camp 6. Seventeen of the nineteen oxygen tanks carried to the high camp were now empty. The implications were clear: A summit attempt by a second party of four would not be possible.

The members of the second party were stunned. Both parties descended to the South Col as Jerstad, Bishop, and Pownall grumbled about the oxygen shortfall. Conjecturing that a two-man assault could work, they rummaged through the tents, counting and collecting oxygen tanks. Bishop was consumed by fulfilling his mission for *National Geographic*—to return with images, victorious—but he was equally keen that a Khumbu Sherpa reach the top, as well—proving that at least one Sherpa from Nepal could match the two Darjeeling Sherpas who had climbed with the first party.

For Pownall, however, something didn't feel right. A similar intuition had visited him in the Icefall, a few days after Jake's accident. Pownall and Gil Roberts had stayed at Camp 1, at the top of the Icefall, and were about to organize a work crew to improve the route through it. Just before embarking, Pownall asked that they all wait for thirty minutes—though he didn't know why. When they finally got up to leave, they heard a loud roar: A massive section of the upper Icefall collapsed on itself, like a breaking surf.

On the South Col, their decision was about to be made for them: The uncertain task of staging a two-man summit attempt was turning into a rescue operation. Well behind the others, Dyhrenfurth had descended to the South Col, twice stopping to sit or lie down while crossing the two-hundred-yard expanse to the tents. He arrived at Camp 5 in a state of near-total exhaustion. All elected to descend to Base Camp.

For Bishop and Jerstad especially, it was difficult to leave the South Col, and their lifelong dream, behind; they felt themselves pulled backward—upward—by the nagging thought: *So close, and yet so far.* Everest doesn't offer many second chances.

Not far below the South Col, the descending parties encountered Dave Dingman and two Sherpas. They were on their way up, carrying cooking fuel and five full bottles of precious oxygen—just enough for a summit attempt for two. Dingman urged Bishop, Jerstad, and Pownall to return to the Col and go for it the next day. But their time in the death zone had depleted them all, and the weather had deteriorated to near-blizzard conditions. Dingman and the Sherpas dropped their loads and turned around to descend with them.

The previous day at Camp 4, Dingman had been through an ordeal of his own.

With two Sherpas, Dingman had attempted to carry loads to the South Col, but they were turned around by weather and sickness. They retreated to Camp 4. Barry Prather—known as "Bear" for his prodigious size and strength—had remained at Camp 4 that day, asleep in a tent. When Dingman arrived, Prather was sitting up but was cyanotic. His breathing was labored, and his pulse raced.

Dingman recognized the signs of high-altitude pulmonary edema. He administered a heart drug and a bronchodilator, and placed him on oxygen at a sleeping flow. Within half an hour Prather improved. Had Prather pushed himself to the South Col, Dingman reckoned, he would not have survived. Prather sensed this, as well, having witnessed a death from pulmonary edema a few years earlier.

For much of the summer of 1959, Prather had participated in the inaugural year of "Project Crater" on Mount Rainier. Maynard Miller led Prather and a small team in a study of the mountain's glaciers, the regional climate, and human physiology. Their base was a tented camp 500 feet from the edge of the summit crater, at 14,200 feet. For a period of two months, team members crawled through rabbit hole–like entryways beneath the plug of ice that sits within the wide mouth of the crater, tracing a network of spectacular ice caves shaped by active steam vents known as fumaroles. They collected temperature data from the mud and sulfur vents, establishing baseline data for exploring the theory that the mountain might be heating up.

In late August, disaster struck. Calder Bressler, a geology professor at Western Washington State College, was invited to visit Project Crater. Bressler, an accomplished climber, had no trouble reaching the summit. During his second night at the camp, though, he was in severe distress. A radio call to a physician in Tacoma suggested pulmonary edema. The professor was given bottled oxygen, but by the next afternoon he fell into a coma.

Pilot Harold Horn, who had been air-dropping supplies to Project Crater all summer, quickly geared up his plane to deliver additional oxygen. Hoping to make a drop before nightfall, Horn and a passenger circled the summit crater. The plane disappeared from sight, and radio contact ended.

Bressler's condition worsened. There was little the team could do for him, and he died the next day. Meanwhile, Project Crater was buried by a multiday storm. When the weather cleared, a search plane spotted a wreck on a snowfield near the summit. The pilots guided Maynard Miller and Barry Prather to the site. By the time they arrived at the crash, the wreckage was nearly buried in snow. The bodies of Horn and his passenger—which would have been nearly impossible to remove—were left on the mountain.

On Everest, the climbing parties descended toward Camp 2, sharing Whittaker's and Gombu's feelings of achievement, and some twinges of disappointment. At Base Camp, Al Auten fired up the radio. He was able to hail a ham operator in Ceylon and ask that he relay a message to Kathmandu. Auten enunciated a coded message into the radio's handset: *Two mail runners left Base at 1300 hours on May one.*

Expedition historian Jim Ullman—who attended the radio calls in Kathmandu—immediately understood the meaning, and adjourned to the Hotel Royal to hold a press conference. He formally announced that the expedition had *placed two climbers on Everest's summit at 1 p.m. of May 1.* The expedition still hoped to place several more climbers on top, he stressed, and only then would they reveal the names. Dyhrenfurth had insisted, and the team concurred, that disclosure of the names of summiters would be delayed until all of the attempts were concluded. He didn't want the ones who were first on top to be glorified at the expense of any later climbers.

A host of reporters jumped into action, including Elizabeth Hawley of Reuters, who had become a fixture in Kathmandu press circles. She made a beeline for the telegraph office at the Indian Embassy—the only telegraph facility in Nepal at the time. The telegraph window was attached to a building in the embassy's lushly treed compound; a number of small chairs and tables were arranged on the covered porch outside. "My assistant carried my typewriter," Hawley said, describing her routine. "And I would sit down and type the message onto the telegraph form and place it in a tray outside the window. A peon collected the messages and took them around to an office at the back entrance of the building, from where they would be sent out by Morse code. The UPI stringer sometimes intercepted the peon during his circuit, and I would catch him reading my dispatches."

At seven o'clock the next morning, Base Camp heard President John F. Kennedy's congratulations to the team broadcast over the BBC.

On May 5, 1963, Dyhrenfurth and Ang Dawa descended to Base Camp, a day behind the rest of the descending South Col team members. They were tired but upbeat.

Unsoeld and Hornbein were there to welcome them, anticipating that Whittaker and Gombu's success would finally free up Sherpas, oxygen, and other resources for a focused attempt on the West Ridge. The time had come to engage the expedition's second goal.

Once again, the West Ridgers perceived a shift in the mood at Base Camp.

Several Sherpas had departed for villages down valley. Whittaker and others who had climbed high on the South Col route were keen to depart for home. "Most of the Sherpas have just about had

it," Dyhrenfurth said—which was true of the Sherpas who had descended with him. "They can't understand why we would try to climb
the mountain from another side when it has already been climbed via
the South Col." Some of the Sherpas at Base Camp were sick. Mission
fatigue—with a touch of homesickness—had settled in.

Tom Hornbein sensed that Dyhrenfurth wished the West Ridgers
would call off their attempt, saving the leader from a difficult decision.
The expedition was already a success from the world's perspective;
they could all go home without risking more lives. At the same time,
Hornbein and Unsoeld's persistence resonated with Dyhrenfurth. An
addicted adventurer himself, he recognized and respected the impulse
in others.

Healthy skepticism about the West Ridge was understandable,
considering how little progress had been made on that route. The first
reconnaissance had ended on April 13, more than three weeks earlier.
The West Ridgers had continued to work on the winch and to ferry supplies to the higher camps, but made limited headway. "Team after team
trudged to Camp 3W to tinker with the winch," Unsoeld said, sum-
marizing the struggle. "Team after team trudged back again, beaten by
various combinations of kinking cables, submarining sleds, and inert
engines." Emerson and Unsoeld had even tried a hand winch—the
kind used for hauling boats onto a trailer. It had briefly moved eighteen
oxygen bottles weighing 250 pounds, but was slow, tedious labor for
four men. "Never has so little been accomplished by so many," Barry
Corbet confirmed. The practical-minded Sherpas decided that it was
easier to heft the supplies onto their backs and simply carry them.

Hornbein referred to the three weeks after the reconnaissance
as "the lost weekend." They nearly lost some Sherpas, too. One afternoon, four Sherpas had settled into their tent at the load dump site
below Camp 3W. They'd just begun cooking when a small avalanche
swept the tents, with the Sherpas inside, one hundred feet down the
slope. Miraculously, most of the snowslide blew over them, depositing
them in a gully rather than burying them. No one was injured. They
cut their way out through the tent fabric, but their crampons and ice
axes were swept away. Spooked by the experience, the Sherpas descended to Camp 2.

More than anything, the West Ridge effort would need oxygen. When Dyhrenfurth was above the South Col, he had struggled with the altitude. Bottled oxygen was crucial in getting him off the mountain alive. But its seemingly cavalier use at the high camps had made the West Ridge crew nervous. Hornbein and Emerson had planned for oxygen to be used above Camp 4 on both the South Col and West Ridge routes. They *hadn't* planned for it to leak from Ang Dawa's regulator, nor for it to be used in the tents during cooking and resting periods. And they hadn't planned for Sherpas to rely on it while descending (aside from the summit back to Camp 6).

In a roundabout way, though, the oxygen overuse fiasco may have worked in the West Ridge's favor. If the seventeen bottles of oxygen had *not* been consumed on the South Col route, the second party of four might have made it to Everest's summit, as hoped. Success on the South Col by two parties would have left the expedition with even less motivation for a third excursion, to the West Ridge.

But that sort of logic—and intangibles such as fortune or fate, for that matter—meant little to Tom Hornbein. He was unstoppable. "You could not have pulled Tom, or Willi, off that mountain—even if everyone else left," Dave Dingman remarked. Team members viewed Hornbein and Unsoeld's dedication to the West Ridge as mysterious, inspiring, or pathological—or some combination of those. What kept them going? Dingman, for one, had been in the mountains long enough to understand. The West Ridge wasn't about conquering a peak or attaining glory. It was an excuse, and a venue, for taking on a challenge. The West Ridge, and mountaineering, were the means, not the ends.

Hornbein and Emerson buried themselves in updating the logistics once again. Just enough oxygen remained—twenty-six full bottles— for two teams of two on the West Ridge, plus another two-man team on the South Col. There would be no room for waste, error, nor acts of God (nor acts of other deities—including those in Willi Unsoeld's Hindu and Buddhist pantheon, which he suspected were at play).

Hornbein and Emerson—the gnomelike experimenter and the cerebral sociologist—presented their findings to the rest of the expedition. The team held a vote (this time, all were present), and it was decided that a small party could attempt the West Ridge, traverse the summit, and try to descend via the surely easier South Col route. Synchronized with the West Ridge attempt, another small party would climb via the South Col—and be well positioned to support the descending West Ridgers. A summit rendezvous would be ideal— the photo ops alone would be spectacular—but was not something to count on.

Dave Dingman liked the plan. "I'd felt bad about reneging on the West Ridge, and this was my chance to make amends." He might also get a shot at the summit in the process, "though this would require that the summit climbers came romping down to the South Col without any need for assistance, which seemed unlikely."

Jerstad and Bishop were also enthusiastic. Indeed, it may have been their own abiding summit hopes—via the South Col—that kept the West Ridge discourse going. "In that sense, they probably saved our ass," Hornbein said, "or at least our opportunity to keep trying. Acting as the support team for our West Ridge traverse also served their own interests."

The new plan would have to be executed with surgical precision and would need a transfusion of good luck, as well. "We seem finally," Hornbein wrote to his wife, "to have come alive."

Tom Hornbein retreated into the role of mad scientist, and devoted all of his energy to organizing loads and to recruiting every spare Sherpa he could. Barry Corbet was in superb shape. Al Auten was also a strong, consistent climber. Unsoeld's strength remained at its near-superhuman level, blunted only by nagging hemorrhoids. Of the West Ridge quintet, only Dick Emerson was operating at a subpar energy level, though this was offset by his good humor and quiet, stubborn determination.

While resting at Base Camp, Hornbein and Unsoeld had been able to maintain their weight—a promising sign for their West Ridge effort. Many climbers lose their appetites at high altitude; Hornbein himself had shed twenty pounds while climbing Masherbrum, in Pakistan.

"Eating is not a function of appetite," Unsoeld remarked, "but of will. Hornbein and I had a pact: We swore to eat until we died. The theory is that your metabolism is so blasted by lack of oxygen that you have to maximize your throughput in order to get the nutrients." After a large dinner—and a dessert of anybody's leftovers—Unsoeld said that they would "stagger back to our tents to sit dazed and breathless on our sleeping bags, barely able to bend over." They learned to deal with this situation by untying each other's boots.

Dick Emerson had the opposite problem: The sight of food triggered a gag reflex. Emerson would lose more than fifty pounds by the end of the expedition.

On May 6, 1963, Willi Unsoeld and Tom Hornbein saddled up their packs, walked out of Base Camp, and stepped into the Icefall. After their respite at 17,800 feet, Unsoeld recalled the weird sensation, when climbing with a heavy load at high altitude, of inhaling as many as eight deep breaths for every step. "Your eyes blur—they simply go out of focus—and after several heartbeats, which you can see pulsing in your eyes, your vision flips back into focus." They arrived at Camp 2 just before dark.

Ang Pema, the energetic Sherpa who had been injured in the Icefall collapse that killed Jake Breitenbach, joined Unsoeld and Hornbein on their climb to Camp 2. Jimmy Roberts kept a close eye on the Sherpas, and he had told Ang Pema to relax for the duration of the expedition. But now Ang Pema was back at it, carrying loads through the Icefall. That morning, he had even fallen into a small crevasse, near Jake's resting place, and crawled out by performing a "self-rescue."

He had been into a crevasse another time, too, when something caught his eye. A climber—fed up with Emerson's diary and its tedious daily survey questions—had thrown his copy of the blue notebook into a crevasse in the Icefall. Ang Pema, alert and industrious as always, climbed down and retrieved it. He returned it proudly to the proper owner, whose name was embossed on the cover.

Jim Lester, the nonmountaineer psychologist, had battled his own fears and lack of experience to make it to Camp 2. Surmounting the

Icefall and strolling through the Western Cwm had triggered a re-awakening in him, and his notebook began to fill with observations that drifted away from scientific objectivity. He was turning reflective and lyrical.

Lester spent two nights alone at Camp 2, and as the sun set he wandered a few yards from camp. The moon rose directly over Lhotse, and he watched it cast a silhouette of the peak on the huge, silver screen of Everest's Southwest Face. He described an other-worldly timelessness, as the terrain seemed to melt and flow with the moon shadows that moved in stately procession toward the lower end of the Cwm.

"I had the feeling that I had seen a spectacle, which I was never meant to see, of the earth and moon enjoying each other. Should I be stranded alone here in the Cwm, unable to move down, I would prob-ably meet my death without panic, giving myself up to the overwhelm-ing spirit of the place."

On the West Ridge route, Barry Corbet and Al Auten were already high above Camp 2, visible as tiny specks on the skyline. Corbet swore that this would be their last attempt to get the winch going. But recur-ring dumps of snow had multiplied the avalanche hazard along the winch line below Camp 3W, and the wind speed was increasing daily. On May 9, 1963, they remained in their tents. "Four of us consumed a bottle of brandy," notes Corbet's diary, "which apparently was enjoy-able." For three more days, an ominous mushroom-shaped lenticular cloud cap seethed over Everest's summit.

May 13 dawned cloudless, and the air was filled with particles of crystalline moisture. At Camp 2, Hornbein and Ang Nyima geared up and headed off toward 3W. They found Unsoeld at the bottom of the winch line. The three climbers escorted a loaded sled as it moved successfully, though hesitantly, up the slope. Exhausted from carry-ing their loads and wrestling with the recalcitrant sled, they collapsed gratefully into the tents at 3W.

Despite all the obstacles, Camp 3W was now stocked with enough supplies to stage an assault on the West Ridge. Fifteen Sherpas had also arrived. Tashi was the most experienced of them and, at fifty-two, the oldest. The West Ridge idea fascinated him, and he had prodded and humored the other Sherpas into sticking with it. When speaking with the sahibs, he used his respectable English vocabulary to combine words in refreshingly hilarious, syntax-free sequences. ("Go to back," for instance, was Sherpa-English for the verb *to return;* "Isn't it?" formed the question *Is that right?*) Tashi adopted the role of father figure for some of the sahibs and enjoyed chattering away while absentmindedly peeling skin from Hornbein's sunburned nose.

Chapter 19

Synchronized Climbing

At times we were two groups playing different tunes.
The ascent of Everest, much like any jazz performance,
combined tradition with innovation without ever
knowing how it would end or exactly how it would get
where it was going. In short, it was mountaineering as
any mountaineer would have it.

—Dick Emerson

Norman Dyhrenfurth was feeling some pressure. The porter grapevine had reached Kathmandu with the rumor that an American sahib named "Jim," along with a Sherpa from Darjeeling, had climbed the mountain. The Nepal and international press was pushing him to formally release the names of the first summit team. "As with Hillary and Norgay in 1953, all our efforts at stressing the *team* effort were largely in vain," Dyhrenfurth said. "Everybody contributed, and everyone worked together. There were the men who first reached the South Col, those who were first to open up the Icefall, and others who did many hard and thankless jobs. This is a team effort, and I'll be damned if we're going to have one or two heroes."

To quash any further rumors or leaks, Dyhrenfurth relented and the team grudgingly agreed: During the May 9, 1963, evening radio call they released Jim Whittaker's and Nawang Gombu's names. Summit photos, which existed only as latent images on exposed film, would have to wait to be developed at the *National Geographic* labs in Washington, D.C. A runner was already spiriting the rolls back to Kathmandu.

Lute Jerstad and Barry Bishop were anxious to get back on the mountain. Their adrenaline had been pumping for more than a week—ever since early May, when the oxygen high jinks at Camps 5 and 6 had cheated them out of a summit attempt.

"We'd vegetated and stewed and chomped at the bit, and became quite psycho over the weather," Bishop said, describing their time at Base Camp. "Flitting through our minds were fearsome questions: Do we still have the strength? Will our desire give out?" Bishop had been fighting a sinus infection and was recovering from a possible torn muscle over his rib. He was also on penicillin to prevent pleurisy, a painful inflammation of the lining of the lung. "When something like this persists, you wonder if you have TB or if the valves in your heart are giving out, or if you're losing a lung. You get used to being a hypochondriac." Especially when exhausted, all of the climbers at Base Camp risked picking up germs—from one another, and also from the mail runners and firewood carriers arriving from down valley.

It was time to synchronize the dual ascents. On May 13 Bishop and Jerstad set out from Base Camp, carrying items that might provide a motivational boost: flags of India, Nepal, the United States, and the National Geographic Society. Jerstad wore a plaid shirt that had brought him luck on previous climbs. Despite their afflictions, they were fully acclimatized to the altitude—which Jerstad demonstrated by fluidly reciting Kipling's "Gunga Din," followed by a Robert Service poem, "The Cremation of Sam McGee," as they powered through the Icefall.

Maynard Miller's boulder-injured foot had recovered, and he had moved his glacier research operation up to Camp 1. Jerstad and Bishop spent the next day helping him deploy a seventy-five-foot-long wire ladder down the side of a crevasse. While hanging from the ladder Miller proceeded to bore into the tree-ring-like annual layers and extract ice core samples for the labs at the University of California.

This was the third time that Bishop and Jerstad had traveled up the Cwm to the higher camps, and they were disheartened to see that new snow had buried much of the route. The weather was warming— the monsoon would soon arrive—and a blistering sun reflected from the snow-plastered valley walls. Every inch of their skin was covered with clothing or white titanium oxide, as sunscreen. Bishop fashioned a nose protector from a piece of tin wrapped in adhesive tape, and fixed it onto the bridge of his goggles. They walked into Camp 2, Advance Base Camp, looking like animated scarecrows.

On May 18 Bishop and Jerstad continued toward Camp 3 with four Sherpas. Bishop broke trail, his boots plunging a foot deep in the new snow with each step.

Something wasn't right at Camp 3. A recent avalanche on the Lhotse Face had buried the tents in snow and ice. The aluminum frame of the four-man tent had been sheared clean off. It took three hours to dig out the other tents and locate the fuel cylinders and oxygen bottles. They repaired one tent, but the Sherpas felt it would bring bad luck to sleep in the mangled remains of the four-man. Bishop and Jerstad volunteered to spend the night in the wreckage.

After a sluggish start the next day, they turned their oxygen to a medium flow and began the 2,000-foot climb to Camp 4, at 24,800 feet on the Lhotse Face. Bishop plowed into the steep, snowy slope in front of him—sometimes face-first. Like a mechanical ditch digger, he carved out a small void in front of him, packed the snow beneath his feet until it held his weight, moved a half step forward and upward, then repeated the effort.

The words of a Hindu holy man—a yogi Bishop had met in India in 1961—helped impel him through the exhausting work. "One day, Lila and I were standing in front of an office in Jaipur, in Rajasthan, when a holy man grabbed me. He took my right hand and began to stare at it. In English, he explained that the mole on my right hand—on the pad of my palm, under the fifth finger—was an auspicious mark. 'You must have other such moles on your back, your chest, and your foot,' he said. Then he told me exactly where they are."

Bishop was astounded. The yogi told him that within two years— before the first of July, 1963—he would realize his dreams and achieve his goals.

"I didn't think about it again until I was asked to join this expedition. But I thought about the yogi all the way up the mountain— especially after our aborted attempt in early May. We in the West have applied our efforts in other directions," Bishop added, "and have

The American Mount Everest Expedition team converged for the first time near Mount Rainier in September 1962 and attended the Seattle World's Fair. (Missing: Willi Unsoeld, Col. Jimmy Roberts, and Nawang Gombu, who were already in Nepal, and Tom Hornbein, who had not yet been released by the navy.) *James Ramsey Ullman Archive/Princeton University*

Guides of the Exum Guide Service at Lupine Meadows in the Grand Tetons, 1959. Left to right: Jake Breitenbach, Bob French (Barry Corbet's brother-in-law), Al Read (later co-owner of Exum Mountain Guides), Barry Corbet, Ed Exum, Glenn Exum, and Willi Unsoeld. *The Exum Collection*

LEFT: Jake Breitenbach on the South Buttress of Mount Moran in the Tetons in the late 1950s, on a climb with Barry Corbet. *Barry Corbet*

The porte cochere of the
Hotel Royal, Kathmandu,
1963. *James Lester*

The vegetable market in
the center of Kathmandu.
*The American Mount Everest
Expedition/David Brower
Archive*

The bulk of the expedition's nine hundred loads of gear and supplies were packed and boxed in Seattle, shipped through Calcutta to Kathmandu, and were carried eighteen days' walk to Base Camp by porters. *Richard Emerson*

BELOW: Loads pile up at the yak pasture of Pheriche, at fourteen thousand feet, three days' walk below Everest Base Camp. *The American Mount Everest Expedition/David Brower Archive*

Dr. Gil Roberts extracts the tooth of an expedition Sherpa.
James Lester

Dr. Dave Dingman vaccinates an expedition Sherpa against
smallpox at Everest Base Camp. *Barry Bishop/National
Geographic Stock*

Near Camp 1 at the top of the Khumbu Icefall, Maynard Miller descends a wire ladder to extract ice cores from layers of the Khumbu Glacier. The Lhotse face and peak are visible behind, at the head of the Western Cwm. *Maynard Miller*

BELOW: Jim Whittaker, Sir Edmund Hillary, and Norman Dyhrenfurth confer in Namche Bazaar. *James Lester*

Tom Hornbein, Al Auten, and Barry Corbet salvage supplies and tents following the storm at Camp 4 West. The Rongbuk Glacier in Tibet is visible below them.
Willi Unsoeld/Courtesy of Jolene Unsoeld

Climbers below Everest's Southeast Ridge, at about twenty-seven thousand feet, headed to Camp 6, April 30, 1963.
James Lester

Jim Whittaker, moments after planting the American flag on the summit of Everest, May 1, 1963.
Nawang Gombu/National Geographic Stock

Tag teams of Sherpas carried Barry Bishop and Willi Unsoeld, who suffered frostbitten toes, from Base Camp to Namche Bazaar. *The American Mount Everest Expedition/David Brower Archive (left); James Lester (right)*

The team at Namche Bazaar, following the expedition. Front row: Will Siri (gray cap), Norman Dyhrenfurth, Barry Prather, Nawang Gombu. Middle: Dave Dingman, Barry Bishop, Willi Unsoeld, Tom Hornbein, Lute Jerstad, Dick Pownall. Back: Col. Jimmy Roberts, Gil Roberts, Maynard Miller, Jim Whittaker, Jim Lester, Al Auten, Knut Solbakken (helicopter pilot), Dick Emerson, Barry Corbet, Dan Doody. Missing: James Ramsey Ullman (historian). Moments after this photo was taken, Barry Bishop and Willi Unsoeld were loaded into the helicopter and flown to the Methodist hospital in Kathmandu to be treated for frostbite. *Thomas J. Abercrombie*

Nawang Gombu presents a *kata* blessing scarf to President John F. Kennedy at the White House on July 8, 1963. The team gathered for the presentation of the National Geographic Society's Hubbard Medal to each member and five Sherpas. Melville Bell Grosvenor, president of the society, is standing at left. *Abbie Rowe/National Park Service*

In the summer of 1963, the Department of State sponsored a goodwill tour of the United States for five of the expedition Sherpas and the liaison officer. Jim Lester drove them across the country in a donated station wagon. *James Lester* RIGHT: Following the expedition, Barry Corbet was hired as a model for this composite image, which ran as a full-page advertisement in national-circulation magazines in 1964. Everest's West Ridge can be seen in the background, and the North Face, in Tibet, is to the left. The Hornbein Couloir is the prominent vertical cleft in the North Face, just below the summit.

In 2003, a reunion of Everest expedition survivors was held at Barry Corbet's home on Lookout Mountain, Colorado. Left to right: Al Auten, Dave Dingman, Norman Dyhrenfurth, Nawang Gombu, Tom Hornbein, Jim Whittaker, Jim Lester, Barry Corbet, Dick Pownall, Maynard Miller, and Paco, Corbet's muse for his editorials in *New Mobility* magazine. *Muffy Moore*

neglected the inner self—neglected what the human mind is capable of." Any fear that he might crumble, he felt, was fleeting. *National Geographic* was counting on him. He had a job to do.

The West Ridgers, meanwhile, scrambled to keep pace with the South Col's fast-track climbing schedule. Jerstad and Bishop had stressed that they didn't want to sit through a good weather window and forfeit a summit attempt while waiting for the West Ridgers to catch up. Pressure seeped into Camp 3W with every radio call from Base Camp. Dyhrenfurth reminded the West Ridgers of their built-in deadline: Porters had been summoned from down valley and would arrive at Base Camp on May 25. They were scheduled to evacuate the mountain the following morning.

The West Ridge group was making respectable progress. The afternoon of May 15, 1963, Tom Hornbein and Willi Unsoeld left Camp 3W and climbed along the West Shoulder to the level site they had found for 4W—a hundred-foot-long shelf directly at the base of the rocky buttress of the West Ridge. They erected their two-man tent about thirty feet from the near-vertical drop into the Western Cwm, climbed inside, and untied each other's boots—the technique they'd perfected after overeating.

"It was a tremendously wonderful feeling to have finally established a tent at the site of what we had plotted a month before," Hornbein wrote to his wife. "The most beautiful spot in the Himalayas—right on the edge, overlooking the South Face and straight across at the summit of Nuptse, up at the summit of Lhotse, across the North Face of Everest, down the Rongbuk Glacier."

Unsoeld recorded his dreams in the blue diary that Emerson had given each of them: "I watch her walk by in the street, and her feet are only ½ as long as the black slippers she wears," he wrote of the old girlfriend who had appeared to him the previous night.

As the two men closed their eyes, a tiny object passed overhead, appearing like a moving star to those who could see it. Astronaut Gordon Cooper, beholding the Himalaya from his Mercury space capsule, may not have imagined the fellow adventurers who were nearer to him than any other humans on earth.

The next morning, Hornbein and Unsoeld left their glorious perch at Camp 4W and traversed onto the north side of the mountain. They hoped to find a site for Camp 5W at the bottom of the long, snowy chute that they had seen in aerial photos and partially glimpsed from below. One of the climbers referred to it as "Hornbein's Couloir," and a version of the name stuck.

They couldn't see much. Blowing snow curtailed their visibility just as they reached the base of the couloir. They returned to Camp 4W, arriving just before dark.

Barry Corbet, Al Auten, and four Sherpas had also arrived at 4W, carrying loads and two additional tents. They gathered to discuss the couloir route and whether it might offer a safe and level site for Camp 5W. An equally uncomfortable question concerned a site for Camp 6W—the final assault camp—which they hoped to establish at a point no lower than 27,500 feet.

Feeling tired but strong, they sang a song or two, then climbed into their tents—four Sherpas in a four-man tent, Barry Corbet and Al Auten in another, and Unsoeld and Hornbein in the smaller two-man tent.

Around nine o'clock that night, the wind began to accelerate. "As I fell asleep," Unsoeld recalled, "I was wondering: Just what *made* this campsite level?" Each brief period of quiet—as if the wind were drawing in a deep lungful of air—was interrupted by increasingly furious gusts that hammered the tents. Around midnight, a powerful gust wedged its way beneath the higher-profile four-man tents. It literally levitated the tents—with the climbers and Sherpas inside—and began to carry them downslope.

"It sounded like a dozen freight trains crashing," Corbet said. "There was nothing to do other than helplessly try to execute a self-arrest with our fingertips through the floor of the tent." Auten was terrified by not knowing what direction they were moving. To their immediate southwest lay the four-thousand-foot drop to Camp 2 in the Western Cwm. On the other side of them, it was seven thousand feet to the Rongbuk Glacier.

A single tremendous gust slammed into them. Now upended, the climbers, stoves, clothing, and oxygen bottles tumbled down the slope like clothes in a washing machine. They came to rest 150 feet away. During the maelstrom, the tent with Corbet and Auten was nearly destroyed. A hole was torn in the floor, and the aluminum frames were wretchedly bent.

Al Auten scrambled out through the floor hole—now above his head—and saw that little was preventing them from being blown even farther downhill. Both tents were still attached to each other. Corbet and the Sherpas signaled from the mass of wreckage that they were all right, if in shambles. Auten judged they had best remain in the tents as human ballast. Confronting the blizzard, he fought back a flapping frenzy of fabric and crudely stabilized the mess. In total darkness, he hunkered into the gale and battled his way to the two-man tent, which had remained in place on the ridge.

A few moments earlier, Unsoeld had said to Hornbein, "I had the weirdest dream."

"'You mean the one where the head comes in through the door?'" Unsoeld recalled Hornbein saying.

"Yeah . . . *that* one."

A moment later, Auten's head burst through their door. *"We've blown away—we seem to have lost our tents!"* he shouted over the wind to Unsoeld and Hornbein. He was wearing two left boots, all that he could find.

Incredibly, Hornbein and Unsoeld had slept through the storm. They groggily roused themselves, found flashlights, and gathered ice axes and ropes. "Our headlamps lit the swath of snow planed flat by the sliding tents," Hornbein wrote. "Only then did we appreciate the power of the storm, and imagine the horror of suddenly waking to find your tent sliding across the snow, accelerating in a headlong journey to Tibet." Auten, exhausted, remained in the tent on the ridge.

They anchored the wreckage with ice axes and lashed it with ropes. Corbet could now leave his and Auten's tent without fear of it blowing off into space—though he decided to stay put until morning. One bent tent spar flourished a ragged section of fabric that flapped furiously in the gale like a flag of surrender. Having done their best to help, Hornbein and Unsoeld fought their way, without oxygen, back up to their two-man tent.

High winds and powerful gusts continued throughout the next morning. One gust forced open the zipper to Hornbein and Unsoeld's tent—altering its aerodynamics. Hornbein, who lay on the windward side, found himself being elevated. Afraid to move—because of his body's critical role as ballast—he awakened Auten, who woke up Unsoeld. Unsoeld was able to close the zipper. Eventually they could sit up. Each of them planted their backs against a corner of the tent, and were buffeted by the assailing wind.

"I wondered what I was doing here," Hornbein wrote, "what insanity had led me to become trapped in such a ridiculous endeavor. The thought was rapid, cathartic: Anybody so stupid *deserves* to be in a place like this. All three of us were aware of our tenuous hold on the hillside. But what could we do, besides make light of it?"

At the morning radio call, Hornbein and Unsoeld learned that Barry Corbet and the Sherpas, who also had a radio, were secure: They hadn't been blown to the Rongbuk Glacier. The Sherpas crawled out and, unnerved by the precipitous slope immediately below, announced that they were retreating to 3W. Not a bad idea, the climbers figured. They prepared to do the same, though simply standing in the wind was a struggle.

From the two-man tent on the ridge, Unsoeld spoke with Camp 2 over the radio. He listened patiently during brief lulls in the staccato flapping of the tent cloth as Barry Prather, the easygoing farm boy from Washington State, drawled about low pressure zones reported over Afghanistan and the Punjab. At that moment, a sudden gust tore away the guy lines on the tent, which began to slide sideways off its tenuous snowy platform.

"We're on our way . . . ! We're headed over the brink!" Unsoeld shouted into the radio, as if bidding a final farewell.

Tom Hornbein was closest to the entrance, and his reaction was immediate. He lunged for the tent door, unzipped it, and grabbed an aluminum snow stake lying outside. With his upper body outside the tent, he jammed the stake into the snowpack and held on. At the same time, he splayed his legs inside the tent vestibule to entangle it—anchoring the whole affair with a nonstandard sort of self-arrest.

Barry Corbet, who had joined them that morning, jumped out over

Hornbein. He began piling food boxes and oxygen bottles on sides of the tent. Unsoeld scrambled out next, continuing to narrate the developments over the radio—though by this time its antenna had busted off. Like a manic sportscaster, he was both immersed in the action and separate from it.

Once the smaller tent was secured, the four climbers descended 150 yards to salvage Auten's and Corbet's ice axes from the wreckage of the two tents. As Corbet dug inside, Unsoeld watched a sleeping bag shoot from the tent and head straight upward, like a kite. "At any moment the whole mass of fabric might cut loose, envelop Barry, and take him with it," Unsoeld said. They secured what they could and filled their packs, but had lost their oxygen masks, first aid kit, down gloves, mattresses, and sleeping bags.

The men struggled back down toward Camp 3W as snow filled their goggles. At times, the wind fairly lifted Unsoeld from the mountain as he clung to his ice ax like a pennant to its mast. Only when they crossed over the ridge and escaped the wind's onslaught could they begin to gather themselves and think.

Hornbein halted a hundred feet above Camp 3W to wait for Unsoeld, who pulled up exhausted, his face coated in rime. "As we sat there," Hornbein recalled, "the realization came that we were finished, demolished, nearly blasted off the mountain. I felt no gratitude that we had escaped with our lives—only awe at the power unleashed on us, and a dissatisfied finality to all our dreams."

At Camp 3W, the survivors straggled in from 4W. They were greeted by Dick Emerson, who had arrived a few hours earlier. He'd been resting at Camp 2—persisting in his endless mission to gain weight while fighting a net loss from diarrhea. He didn't want to miss the action and was determined to climb up and offer support.

Emerson had been largely oblivious to the storm. The morning before, he told them, he'd started out from Camp 2 alone, despite the risks of solitary travel. By midafternoon he realized that he wouldn't reach 3W before dark. He could forge onward, arriving at 3W exhausted and in darkness; or he could turn back and reach Camp 2 by evening. There was a third choice: He could bivouac.

"I think I *wanted* to bivouac, but I don't know exactly why," he wrote. Emerson had no sleeping bag but was carrying an air mattress and adequate down clothing. When he reached the load dump, he located the crevasse he had explored while unsnagging the winch cable and remembered that it could provide emergency shelter. The oxygen bottles at the dump would aid in sleep and protect him from frostbite.

With two bottles tucked in his pack, Emerson rappelled thirty feet into the crevasse. In darkness, he chopped and compressed snow, building a sleeping platform at the point where the crevasse narrowed. Then he set up the air mattress (remembering to remove his crampons), donned every bit of his clothing, adjusted the oxygen regulator, and lay down. The wind picked up. Snow drifted into the crevasse and began to cover him—nicely insulating him in the process.

"I was awakened by the cold around my eyes, where powder snow had sifted in. I was thoroughly warm otherwise, but slowly realized that I'd been buried. I rose to my feet, cradling the oxygen bottle like a baby in one arm. I remade my bed and—listening to the wind roaring past my cavern—immediately fell back to sleep."

In the morning, the wind was still howling. Snow billowed into Emerson's crevasse, sufficient to seal the opening and block the light. He clawed his way upward, and emerged to discover that the sky was blue and the weather mostly stable.

He continued climbing toward 3W as a ground-level blizzard scoured his face. Inching forward between gusts, he drove his ice ax into the snow with each step. The wind tore away the air mattress, which he'd strapped onto his pack in a partially inflated state. He last saw it gaining altitude in a westerly direction. His own feet weren't visible through the snow blowing along the surface, but he could see Camp 2, below. Camp 2 could probably see him, too. As long as he was moving upward, they would assume that he was all right.

Chapter 20

A Wild Idea

To put yourself in a situation where a mistake cannot necessarily be recouped, where the life you lose may be your own, clears the head wonderfully.

—A. ALVAREZ, FOREWORD TO *The Games Climbers Play,* KEN WILSON, ED.

RELIEVED TO BE OUT OF THE WIND, THE SURVIVORS OF THE DESTRUCtion at Camp 4W gathered whatever shreds of nutrition and sleep they could. Together, they quietly absorbed the obvious: The West Ridge attempt was over.

For one thing, there weren't likely to be any Sherpas to carry supplies for them; the four who weathered the storm had descended, with no wish to return. And the West Ridgers couldn't ask Bishop and Jerstad, who were steaming toward the South Col, for a postponement beyond May 22.

"No one seemed to think we had a chance, now—especially after the wind had swept away one camp, and an avalanche another," Barry Corbet said. Hornbein agreed, and felt that to be off the mountain once and for all was the only goal with any meaning. If they were to descend now, Dick Emerson pointed out, popular opinion would regard their decision as exquisitely rational.

Another force was at work, though—an irrational, magnetic force—drawing them upward like a reverse kind of gravity. During nearly two months on the mountain—and many more in thinking and preparation—a pathway up the West Ridge had been grooved in their psyches.

Unsoeld had long been intrigued by Hornbein's calculating, scientific mind. "That night, Tom couldn't sleep," Unsoeld said, "which was always a dangerous development." Hornbein felt that their mission simply wasn't complete. First off, many of the basic supplies, such as food and fuel and oxygen, were sitting amid the ruins of Camp 4W.

In the morning, Hornbein presented the plan he'd concocted during the sleepless night: They would eliminate Camp 6W altogether. To pull this off, they'd begin by recruiting any available Sherpas, then scavenge Camp 3W for equipment and tents to replace the wind-shredded mess at 4W. From 4W, they would send a reconnaissance team—followed by Sherpas carrying loads—as high as possible up the "Hornbein Couloir." This high point would be their final assault camp, 5W. The next day, a single summit team of two would push off from 5W and make one last, valiant shot at the summit.

"Tom had it figured out," Unsoeld said. "How many porters we would need, what we could do without, how the oxygen situation stood. Tom's insomnia was always very productive. And in our weakened condition, it was difficult to distinguish fanaticism from genius. Obviously, it was a kind of hypoxia."

The new plan would result in three team members working in support of one two-man summit party—rather than a *single* member in support of four summit climbers, as configured earlier. The West Ridgers agreed that it seemed worth a try—though it would take a couple of days to regroup. For the moment, they preferred to lie in their sleeping bags, eat, and read. By radio, they asked Base Camp if any Sherpas could be talked into joining them at 3W.

Dick Emerson, who was in no shape to go for the summit himself, urged that they discuss the summit team. He led off by nominating Unsoeld and Hornbein, pointing out that they had toiled on the route more than anyone. Besides, they had painstakingly earned a belated, grudging respect from most of the South Col climbers—for their tenacity if nothing else.

Unsoeld wasn't so sure about himself. He had been strong

throughout the expedition, but felt run down from a succession of struggles—messing with the winch, climbing high in search of Camp 5W, surviving the storm, and hemorrhoids. He felt Barry Corbet should have a turn. In their six weeks on Everest, Corbet hadn't experienced a single day of real climbing, of pushing a route over new terrain. Instead, Corbet had humped loads, sweated and swore over the winch, and waited restlessly at Camp 2.

"You two have been climbing together," Corbet countered to Unsoeld and Hornbein. "You know each other, and you'll make the strongest team. What's more, you're both just about over the hump. This is my first expedition. I'll be coming back someday."

It was decided: Corbet and Auten would head out in advance to find a site for Camp 5W, and the others would follow. If either Hornbein or Unsoeld were flagging, Corbet would jump in to replace them.

All of the arguments, suspicions, and jockeying over the two routes were now beside the point. A hidden hand had spirited the West Ridgers through a gauntlet of physical, political, and meteorological obstacles, delivering them to this point in space and time. They felt strong and were poised high on a new route up the world's tallest mountain. They had just enough time and support for one final shot at the summit.

Dick Emerson was both witness to and participant in this live-action test of his sociological hypothesis. The outcome of a much-delayed, storm-ravaged, underequipped, and ill-supported attempt on the West Ridge couldn't be in greater doubt. At the same time—*or as a consequence*—the level of Hornbein and Unsoeld's motivation had reached a high point. It was just as Emerson had predicted.

Uncertainty increases motivation.

The corollary to this theory, Emerson could see, was also at work: *Information exchanged serves to maximize uncertainty*. In all their wild speculations about the future—whether optimistic or pessimistic—they favored scenarios in which the outcome remained squarely in doubt.

Willi Unsoeld expressed his own version of the hypothesis: "Someone once said that Himalayan mountaineering is ninety percent boredom, interrupted by flashes of sheer terror. Every now and then we started looking for sheer terror, just to liven things up."

Back on the South Col route, Lute Jerstad and Barry Bishop were pushing slowly upward. Before they'd left Camp 2, the radio had buzzed with news of the 4W storm. The West Ridgers, they learned, had downgraded their summit chances.

Jerstad and Bishop didn't have the leisure to wait for another update; they would have to forge onward. It took them nearly five hours to reach Camp 4, and another hour to exhume the tents from beneath a thick quilt of new snow. When the sun set, the temperature plummeted. They crawled into their bags, making room for boots, water bottles, radio batteries (to keep them from freezing) and wet socks, which would be dry by morning. Add the walkie-talkies, camera gear, oxygen tanks, regulators, and inevitably spilled meals, and the tents devolved into glorious havoc. Bishop invoked "Bishop's Law of Mountain Living": The level of bedlam in a tent is squared by the addition of a single person.

Their haul to the summit had begun. They'd begun sleeping on a trickle of oxygen and would soon be climbing on it. Everything counted now: hydration, diet, oxygen (enough, but not too much), health, mood and—especially—time.

To boost their spirits, Jerstad and Bishop spoke of wives and hot showers and civilization and rounds of beer at the Yak and Yeti Bar. Jerstad longed to see his wife, Paula, and their new baby, Joanna. He was pushed upward, he admitted, partly by a desire to send them a telegram saying that he'd climbed Mount Everest—because it would mean that he was coming home. Bishop had been presented a handkerchief by a little girl living next door in Bethesda, Maryland, and he had promised he would carry it with him for good luck—and return with it, too.

On the far side of the Yellow Band, Jerstad and Bishop traversed a perilous slope as chunks of snow and ice zinged down toward them from above. The fixed rope from two weeks earlier was buried in snow, and they wrenched it free. Their immediate goal was the Geneva Spur, a hump of dark stone that served as a gateway to the South Col. Just before reaching the crest of the Spur, they uncovered a treasure trove: the four full bottles of oxygen cached by Dingman and the Sherpas on May 2 when they turned around in the storm.

The Sherpas with them were fully loaded, so Jerstad and Bishop added the four bottles to their own packs—bringing each of their loads to nearly sixty pounds. Concentrating on keeping their balance, they negotiated the tricky, downward traverse toward the South Col.

When Bishop had first climbed to the South Col in late April, drifts of snow lay in the Col's saddle. By May 20, it had been swept clean by steady 30 to 60 mph winds. The three tents looked weary. Bishop and Jerstad off-loaded their packs, then searched for the other bottles of oxygen left on the Col when it had been abandoned, some two weeks earlier.

Three Sherpas straggled into camp, hunched beneath their own sixty-to-eighty-pound loads. Impressively, none of them was breathing supplemental oxygen. As soon as they threw off their packs, they fired up the stoves to melt snow.

Moving in hypoxic slow motion, Jerstad and Bishop wandered over to the historic campsites of the 1953 British and 1954 Swiss expeditions—graveyards of empty oxygen bottles, tent poles, shreds of fabric, fuel canisters, and broken crampons. Bishop deemed it the "world's highest junkyard." They found a full butane cylinder and two full oxygen bottles from the Swiss expedition, and Bishop radioed Dave Dingman to bring up the adaptors they had stocked for just this eventuality.

The Sherpa who had carried the largest load to the Col lay prone in the tent with nausea, a headache, and severe pains in his back and chest. When his breathing became difficult and erratic, Bishop checked his pulse. It had dropped from 120 to 108 beats per minute. They placed him on bottled oxygen, which partly revived him. He had simply carried too much weight. Now, only two Sherpas remained to carry loads to Camp 6.

As the men crawled into their sleeping bags, the wind howled incessantly, enveloping them in noise. They tried to remain economical in their movements, but neglecting even small, normally insignificant details—such as putting their socks and boots in their bags to dry—could put an end to their climb.

Over the radio, Base Camp informed them that the West Ridge team was back on track. They had recovered from the storm and were targeting a summit push on the twenty-second, depending on the success of their upward push on the twenty-first. The weather forecast was promising. Jerstad and Bishop were encouraged by what seemed to be a confluence of clear skies, hard work, good timing, and incredible luck—so far.

Just after sunrise the next day—May 21, 1963—Jerstad and Bishop crossed the South Col. They began chopping steps up the triangular face that leads to the Southeast Ridge. By the time they reached the tents at Camp 6—it seemed to take forever to get there—the intense sun and breathless climb had warmed them. Their two Sherpas dumped their loads and partially full oxygen tanks, then descended to the South Col. The two Americans turned off their oxygen to conserve the life-giving gas, and shoveled away at the partially buried tents. Every few minutes they collapsed on the snow in exhaustion.

While melting snow for water, Jerstad knocked over the pot. He started over. Then the stove ran out of fuel. Frustrated and underfed, he and Bishop climbed into their bags. To save time, they didn't remove their boots and overboots; in the morning, the process of suiting up their lower legs could take over an hour.

Bishop had been drained, physically and psychologically, by the climb, the clearing of snow, and the mishaps in the tent. Now he was suddenly gripped by intense, nauseating claustrophobia and loss of equilibrium. Unable to lie down or sit up, he twisted his body and propped his head at an awkward angle.

"He had a wide-eyed, wild look," Jerstad said, "and told me that he thought he was going crazy." A higher flow of oxygen helped—but Bishop feared that his dizziness, and probable lack of sleep, would affect their chances to reach the summit the following day.

Chapter 21

A One-Way Round Trip

I believe that no man can be completely able to summon all his strength, all his will, all his energy, for the last desperate move, till he is convinced the last bridge is down behind him and that there is nowhere to go but on.

—HEINRICH HARRER

"I'M DELIGHTED BY YOUR PLAN," DYHRENFURTH TOLD UNSOELD OVER the radio from Base Camp. "This is exactly what we were going to suggest: that only two men make the attempt. All I can say is, you've had a lot of tough luck. You've worked awfully hard, and we're two hundred percent with you."

The tide had turned. The 1963 American Mount Everest Expedition was a single team again. Some members were within striking distance of the top, and all were on the cusp of going home—regardless of the outcome. Until now, Dyhrenfurth hadn't fully committed to the West Ridge effort out of concern that it might jeopardize their larger mission. Yet it had been Dyhrenfurth, after all, who'd first unrolled the oversized photographs of the West Ridge at Tom Hornbein's home in San Diego—planting the seed that was now, finally, about to bear fruit.

One layer of uncertainty was peeled away when, on May 19, 1963, five Sherpas arrived at Camp 3W. The veteran among them had corralled four other Sherpas who hadn't seen much work on the South Col route, and they were eager to prove themselves in a grand, triumphal push. The effort would be time limited: In a few days the expedition would literally run out of oxygen. And the porters were on their way to clear out Base Camp.

"I hesitate to put the words on paper," Hornbein wrote to his wife, "but as it stands now, health holding up, Willi and I will make the first shot. Outside of a deeply annoying cough, I find myself capable of going surprisingly well, even able to keep a fairly competitive pace with the great Unsoeld, and no less motivated toward our mutual goal. I only hope I hold up—and Willi, too, for nothing could be more perfect than to climb to the top together."

The five West Ridgers and an equal number of Sherpas were soon on their way back to Camp 4W, moving quickly on wind-hardened snow under auspiciously clear skies. Then Unsoeld stopped. He'd left a lens filter at 3W. He felt that his photographs would be unusable by *National Geographic* without it. He returned to Camp 3W to retrieve it.

For an hour, Hornbein sat alone on the West Shoulder as the sun shone through a thin layer of clouds. He removed his oxygen mask and mittens, and gazed at the remarkable world of snow and ice below, luxuriating in a feeling of smallness. "I thought about my wife, my four girls, and my young son, half a world away, and I wondered if they could imagine or sense that I was thinking about them up there. . . . We also knew that the thing that had brought us to the West Ridge in the first place would not let us go."

The West Ridgers pitched two large tents on the patch of level ground at Camp 4W—exactly the spot they'd been blown off a few days earlier. This time, they added abundant anchors. The aluminum snow pickets that had held the flattened two-man tent were still in place, the frayed stubs of its doomed guy lines attached. "We took pictures of these," Unsoeld said, "to send to the manufacturer when we got back—to show him that he still has a way to go in tent design and construction." Al Auten couldn't decide whether he should contribute his ice ax as an additional tent anchor—or take it to bed with him in the event he would need to make a self-arrest through the tent floor.

Their elaborate defenses against the wind may have conjured the unusual tranquillity at 4W that night. Higher on the mountain, the low roar of the wind persisted, like a deeply toned organ summoning a divine and infinite power. After dark, though, even those high-altitude winds subsided. The climbers' rest was peaceful, aided by a judicious flow of oxygen.

The weather held into the morning of May 21. Barry Corbet and Al Auten took the lead along what they called the Diagonal Ditch, an uphill traverse onto the North Face, and ultimately to the base of the Hornbein Couloir. An hour later, five Sherpas prepared to follow. One energetic Sherpa picked up a load that weighed at least fifty pounds.

"Very heavy load, sahib," he remarked to Dick Emerson. "Can't carry this high." He set the pack down and paused to ponder it. Before anyone could respond, he shouldered it again. "Oh, well. Last carry—I take." This would be the final uphill slog of the expedition, and he wanted to go home satisfied after a long and hard last day. "All good Sherpas down at Base Camp, all bad Sherpas up at 4W," he explained. A round of laughter affirmed his meaning: The sensible ones had stayed below.

Hornbein, Unsoeld, and Emerson—the 1960 Masherbrum triumvirate—departed shortly after the Sherpas. They traversed toward the North Face on the pleasurable, hard-packed snow of the Diagonal Ditch. Dick Emerson carried a spare bottle of oxygen as well as the bottle he was breathing from.

"Dick—for God's sake, get rid of that bottle!" Unsoeld said sympathetically. He felt that Emerson had no business being up there. Dick hadn't thrived with altitude and was propelling himself along on willpower alone.

"No, no—I'm here because you guys need the spare bottle."

"Dick," Unsoeld said, "we asked you to come this far with us today because we love you." As long as he could, Emerson was sticking with the pact they had made on Masherbrum in 1960: all of them or none.

They reached the base of the Hornbein Couloir at one in the afternoon. This was to be Emerson's high point. He would wait here for Corbet, Auten, and the descending Sherpas, who were now far above them. They rested for a few minutes and shared a quiet, nearly tearful moment. It was unclear who was more worried about whom.

It didn't matter. Favorable luck, strange omens, obstacles, and arguments be damned. The dazzling, vast unknown—a key threshold to the uncertainty that Emerson had been diligently studying—was beckoning them forward and upward. This was no longer an academic exercise.

Hornbein and Unsoeld reshouldered their packs and began climbing the snowy defile of the Hornbein Couloir. A few hundred feet up, they glanced back. Emerson sat on a ledge below, looking unimaginably alone.

The couloir steepened to forty-five degrees. They were grateful for the steps that Barry Corbet had carefully cut ahead of them—much needed by the heavily loaded Sherpas who had limited experience on steep snow slopes. He was still carving steps, far above, judging by the chunks of ice that came whistling down the shooting gallery–like couloir. When larger pieces headed their way, they ducked behind outcrops for refuge.

Around 4 p.m., Hornbein and Unsoeld looked up to see Corbet and Auten sitting on a small shelf at the base of the Yellow Band: a layer of light-colored, rotten sedimentary rock also found on the south side of the mountain. If this was the intended camp, Unsoeld fretted, it had better be at least twenty-seven thousand feet—or the next day's climb to the summit, and a timely descent, might be impossible.

"Twenty-seven thousand, two hundred twenty-five feet," Corbet sang out, reading from his altimeter as Hornbein and Unsoeld approached. The ledge, just eighteen inches wide, was the only conceivable site for Camp 5W they could find. Above them the couloir narrowed and steepened. Below, the slope fell away at a sustained fifty-degree angle.

When the Sherpas arrived, there was no room for them to sit or to put down their packs. With extreme care they unloaded the oxygen bottles and boxes, then passed them hand-to-hand to the widest part of the ledge to be stacked and balanced. The oxygen was so tightly rationed that the loss of even a single bottle could have ended the climb.

The rookie Sherpas had completed the most demanding and technically difficult carry of the entire expedition. Barry Corbet, Al Auten, and the Sherpas would have to head down promptly in order to grab Emerson and reach Camp 4W before nightfall.

Corbet uncoiled a 120-foot length of rope and joined it to a similar length they had used on the way up. He speared the shaft of his ice ax deep into the snow, wrapped one end of the rope around it, and threw the end of rope down the couloir. The Sherpas would have to clip their carabiners onto the rope, and use it as a hand line. Auten went first, to look for a secure stance where he could wait and collect the Sherpas as they came down.

Then Corbet sent the Sherpas. "Just like Mount Owen," he shouted over to Unsoeld—invoking the snowy chute of a peak in the Tetons they had both guided. Corbet was the last to go. He threw the top end of the rope down the couloir, withdrew his ice ax, turned to face the slope, then began descending. In his shirt pocket sat a photo of the year-old son of his brother-in-law. If he reached the summit, he had planned to toss the bust of Chairman Mao down the North Face and leave the photo in its place.

Next time. Corbet's oxygen mask hid tears. He had just reached the highest point of his climbing career, but mainly he harbored a private fear for Unsoeld and Hornbein, his friends and mentors. Losing Jake was more than he cared to endure for one expedition.

When the Sherpas arrived at Auten's position, he kept them clipped into the rope. After Corbet arrived, he threw the top end of the rope down below them, anchored the new top end, and Corbet descended first over the next stretch. In this manner they alternately flipped the rope, end over end, descending 2,100 linear feet to the bottom of the Hornbein Couloir. "The Sherpas had never seen such a thing," Auten noted, "In half an hour they descended what had taken them most of the day to climb up."

Partway down the couloir, one Sherpa slipped and began to slide on his back, adjacent to the rope. He accelerated quickly but twisted onto his stomach and grabbed the line. He caromed into another Sherpa, who had been descending thirty feet below him. The two Sherpas carried on in a tangle before coming to a stop, unharmed.

Corbet was the last man out of the couloir, glissading along with his back to the mountain—making turns on the snow with his boot edges, as if on skis. But fatigue was making him clumsy, and he slowed down—uncertain he would have the strength to make a self-arrest should he fall.

Dick Emerson was waiting at the bottom of the couloir. The men started on the long traverse to the Diagonal Ditch and back to Camp 4W. Emerson was stricken by a spell of weeping, possibly fueled by the long isolation at this impossibly remote outpost. "And perhaps," Corbet surmised, "in great hope and fear for Hornbein and Unsoeld; or maybe Jake's death had culminated for him in this intersection of us all." They picked their way through fading, eerie light, walking the last stretch to 4W in darkness.

"As I lay in bed that night," Emerson wrote, "I reviewed the work we might have to do during the next two days if Unsoeld and Hornbein got into trouble. None of us talked about such matters."

Up on the narrow perch of Camp 5W, Unsoeld and Hornbein began digging out a platform and pitching their tent. Their oxygen now turned off, they hacked away for an hour, careful not to dislodge ice that would fall on the descending climbers. After one brief burst of impatient chopping, Hornbein's vision dimmed. He slowed his pace, and his vision returned as more oxygen flowed to his brain.

The tent sat at an awkward angle on the platform, its outer eighteen inches hanging over the precipitous Hornbein Couloir. They placed heavy items in the uphill side of the tent, and anchored the guy ropes with a piton they drove into the delaminating rock of the Yellow Band. Hornbein hoped this "combination of ineffectual measures" would keep the tent from sliding off the mountain.

Cramped and contorted, Hornbein prepared chicken noodle soup, reconstituted freeze-dried crab in tomato sauce, crackers, and jam. Dessert was a can of grapefruit segments. Butane gas cylinders and water bottles, which could not be allowed to freeze, were piled into their sleeping bags with them. They wore all their clothes except their boots, which were recruited to support the sagging outer edge of the tent. Since Unsoeld outweighed Hornbein by twenty pounds, he slept on the uphill side, next to the rock face.

Teetering on their ledge, higher on the planet than any other humans, Hornbein dutifully wrote an entry on pages torn from his blue diary. Then, as an idle experiment, he removed his oxygen mask and wrote a letter to his wife, to record hypoxia's effect on his coherence and penmanship.

The men slept well, despite their precarious roost. When the supply of sleeping oxygen ran out at 4 a.m., Hornbein awoke and fired up the stove to melt snow for soup, cocoa, and coffee. He cross-checked their climbing gear, then affixed his crampons inside the tent. Unsoeld cautioned that he risked puncturing the air mattresses. "I told him this was of scarcely any importance," Hornbein said, "since, in any case, we would descend by the other side." This raised the issue—which they hadn't discussed—of what would happen if they needed to turn back. Up was the only direction they had really thought about.

They hooked up to fresh oxygen bottles, but Unsoeld's developed a leak. Hornbein swapped his regulator with Unsoeld's, but it still leaked. "It doesn't sound serious," Hornbein said hopefully. If needed, they might be able to share a single bottle between them, using the T connector designed for sleeping. The hose, however, was just three feet long; climbing in that manner would require moving in lockstep. They had little choice but to continue, and abandon their tent, sleeping bags, and remaining food. Hopefully forever.

The going was difficult from the outset. Unsoeld led, but his crampons wouldn't hold on the loose snow. He cut steps, sending an endless cascade of sugary snow crystals onto Hornbein. The fifty-five-to-sixty-degree pitch of the couloir was relentless, offering nothing to sit on or lean against. They climbed one at a time and conserved oxygen by turning it off while securing each other—with dubiously shallow ice ax belays. Hornbein arrived at each of Unsoeld's belay positions entirely out of breath. He checked his regulator, which was set at a flow of two liters per minute, yet the bottle remained nearly full.

A few hundred feet above their camp, the couloir narrowed gradually into a crack the width of a man's body, forcing them to climb sideways so their oxygen bottles would fit. They next faced a cliff sixty feet high—a long pitch of technical rock climbing. But the Yellow Band consisted of rotten, downsloping slabs, with few firm cracks for the placement of pitons. The unnervingly slick texture of the rock provided some purchase for crampons, yet the climbers felt they might slip at any moment.

Unsoeld offered the lead to his partner. Hornbein muttered that he didn't like the looks of it, but began climbing. The first move required a long step up to a steeply sloping slab, on which he had to trust that the points of his crampons would hold him. There were no handholds at all.

Hornbein disappeared above. For a long time Unsoeld detected no movement and was close to dozing off—the result of sleep deprivation and shutting off his oxygen. "Then I heard a hammer—the first piton ever driven into Mount Everest. I thought, *If Tom is driving iron, it has got to be a bear.*"

But the piton strikes—*bong . . . bong*—did not emit the clean, bell-like ring that would have signaled a firm placement. The rock was crumbling around the piton.

Hornbein tried to climb higher but was stymied. He rigged a rappel from the sketchy piton, and slid down the rope like a giant spider, nearly landing on Unsoeld. He told Unsoeld that he couldn't go higher. Then he realized he hadn't turned up his oxygen flow, which would have boosted his acuity and strength.

"Tom . . . If you couldn't do it, what chance do I have?"

"No—you won't have any trouble. Just increase your oxygen flow."

Unsoeld quickly reached the point where Hornbein had placed the piton. He removed his mittens, cranked up his oxygen flow to four liters per minute, and climbed bare-handed, worming his way up. Arriving at a ledge, he sat and belayed Hornbein, who followed up rapidly.

Air had been hissing from Unsoeld's regulator for six hours, and his tank was empty. "I had been going very well on a flow of two liters, hyperventilating on the difficult parts," Unsoeld said. "We had wondered how you'd know when your oxygen ran out. I can tell you. My guts just drained out of my abdomen and trailed behind me."

Unsoeld switched to his second tank. This one didn't leak.

At the top of the rock pitch, they entered an area of blue-gray limestone at a more gentle angle. This was the upper edge of the

Yellow Band, at twenty-eight thousand feet. The summit was just over a thousand feet above them. Now they faced a real problem: It was three thirty in the afternoon, and the shadows were getting longer.

They sat on a cluster of rock slabs, their first real rest of the day. "Well, it looks like we have a decision to make," Unsoeld said. They would have to go on or turn back. Unsoeld didn't press Hornbein for a response. They knew that their decision had been made long before.

"I looked down," Hornbein wrote. "Descent was totally unappetizing. Too much labor, too many sleepless nights, too many dreams had been invested to bring us this far." There was also no avoiding the truth: A descent via the West Ridge, along the route of their ascent, would be problematic. The rock was rotten—Everest is a heap of uplifted ocean sediments—and a piton hammered into it could not be relied upon as a solid anchor for a rappel. Climbing down over steep terrain, as every mountaineer knows, is more difficult and dangerous than ascending.

The summit was located on their easiest route home, and it was tantalizingly close. Unsoeld pulled out the radio and called Base Camp. "We're sitting at the top of the Yellow Band," he said to Jim Whittaker, "and it would be too difficult for us to descend. There are no rappel points. So tell Dave and Girmi Dorje that it's up and over for us. We may be kind of late, so keep a candle in the window."

Whittaker confirmed that Dave Dingman and a Sherpa were supposed to be waiting in support on Everest's far side, at Camp 6 on the Southeast Ridge. He had no update on Bishop and Jerstad's summit progress.

"If it's not going to pan out, you can always start working your way down," Whittaker said over the radio, concerned that Hornbein and Unsoeld might be forfeiting their only safe exit strategy. Unsoeld and Hornbein glanced at each other: Reconsidering was no longer an option. They told Whittaker they would keep that in mind and agreed to check in on the radio an hour later.

They had drifted to the east and decided to traverse back toward the crest of the West Ridge. The ridge itself wasn't visible, but they were confident that it lay beyond the skyline to their right. The slopes above presented a puzzle, however, and they hadn't really located themselves. It was one thing to absorb an image of the route from photographs—but here on Everest's sheer immensity, they were like fleas on an elephant, with little to take their bearings from.

They hailed Whittaker on the radio again, and asked if he could describe the configuration of the West Ridge from the summit. His view of the terrain immediately below had been limited, Whittaker said, but he had seen a snowy ridge that appeared distinctly climbable.

The description didn't fit with anything Unsoeld and Hornbein could see in their rocky world. "The main thing that we got out of these contacts," Unsoeld said, "was the reassurance of Jim's voice. I had great difficulty in keeping my own voice steady, just from the fact that he was talking to me. We were extremely emotional at this point." Hornbein was struck by the odd sensation of holding a chatty conversation with folks below while functionally disconnected from that world. Base Camp was there, but he and Unsoeld were here— untethered, on their own. They might as well have been on another planet, or in an orbiting Gemini capsule.

"Home, life itself, lay only over the top of Everest and down the other side," Hornbein wrote. "Suppose we fail? The thought brought no remorse, no fear. Once entertained, it hardly seemed even interesting. What now mattered most was right here: Willi and I, tied together on a rope, and the mountain, its summit not inaccessibly far above." Hornbein admitted to some anxiety, but this was overshadowed by a feeling of calm and of pleasure at the joy of climbing.

They knew they needed to keep moving up, seeking out the path of least resistance. They negotiated downsloping slabs, flaking rock, and snow gullies, then reconnected with the crest of the West Ridge for the first time since they had left camp the day before. Everest's South Summit was now visible, directly across the Southwest Face. Leaning over the ridge, they peered down at Camp 2 in the Western Cwm, a mile and a half below.

The wind at the crest was brisk, but the rock felt solid. They removed their crampons and climbed on the lug soles of their reindeer boots, grateful to find handholds big enough to accommodate their mittens. For three rope lengths, they moved easily upward along the narrow ridge. Hornbein delighted in the boost he felt from being thirteen pounds lighter; he'd jettisoned his spent oxygen bottle.

At the top of the rocky stretch they reattached their crampons and continued slowly upward on wind-hardened snow. "To our north, it was a sheer drop of ten thousand feet into Tibet," Unsoeld recounted. "And to the south, to our right, it was seven thousand vertical feet into the Western Cwm. So as we climbed, we leaned a little to the right."

Chapter 22

The Vast Unknown

Happiness can be understood only by understanding
pain and remorse. Well-being is felt after one has been
tempered by fire and cold. So the world below is
understood by being compared to the world above.

—LUTE JERSTAD, IN A LETTER TO JIM
LESTER, JUNE 5, 1964

MOST OF THE PLANET LAY BELOW THEM. WILLI UNSOELD RAISED
his head—and stopped. Ahead of him, the Northeast Ridge and
Southeast Ridge converged on a small dome of snow. Something else
stood out.

"Forty feet ahead was the American flag, shining in the slant-
ing rays of the sun and flapping wildly in the breeze. It was wrapped
around the picket, and frayed at the edges. It made quite an impact on
our very impressionable minds."

Tom Hornbein was a short distance behind. "Willi . . . stopped,
coiled the rope, and I wondered why he was standing there," he wrote.
"I came climbing up and joined him and looked ahead. I kept telling
myself: *It can't be the summit; it's too near.*"

With thoughts and feelings shared but unspoken, Hornbein and
Unsoeld hugged. It was 6:15 p.m. Together, they walked the remaining
forty feet to the peak.

"We felt the lonely beauty of the evening, the immense roaring silence of the wind, the tenuousness of our tie to all below," wrote Hornbein. "There was a hint of fear: not for our lives, but of a vast unknown

which pressed in upon us. A fleeting feeling of disappointment—that after all those dreams and questions, this was only a mountain top—gave way to the suspicion that maybe there *was* something more, something beyond the three-dimensional form of the moment. If only it could be perceived."

Sunset bathed the summits of Makalu and Lhotse and the distant high valleys in amber light, and they took photographs. Unsoeld laid a crucifix, wrapped in a silk blessing scarf given him by Nawang Gombu, at the base of the flag. He tied another *kata,* this one from a Sherpa relative, to the stake. Then he said a brief prayer of gratitude for the nature of the world in which we live, and for mankind's ability to appreciate it.

"Buddhist prayer flags and ceremonial scarf, the American flag and the cross of Christ, all perched together on top of the world—supported by an aluminum picket painted Survival Orange," Unsoeld wrote. "The symbolic possibilities rendered my summit prayer more than a trifle incoherent." He also unfurled the pennant of the Oregon State University Mountain Club; he had met his wife, Jolene, on a club outing.

Finally, the two men spoke a few words to each other through their oxygen masks, above the roar of the wind: "Mostly an emotional expression of how close together this climb had brought us," Unsoeld recalled. "It was a testimony to interpersonal relations, rather than to overcoming a great mountain. We spoke also of the disappointment of having to leave behind Barry Corbet, who was obviously capable of making the summit as well."

Willi Unsoeld and Tom Hornbein were only halfway home. Instead of luxuriating in the dramatic scene, or in a sense of glory, they turned to the urgent task of getting themselves off the mountain.

The odds, and the setting of the sun, were not working in their favor. But for Hornbein, there was also a profound intuition at play. "The prospect of descending an unknown side of the mountain in the dark," Hornbein wrote, "caused me less anxiety than many other occasions had. I had a blind, fatalistic faith that, having succeeded in coming this far, we could not fail to get down." As the Tibetan Buddhists say, if you are doing all that you humanly can to improve your situation, then there's no reason to worry.

Moments after they departed the summit, Hornbein removed his oxygen mask, lay it on the snow, and banged on it a few times with his ice ax—dislodging the accumulated ice that threatened to block the flow of oxygen. Then he looked to his left and saw the massive summit cornices stretched like ghostly hands over the abyss of Everest's Kangshung Face. He also saw something that encouraged and half surprised him: fresh footprints, leading down the ridge.

Lute Jerstad and Barry Bishop had reached the summit. Hornbein and Unsoeld knew nothing of where they were or what had happened to them; they presumed that Jerstad and Bishop had already descended and arrived at Camp 6. They would soon learn more—sooner than they expected.

Not far below the summit, Unsoeld stopped to call Camp 2 on the radio. He reached Maynard Miller. They had reached the top, he told Miller, and were now descending toward the South Col. To Miller's astonishment, the next words from Unsoeld that came over the airwaves were from Robert Frost: "I have promises to keep. And miles to go before I sleep." Home was a near-impossible distance away.

Hornbein belayed Unsoeld down the ragged, vertical stretch of the Hillary Step. As Hornbein prepared to follow, his oxygen tank banged against a chunk of ice, setting off a tremendous hissing noise. He feared the regulator was damaged, and yanked on the rope to halt Unsoeld, who was at that moment traversing the knife-edge ridge between the Hillary Step and South Summit. Hornbein's vision dimmed as he felt for the regulator. Thankfully, it had merely been loosened, and he was able to retighten it.

They could bivouac for the night in the protected saddle at the base of the South Summit, Hornbein pointed out. Unsoeld was set on forging ahead. "It wasn't entirely rational, this feeling of mine," said Unsoeld. "I mean, you don't get down a peak this size in one night. Yet I still had this conviction that we had to get down as far as possible."

Gaining the crest of the South Summit, Unsoeld and Hornbein looked out at the peaks of Lhotse and Makalu, highlighted in alpenglow. Behind them, Everest's summit was rinsed in a cold golden light. They moved on.

At times they plunge stepped through soft, deep snow, then trod carefully over snow-plastered rock that offered nothing for their ice axes to grip. Jerstad's and Bishop's tracks faded, then reappeared just as Hornbein and Unsoeld drifted off route. A fall would likely pull both men from the mountain. Then Unsoeld's last tank of oxygen ran out.

They plodded onward. The light on Lhotse and the South Col faded to streaks and silhouettes, then dissolved into a great, singular blackness. There were no higher peaks or atmospheric haze to reflect residual light, and they were absorbed into the native darkness of the stratosphere—into a dreamlike world that awakened their senses of hearing and touch. Only camera flash–like reflections on the snow— from distant bursts of heat lightning—remained to guide them. One week earlier, from *Faith 7*, Astronaut Gordon Cooper had similarly marveled at the constellations of flashes from thunderstorms across the plains of northern India.

They could feel the slope steepen.

"Willi!" Hornbein suddenly shouted. Hornbein had stepped off a small cornice of snow and dropped several feet. The rope snapped taut on Willi, and he threw himself on his ice ax, executing an abrupt, static belay—the kind that can result in broken ribs. Once Hornbein had secured himself, Unsoeld descended to him. Then Hornbein extended his ice ax and arms, and helped Unsoeld over the cornice. It was a big enough drop to launch an unwary climber onto the treacherous slope below.

The beams of their flashlights dimmed to a faint glow almost immediately after they were switched on, and their retinas only captured faint imaginations of footprints or ice ax holes. Whittaker had warned them to avoid heading to the left as they descended the Southeast Ridge. Fine. A series of buttresses, separated by menacing gullies, tended to draw them off to the right. Unsoeld tried a short foray in that direction, then overcorrected to the left—until he felt his ice ax punch through the thin crest of the ridge.

The wind picked up and battered them in sharp, unpredictable gusts. Just as they braced themselves for the next one, a gust would strike from the other direction.

They hoped that Dave Dingman was climbing up from Camp 6 to guide them down, but Unsoeld suspected that Dingman wasn't about to go rollicking around looking for climbers at that time of night. He wouldn't know the terrain any better than they did.

From a strobe of lightning, Unsoeld glimpsed tracks on the ridge directly below them. They shortened the rope connecting them to fifty feet, which made conversing easier. The snowy stretch of ridge turned to rock. Guessing that they might be near Camp 6, they yelled into the darkness, hoping that Dingman and the Sherpa with him might hear them.

Silence. A few moments later, both swore they heard a distant, humanlike sound. They agreed it was the play of the incessant, irritable wind. Then they heard it again. *"Helllooooooo . . ."*

"We started yodeling," Unsoeld said. "It's the first time in my life that I've used the international distress signal of three yodels in succession." They yelled and yodeled several more times. Again, silence. Just as they began to move again, they heard shouts, but couldn't understand them.

Why aren't they shining a light? Unsoeld and Hornbein wondered. *Are they just lying around in their tent?* Unsoeld flashed his weary light, but saw nothing in response. Then, oddly, the voices called for *them* to shine a light.

Puzzled, they continued.

More calls cleaved the darkness. "It must have been Camp 6, because the voices hadn't moved," Unsoeld recalled. He was able to triangulate the sounds as coming from their left. Their spatial orientation was dependent entirely on sound; they had no visual cues to work with.

Two dim, black blotches slowly appeared, though they couldn't estimate their distance. Suddenly, Unsoeld fell into a shallow crevasse. He came to rest with its edge at shoulder level. "There's a crevasse here!" he shouted.

A different voice—closer now—responded calmly. "You're right on route. Keep coming." Unsoeld crawled from the crevasse, and within moments he and Hornbein were upon the voices. The men threw their arms around each other's shoulders and pounded each other on the backs. *"Who is it? Who are you?"*

It wasn't Dave Dingman at all.

"It was Lute Jerstad and Barry Bishop," Unsoeld said. "And they were as lost as we were."

Unsoeld and Hornbein saw that their teammates might need even more help than they did. Jerstad and Bishop were clearly at the ends of their ropes.

Jerstad and Bishop's day had begun, like Hornbein and Unsoeld's, before sunrise. Rousing himself in the predawn darkness, high on the Southeast Ridge, Bishop foresaw that he was going to have an "off" day. He just wondered *how* off. Jerstad lit one butane stove and began melting snow. While replacing the empty cylinder on the other stove, he neglected to close the valve. Over the howl of the wind, he didn't hear the hiss of leaking gas.

Butane slowly filled their tent—until the flame from the other stove ignited the gas in a terrifying explosion. The blast blew Bishop's oxygen mask from his face, singeing his beard and eyebrows. Jerstad's beard caught fire, and the tent was engulfed in flame and smoke. Jerstad tore at the tent door while Bishop lunged for the vent at the rear of the tent. Reaching through a hole in the tent liner, Jerstad found the zipper to the entrance and flung himself outside. His momentum nearly carried him over the ridge and down toward the South Col. Bishop ejected right behind, landing on top of him.

Propped on their hands and knees at 27,450 feet, they gasped for air for several minutes before they could begin to breathe normally. It took a longer time—unknown minutes—for Bishop to gather his wits and piece together what had happened.

Bishop was rattled. He looked up at the indigo sky. Could they go on? The incident had set them back severely. Then Bishop thought of the Indian astrologer. He resolved that neither fire nor sleep deprivation would cheat them of the summit. Fulfillment of his dreams had been written ahead of time on his destiny, the yogi had explained.

At 8 a.m., wearing fifteen pounds of clothing and carrying forty-five-pound packs, they departed. Switchbacking upward, they drifted in and out of Whittaker's and Gombu's tracks, taking four or five breaths for every step. Four hundred feet below the South Summit the route steepened, and they paused to nibble on some rum fudge—a high-calorie snack the British expedition had found palatable at high altitude. They also changed oxygen bottles, relieving themselves of thirteen pounds each. The few atmospheres of pressure remaining in Jerstad's tank might be useful on the descent; he left it on a rock ledge at their feet.

When they stood, Bishop's crampons caught on the tank that Jerstad had just placed there. He took a backward header into open space. Again, Bishop found himself about to rocket toward the South Col. Twisting in midair, he landed on his stomach, did a self-arrest (without an ice ax), and slid to a halt a few yards below their resting spot. Jerstad dove after him. The effort exhausted them both.

Jerstad, feeling stronger than Bishop at this point, took the lead. They were now sucking six breaths with every step, craving oxygen, but they rationed the gas in their bottles to a modest two and three liters per minute. "If you were at sea level and felt as lousy as we did," Bishop said, "you would check yourself into a hospital." The weather, at least, was holding. Bishop calculated that if they could endure the pain and maintain their snail's pace, they might reach the summit.

At 2 p.m. they crested the South Summit. On its far side, Jerstad wandered off route and began descending toward Everest's Southwest Face, for no apparent reason. "I don't know what possessed me, but I thought I saw some footprints down there," Jerstad said. "All this time, Barry thought I was completely crazy." Bishop gently tugged on the rope to get Jerstad back on course. (They would later learn that Jerstad had followed tracks that Jim Whittaker made while retrieving his dropped camera.)

At the Hillary Step they worked their way up the narrow space between rock and snow, using their hands, feet, and heads for leverage. Conditions had changed since Whittaker and Gombu had climbed it three weeks before. The deteriorating snow no longer offered easy purchase for their crampons.

Then they saw it: the American flag, framed by the void of space. The half of it that wasn't wrapped around its post was held out as if rigid by Everest's relentless wind. The flag's colors seemed to glimmer like neon against the blue-black troposphere above. "I told myself that even if I had to crawl up there on my hands and knees, I was going to get there," Bishop said. "It didn't hit me right away, but when we were halfway from that last snowy hump to the summit, tears were running down my face."

Fifty feet from the top, Jerstad coiled in the rope as Bishop walked up to him. He placed an arm around Bishop's shoulder and the two of them continued to Everest's summit together, the ninth and tenth humans to reach its top. The time was 3:30 p.m. They collapsed beside the flag and embraced.

Jerstad shot two hundred feet of movie film, the first ever taken on the summit. "I was going to leave pictures of my family there, but I forgot," Jerstad said. "I could never have gotten them out of my pocket, anyway." He had also carried up his parents' beloved copy of the New Testament, but was so fond of it that he decided to carry it back down.

To their south, the plains of India were obscured by a solid layer of pre-monsoon clouds. To the southwest rested Ama Dablam, which Bishop had climbed in 1961 as a member of the first ascent party. It took him a moment to pick out the statuesque, 22,349-foot peak; from their high angle it blended into a tumultuous sea of snow and rock.

It was late in the day. Only a short stretch of the West Ridge was visible, and there was no sign of Tom Hornbein or Willi Unsoeld. They couldn't afford to linger. The time was now four fifteen, and they feared that their oxygen would run out before they could descend the Hillary Step and climb the thirty feet to the South Summit. They reduced their flow to a trifling one liter per minute.

Along the summit ridge, a 60 mph wind blew the rope between them into a horizontal parabola to the east, suspending it above Tibet. As Jerstad made his way downward, Bishop watched the rope catch on one of the giant cornices of snow. He gave a tug, but the signal was absorbed by the loop of rope dancing in space. Jerstad continued to descend. Bishop found himself being pulled toward the edge as the tightening rope sliced into the cornice. Dropping to his stomach, he tugged harder. This time, a chunk of cornice sheared off along the slice—exposing him to the two-mile vertical drop of the Kangshung Face. Bishop hastily untied the rope from his waist, and let it go. He scrambled downslope unroped, then picked up the trailing end of the rope when it snaked back onto the ridge. Bishop quickly retied it to his waist and carried on. Jerstad, still descending, remained blissfully unaware that anything had happened.

To surmount the South Summit required a labored, brutally slow ascent of thirty feet, equivalent to climbing three flights of stairs in ten minutes. From its crest they again scanned the West Ridge for Unsoeld and Hornbein, but saw no movement. Turning, they plunge stepped in slow motion down the Southeast Ridge, taking care not to fall. The gray darkness left them with only a dim outline of distant ridges. Their pace diminished to a crawl.

At 8 p.m., still well above Camp 6, they wondered—as Hornbein and Unsoeld soon would—if they might have to bivouac for the night. Jerstad had skirted a strange-looking crevasse on their way up, a feature that could work as a shelter.

That's when they heard voices and shouts—though they weren't certain, at first, whether the sound was coming from above or below. Gasping for air, they yelled back as best they could. Then they heard more shouts, this time from above them.

"Lute and I realized immediately that Unsoeld and Hornbein had been successful, and they were descending behind us. Even in our ridiculous condition, we were ecstatic." Leaning on their ice axes, hyperventilating in the darkness, Jerstad and Bishop called out to Hornbein and Unsoeld, directing them downward. "By day, they might have sniffed out the route," Bishop said. "But not at night. The route was complex, and they had probably estimated that Camp 6 was much closer than it actually was." That's when they heard a distressed cry: Hornbein or Unsoeld must have stumbled into the same crevasse that Jerstad and Bishop, by daylight, had carefully avoided.

Chapter 23

A Biblical Calm

*We saw each other, but could not see. We felt each
other, but did not feel. We knew each other was
safe, but we knew nothing. Man vanished into
nothingness—but in that nothingness lay the strength
and dignity which man's soul is capable of.*

—Lute Jerstad, at 27,450 feet on the
Southeast Ridge of Mount Everest

Unsoeld and Hornbein found Bishop and Jerstad hunkered
on the rocks. Bishop's feet were beginning to freeze, and the wind
had pierced the perforations of his goggles, frost-nipping his eyeballs.
Jerstad's right eye was almost totally snow-blind, and he had begun to
lose feeling in his toes.

Bishop wasn't sure he could go on. Hornbein removed his gloves
and, with numb and clumsy hands, removed the regulator from Bishop's empty tank and screwed it onto Jerstad's partially full one. He
fumbled to reconnect Bishop's hose. The oxygen helped revive him,
with an additional boost from a tablet of Dexedrine, an amphetamine.

Descending the Southeast Ridge in darkness would be dangerous.
Surviving a bivouac at that altitude was unimaginable. Hornbein overheard such talk and spoke up forcefully.

"We can't stop here. Gotta keep moving." Jerstad and Bishop might
at least recognize the route back to Camp 6—though Jerstad was effectively blind, and Bishop was both depleted and disoriented. Bishop
remained roped to Jerstad, who wielded his ice ax like a blind man's

cane, probing for the edge of the ridge. Jerstad tried to stick close behind Hornbein and follow his elusive silhouette while attempting to get his bearings.

Then Jerstad stepped off the Southeast Ridge—with no one belaying him.

"Lute has a prognathous jaw, and he hooked his jaw on the rope between Tom and me," Unsoeld said, explaining how he inadvertently saved him by pulling the rope taut in what he dubbed a "clothesline belay"—like snagging a plane that has landed on an aircraft carrier. It took Jerstad several minutes to haul himself the few feet back to the ridge.

Jerstad and Bishop stumbled and fell several times. Bishop wanted to sit down for good. Hornbein and Unsoeld pushed and pulled, coerced and cajoled. "We felt like beasts, but the old guiding instincts came to the fore: I'd flay the flesh off his bones to get him on his feet. 'Anybody can walk a hundred feet!' I'd tell him. 'No matter how tired! It's only another hundred feet!'" Zombielike, drawing on his last scraps of will and energy, Bishop kept moving. Jerstad, who had a shred more energy, moved in tandem.

The lower stretch of the Southeast Ridge fans out into a series of snow gullies intersected by rock outcrops. Jerstad knew that they should move away from the ridge and descend one of these gullies, but he wasn't sure which one. Somewhere midslope, they would need to turn sharply left and traverse to Camp 6—but they risked over- or undershooting the junction.

Halting at a relatively level patch of rock, the four men swallowed an impossible truth: There was no choice but to stop and wait for the morning.

No preparation was needed; they simply sat down on the rocky rubble of the ridge and curled up on their pack frames. They were dehydrated, oxygen-starved, and exhausted. It was 12:30 a.m., and they were alone at twenty-eight thousand feet—a thousand feet below Everest's summit, and more than five vertical miles above sea level. If they survived the night, it would be the highest successful bivouac in human history.

Hornbein and Unsoeld huddled together, with Jerstad and Bishop five feet above them. Hornbein's feet were cold, and he untied his crampons and unlaced his boots. Instinctively, Willi Unsoeld, known in the Tetons as the Old Guide, tucked Hornbein's ice cold feet inside his own parka, up against his belly—just as he sometimes did for his charges when guiding in Wyoming. Hornbein felt no sensation of his feet resting on a hairy abdomen—nor any feeling at all.

"Tom asked me about *my* feet," said Unsoeld. "'I'm feeling fine, Tom,' I told him. 'I can't feel a thing.'" He later admitted that, at the time, he was secretly proud of his superior cold tolerance, though on some level he likely knew that such loss of feeling is a dangerous thing. Bishop emptied his pack and placed his own tortured feet inside, hoping to insulate them. But the rock beneath conducted the cold through the aluminum frame to his steel crampons, and from there to his feet, making them even colder. He risked freezing his fingers if he removed the crampons—and wouldn't likely get them back on. For the remainder of the night, Bishop felt no sensation in his toes or feet. His breathing became fast and shallow, worsened by his severe sinus infection. He focused on hyperventilating, deeply and rapidly, which kept him from nodding off and losing awareness of his freezing digits.

The temperature on the Southeast Ridge dropped to minus eighteen degrees Fahrenheit. The four climbers sat shivering, with no energy for conversation. Jerstad wriggled his toes continually, and was able to maintain some feeling. His fingers were too cold to zip up his down parka, so he curled into as much of a ball as he could. Their only chance of survival was if the freezing wind died down.

Inexplicably—on one of the most exposed, wind-scoured ridges on earth—the breezes dwindled to a virtual standstill, leaving them in complete silence. The darkness was total. The only light striking their retinas was the flicker of heat lightning over India—a distant, exotic land of civilization and warmth, more than a hundred miles to the south.

"The night was overpoweringly empty," Hornbein said. "Stars shed cold, unshimmering light. We hung suspended in a timeless void. Unsignaled, unembellished, the hours passed. I floated in a dreamlike eternity, devoid of fears, plans, or regrets. Death had no meaning. Nor, for that matter, did life."

"We had thought that three or four hours without oxygen at that elevation would lead to death or irreparable brain damage," Jerstad later wrote to Jim Lester. "We had pushed ourselves to the limit of physical endurance, then passed beyond it for several hours. Nothing was left. Death does not always come quickly or with great pain. We could have stepped across the bar with little feeling of physical change beyond the pain and fatigue—which we had already felt and transcended, mercifully, by frostbite. We saw each other, but could not see. We felt each other, but did not feel. We knew each other was safe, but we knew nothing. Man vanished into nothingness—but in that nothingness lay the strength and dignity which man's soul is capable of."

Over on the West Ridge, at Camp 3W, Barry Corbet, Dick Emerson, and Al Auten waited by the radio. The only news they had culled about progress higher on the mountain was sketchy and disconcerting.

Kathmandu was also awaiting an update. Jesuit priest Father Moran, the expedition's backup ham radio contact, had joined Jolene Unsoeld and others at the Unsoeld home for dinner. Barry Bishop's wife, Lila, was notably absent; painful joint aches had taken her to Shanta Bhawan, the missionary hospital, where she had been diagnosed with dengue fever.

An hour before dinner, Father Moran had been on the radio with Base Camp. He'd heard the startling news that, though Unsoeld and Hornbein had reached the summit, it was very late in the day and they were descending in darkness.

"It's going to be all right," Father Moran announced with self-assurance to the evening guests. "The winds are going to remain calm."

The gathering suddenly became silent, as they fell into a moment of hopeful prayer. When Father Moran returned to his quarters, he and the other Jesuit priests remained up all night—praying intently that the winds upon Everest be stilled.

"When I heard that Father Moran had pronounced them safe, and then followed up in prayer with the other fathers," Lila Bishop later recalled, "I somehow knew that Barry and Lute would be all right—or at least alive."

———

At a glacial pace, the world around Everest shed its cavelike black-ness. "The high peaks turned battleship gray, and then alpenglow hit the tops—the highest summits first," Barry Bishop said. "A rich golden light with a touch of pink began to descend and paint the lower peaks."

The climbers had neither the energy nor sufficient sensation in their fingers to take photographs, much less change rolls of film. They lingered until the sun struck them, and by 6 a.m. were mildly warmed by its rays—and by the unexpected and sublime feeling of simply being alive on the twenty-third of May, 1963. With numb hands, Hornbein strapped on his crampons.

Unsoeld and Hornbein led, easily finding the route downward. The slope they had descended the night before was the correct one, it turned out—they were within twenty feet of the track Jerstad and Bishop had taken on the way up. They saw several places, however, where an unwary climber could have slid off the mountain and into the darkness below.

As they neared Camp 6, they saw two figures coming toward them. Dave Dingman and Girmi Dorje, one of the strongest Khumbu Sherpas, were heading upward, breathing oxygen. Dingman was flab-bergasted to see four live souls instead of two dead ones. Hornbein and Unsoeld, he realized, must have come from the other side of the mountain; he had heard no news for two days. It would have been im-possible to survive a night exposed at this elevation, certainly, and he had resigned himself to the gruesome task of finding and identifying the bodies of Bishop and Jerstad.

Dingman shared embraces with Unsoeld and Hornbein.

"We're just passing through," Unsoeld quipped to Dingman.

"Tom and Willi explained to me that Lute and Barry, above and behind them, were in much worse shape," Dingman said, "and that we should save our oxygen for them."

"Why don't you go to the top, Dave?" Unsoeld said. "You're getting a good, early start."

"No—we came up to help you guys out."

Dingman and Girmi Dorje *were* carrying oxygen and provisions for a summit attempt, but only in the event they needed to go that far to find Jerstad and Bishop. They were sleep deprived, having kept an all-night vigil at Camp 6, occasionally venturing upward. Even by daylight, Dingman knew, no one could have mounted a rescue effort. Most of the team was at Base Camp, already preparing to depart.

Dingman continued upward, shouting to Jerstad and Bishop to stay where they were. "They didn't recognize me," Dingman said. "They were lying prostrate on a rock shelf, speaking slowly. Their faces were a deep, ashen blue color." He and Girmi Dorje connected fresh oxygen tanks to Jerstad's and Bishop's regulators. After several minutes, a pink color returned to their cheeks and they became more coherent. Within half an hour they were able to move. Miraculously, much of their coordination and climbing skills returned.

Within an hour, all had converged at Camp 6, which Hornbein described as a luxury spa compared to their lodging of the night before. Relishing the freedom to lie down and breathe oxygen freely, they drank every liquid they could: water, tea, lemonade, coffee. Hornbein figured he might as well collect his urine for physiologist Will Siri's exhaustive study, and he peed into the plastic bottle as he was supposed to. Siri would wag his smoking pipe at him if he returned empty-handed.

When they pried off Bishop's boots, his feet were bone white from his toes to his heels. Unsoeld's looked much the same.

The climbers and Girmi Dorje packed up the sleeping bags and abandoned Camp 6 by midmorning, hoping to make it to Camp 2 before dark. The day was brilliant and calm as they methodically descended the snow couloir below the Southeast Ridge. The points of their crampons had worn smooth; when they stepped onto the polished blue ice above the South Col, Bishop took care to connect all ten points of each crampon with the surface, to avoid slipping. After venturing out onto the expanse of the Col, they fought a moderate, wind tunnel–like breeze to reach Camp 5. With their crampons on, they crawled into the larger tent and discussed their frostbite and the plan for descent. One of the Sherpas urged liquids on them.

Dave Dingman led the procession from Camp 5. They crossed the South Col to the top of the Geneva Spur, then descended across the Yellow Band. Unsoeld and Hornbein, on the South Col route for the first time, savored this new aspect of the mountain. They descended through Camps 4 and 3, shedding their outerwear and goose-down summit clothing as they went. The mountain episode of the Everest endeavor was nearly over. Each step downward was a step homeward.

Navigating by flashlight, Dave Dingman in the lead, they arrived at Camp 2 around ten thirty that evening. The rest of the West Ridge team—Emerson, Corbet, and Al Auten—had arrived at Camp 2 that afternoon. They had looked across the Cwm and up at the gargantuan white canvas of the Lhotse Face, and counted the descending dots. Every climber was accounted for. In an emotion-charged reunion, the climbers simultaneously shared their personal accounts of the past forty-eight hours, a virtual lifetime.

Snow-blind in both eyes, Jerstad squinted uncomfortably through a heavy dose of codeine. Dick Emerson topped him off with some Nembutal, a sedative, and Jerstad fell asleep in his lap. Willi Unsoeld's toes had frozen solid and looked like pale granitic marble. A large pot of water was brewing for tea, and he agreed to try the recommended treatment: rapid thawing. He plunged both feet into the pot.

"Afterwards, of course, we drank the water—and didn't even have to use any tea leaves," Unsoeld later quipped. Barry Bishop's feet took the treatment, too. As they thawed, he felt a crushing, migraine-inducing pain spread across his soles, from his heel to his metatarsals.

Dingman and Hornbein had debated whether it was better to thaw frozen digits at Camp 2 or at Base Camp. Oddly, it's preferable to walk on frozen feet than on thawed feet. Once thawed, walking can macerate adjacent living tissue, and a climber should be carried. Bishop and Unsoeld could be carried through the Western Cwm, but not through much of the Icefall. If Unsoeld's and Bishop's total of nineteen frozen toes weren't thawed actively at Camp 2, they would thaw slowly during the night, anyway, which is not ideal.

To get a head start on a rescue, Dingman radioed Gil Roberts at Base Camp and requested a helicopter evacuation for somewhere high on the approach route.

On May 24, 1963, the weary climbers left Camp 2 for the last time. At Camp 1, they stopped to drink water, but their terrific thirst outpaced the capacities of the stoves to melt snow. Glaciologist Maynard Miller scratched his head. He knew precisely where they could find water: in the bottles containing his precious melted samples of ancient ice, drawn from the core layers deep within the glacier. He retrieved several bottles and poured it into their canteens.

Below Camp 1, the climbers entered the Khumbu Icefall. The glacier's movement had accelerated during May, and the route through the deadly maze had been adjusted, sometimes daily, by the team of Icefall Sherpas. Barry Bishop found it eerie to look over at the bamboo wands that had marked the route in March: Some of them were now a hundred yards from the present route and were lodged sideways, like arrows, in broken, uptilted chunks of ice.

One section of the Icefall had shifted and slumped only a day earlier, destroying a crucial part of the route and leaving behind a yawning crevasse with one side higher than the other. To span that section, the Sherpas had rigged a "Tyrolean traverse"—a hundred-foot length of rope pulled taut across the chasm like a tightrope. The line sloped at a forty-five-degree angle. Climbers clipped onto it and—suspended from a sling, with one leg draped over the rope—slid downward across the chasm. The loads were sent across separately.

Jake Breitenbach lay inside the glacier, somewhere, in a jumble of ice blocks. He had been entombed two months and one day earlier. The descending climbers stopped and stood silently in humble tribute. Their mission on Everest was as much Jake's as anyone's. Now they, the survivors, had finished the job.

"I never went past that spot without thinking about my likeable, blond-haired comrade who resembled Dennis the Menace," Barry Bishop recalled. "One steels oneself against thoughts of catastrophe, but not against thoughts of a lost friend."

Part III

Cherishing Mystery

I've had love overflowing, impassionate careers, a life of adventure and everything I have ever wanted. Nothing missed and no regrets. So, dear friends, enjoy the memories, keep them alive, then let them fade when it is time. Live on in peace, health and happiness. Look for meaning where you can and cherish mystery where you can't.

—BARRY CORBET'S FINAL LETTER TO
HIS FRIENDS, MAILED AFTER HIS DEATH
ON DECEMBER 18, 2004

Chapter 24

The Vigorous Life

A lot of people said, "Boy—you were the conquerors of
the highest mountain on earth." But together we added
up to half a mote in the eye of the infinite. Just a speck.
And that's part of the preciousness of it—that you are
no more than a speck in the midst of the immensity.
—WILLI UNSOELD

AT DUSK ON MAY 24, 1963, THE MOUNTAIN'S REMAINING CLIMBERS—
its survivors—stumbled wearily into Base Camp. They huddled in the
mess tent in a scene of fraternal chaos and shed their down jackets
and long underwear as if they were a tired mountain skin. Sun- and
wind-burned flesh peeled away from splotched faces, and pieces of it
snagged in their wiry, matted beards.

The cook tent Sherpas ferried in drinks and food as the Everest
team decompressed. Their stories spilled forth with exhilaration, relief, and a lingering sadness. No longer did they need to speak in the
insistent, loud monotone of their walkie-talkie voices. There would
be no more swell and hiss of the sleeping mask at night, no more
worrying about the next ailment or the last one. The weather and the
delivery of supplies would no longer dictate their lives—nor would the
dreaded Icefall.

"No more straining to size up the possibilities for success," Jim
Lester summarized. "The team was off the field, the game well won."
They retired to their tents to assume what Sir John Hunt, leader of the
British expedition, called "the Everest position": flat on their backs.

It was a good position for reading the last letters to arrive from down valley. A woman's billowing cursive filled one letter to Barry Bishop—from the wife of the U.S. ambassador. She began by relaying the admiration she had witnessed among the Nepalese.

"On May 3," Bishop read aloud, "the Ambassador and I had a group of forty student leaders—boys and girls from the University—for a buffet dinner here. They bombarded us with questions, including asking about the 'bust' of Mao Tse-Tung. When we quoted the official words from the summit party—'No evidence of it'—they laughed knowingly. And when I told them that we liked to think of our American and Nepalese flags flying together that night over Everest, they seemed surprised that both were there, and were very happy."

Her letter carried on about social activities at the Hotel Royal, whetting the climbers' appetites for their return to civilization. "On Monday last we had perfectly delicious goodies left over from the state visit of President Ayub Khan of Pakistan, such as hors d'oeuvres of smoked eel, caviar—and the rare Himalayan pheasant, which was served hot instead of stone cold as it had been at the State Banquet! We drank to the further successes of our Expedition, needless to say."

Departure from Base Camp was scheduled for first thing in the morning—a good excuse for their own celebration. Jimmy Roberts—the beleaguered transport officer, perpetually caught between the Sherpas and the sahibs—was justifiably relieved that it was all over, or nearly so. The remaining beer and spirits flowed liberally—why carry them out? Colonel Roberts did more than his bit to lighten the loads. Jim Lester watched as the cardboard box that Roberts was sitting on gradually gave way under his weight. As he neared the ground, Roberts whispered with a grin, *"Ghastly arseholes!"* then settled into a slumber on the floor.

"It wasn't clear if he was referring to the Americans," Lester said, "or perhaps to the Sherpas, whom he loved like a parent. He had done a magnificent job of organizing and managing our Sherpa workforce, and we didn't need him to love us as well."

The next morning, the sounds of Sherpas laughing and singing bawdy ballads while they prepared loads was a welcome change from the constant thrum of the generator and kerosene pressure stoves. A murmur of conversation also carried over from the glacial moraine at the edge of Base Camp: 275 porters had arrived from down valley and were waiting to be assigned loads to carry out. A rumor spread that there wouldn't be enough loads for all of them. The porters converged on the tents at Base Camp, grabbing for boxes that hadn't yet been weighed and inventoried. A Sherpa wielding a stick with a flail on the end—a local riding crop—was able to hold them off, at least momentarily.

Before departure, the Sherpas began pouring gasoline on the ground around Base Camp, then igniting it for the sheer, kids-setting-off-firecrackers fun of it. Al Auten ended the antics by reminding them that they might need the gas for the generator on their way out.

Colonel Roberts estimated that the Sherpas' record of performance at high altitude would stand for many years. Fourteen Sherpas had carried loads to over twenty-seven thousand feet. Four made it to the South Col three times, eleven reached it twice, and eight more delivered a load there at least once. Beyond this robust record, however, their careful study of the mechanics of an expedition would be even more valuable to them. The younger Sherpas especially were drawn to the team's sense of organization and efficiency, and its use of technology—concepts they'd had little exposure to. And—of practical value for future jobs—they had begun to learn how American sahibs think and act.

The snow that had covered the path below Base Camp had given way to alpine flowers, edelweiss, and stunted juniper. The warmth of spring and the pre-monsoon rains had unlocked the fragrance of the earth, and tufts of brilliant green erupted from rock and rubble. The frozen flat expanse at the Gorak Shep camp had thawed into a small lake. Tiny squalls rippled across its surface.

On the approach march, Jake Breitenbach had often paused on the trail to contemplate the glacial boulders (some as large as two-story houses) that were engraved with Buddhist prayers. After Breitenbach's death, the brother of an expedition Sherpa had erected a platform on the side of a boulder beside the Gorak Shep lake. With a hammer and chisel, using skills he had learned as a monk at the Tengboche monastery, he had incised in bas-relief:

IN MEMORY OF
JOHN E. BREITENBACH
AMERICAN MOUNT EVEREST EXPEDITION 1963

The descending Sherpas, meanwhile, were engaging in a pastime that Breitenbach would have approved: drinking. Virtually none were sober as they negotiated the trail, some walking arm in arm for mutual support. Ang Dawa, who had climbed with Dyhrenfurth above Camp 6, sat by the edge of the lake as another Sherpa splashed water onto his face to rouse him sufficiently so that he could carry on down the path.

Like soldiers in retreat from battle, some of the climbers were in better shape than others. All had lost weight. Willi Unsoeld set out on the approach march at 171 pounds and now weighed 155. Everest had turned Tom Hornbein from a gnome into a grizzled sprite; his weight dropped from 146 to 123 pounds. The team had lost a combined body weight of more than 500 pounds. Ten percent of that was Dick Emerson's contribution.

Most of the climbers had been sick at some point. But—other than Bishop and Jerstad on the day of their climb and night of their bivouac—had they actually pushed their bodies to the limits of human survival? Physiologist Will Siri wasn't so sure. His blood and urine work indicated that the team had suffered mainly from undernourishment.

And frostbite. Bishop and Unsoeld could no longer walk on their thawed feet without causing damage to living tissue—nor without agonizing pain. Eight porters were assigned to carry them to either Tengboche or Namche Bazaar, depending on how far a helicopter could penetrate the valley through brewing monsoon clouds. Each of the invalids was draped over a porter, sitting on a trapezelike seat suspended from their porter's forehead. In tag teams, each porter carried his load about a quarter mile, then transferred it to a fresh man. Their bare soles, like the pads on lizards' feet, reassuringly gripped the terrain. The most sure-footed man had six toes on each foot; he forded the rambunctious Dudh Kosi river with Bishop on his back, water at times up to his thighs, while negotiating submerged rocks that rolled underfoot. On the flat sections they shuffled along at high speed, not wasting energy in up-and-down movement. Unsoeld's four porters competed with Bishop's four, at times racing neck and neck like Roman charioteers. Having survived the mountain, the riders now prayed they would survive the downward journey.

The air grew thicker and more rejuvenating as the team descended, and thinking became clear and vivid. "Questions that any man might have had about himself, or about the group, were for the time being resolved," Lester noted. "We were free to take in the scenery, and to appreciate the glory of going to sleep under the stars." Their camp in the yak pasture at Pheriche—snowed in and unwelcoming during the approach—now seemed bucolic and welcoming. After midnight, Lester looked out over the valley upon the moonlight-glazed snow of the surrounding mountains. He felt like crying at having to leave the purity of such a place.

In an anteroom of the Tengboche monastery, the monks set up a twenty-foot-long table, draped it in a white cloth, and padded the benches with ornate Tibetan rugs. The abbot sat at the head and the team members aligned themselves along the sides, as monks served biscuits and *chang*. The team presented the abbot with a gold Omega wristwatch, and the abbot gave each of them *kata* blessing scarves.

Dyhrenfurth paused at the stupa near the monastery, just as he had in the 1950s, and again felt a swell of regret at leaving the idyllic site. This time, the mountains—including Everest—were enveloped in heavy clouds, making departure easier. He concluded that he had learned a few of Everest's secrets—or perhaps *remembered* them, from the previous lifetimes that he suspected he had spent here.

Bishop and Unsoeld needed a helicopter. Each morning the skies were clear when the sun rose, but by eight o'clock clouds boiled in from down valley, climbed the hillsides, and enveloped them in fog. Al Auten sent a radio message to Kathmandu, hoping that the embassy radio operator, or Father Moran on his ham radio, could hear him. He heard nothing in return.

Two days after departing Base Camp, the team arrived in Namche Bazaar. It was the first time they had showered or bathed in two months, and they changed into shirts and shorts. Several of the team were invited to the home of a Sherpa who was hosting a Buddhist funerary ceremony. A score of monks from Tengboche had taken over the upstairs chapel, and the team was escorted into the altar room. The monks nodded and smiled toward them while sonorously chanting from the 108 volumes of the Buddhist canon, sanctified by reedy horns and the accelerating beats of a large drum.

Dyhrenfurth learned that the weeklong ritual had been commissioned following the death from smallpox of ten Sherpas from neighboring villages. If it hadn't been for prompt delivery of vaccine from Kathmandu, the number would likely have been much higher.

The next day at dawn, clouds again piled up in the valley to the south and washed toward them like an incoming tide. Surely no chopper could make it through to Namche, so the team lounged in their tents. Then at six twenty-five, in near disbelief, they heard the *whacka-whacka* of helicopter blades. The team threw on their clothes and scrambled toward the level shelf atop the ridge overlooking Namche. The helicopter circled over the village, its blades beating the thin air like a disoriented dragonfly. Al Auten's radio message had been received in Kathmandu, and the radio operator understood that two injured climbers were ready to be picked up—though it wasn't clear where. The pilot had been told to look for a cluster of orange tents.

A crowd of Sherpas had gathered, along with the team, and all gave a cheer as the pilot landed. A photographer from *National Geographic* stepped out and began to frantically document the scene. Three Sherpas delivered Unsoeld and Bishop to the landing site in time for a final portrait of the team together in the mountains. Then the Sherpas squeezed them into the chopper.

The helicopter lifted off and skimmed to the right, barely clearing the rocks at the edge of the small plateau. Once over the precipice, it pitched sharply forward and dropped out of view—to gather speed and create lift. Gil Roberts, veteran of mountain medical flights, watched carefully. "A cool cat," he said in a nod to the skilled Norwegian pilot.

Back in Namche, the Sherpas resumed their celebration. Dyhrenfurth, the esteemed leader, was obliged to accept bottomless offerings of *arak* and *chang*. Each full cup was formally presented to him with a dab of yak butter on the rim, as a blessing.

"I couldn't possibly have done all the drinking by myself,"

Dyhrenfurth said. He handed off each glass to a nearby thirsty team member. Many of the Namche Sherpas had been with Dyhrenfurth on his previous expeditions and would stay behind in the village.

From a rainy fifteen-thousand-foot pass, the team dropped down to Junbesi, the tranquil village where the woman with severe burns had been rescued during the approach march. The helicopter ride to Kathmandu and treatment at the missionary hospital had saved her life, though some in Kathmandu grumbled that the mission was no more than an opportunity for rich Americans to show off.

"'In this part of the world, life is cheap. What was a burned woman?'" Dyhrenfurth said, mimicking with disapproval the reaction that had filtered up to Base Camp. He was unapologetically glad that they had done it. The burned woman appeared at the expedition's camp that evening. To express her gratitude, she presented Dyhrenfurth with a bottle of distilled *arak* and a basket of eggs with an iris on top. "She will never win a beauty contest," he allowed. "But it's amazing to see her alive and able to talk—to lead a fairly useful life and be a mother to her son."

One more pass stood between the men and the lowlands. Lute Jerstad's toes were now in bad shape and he, too, needed to be carried— a tough job in the muddy river valleys. He cringed at the image of his feet colliding with trailside boulders while being carried along, and he rode a horse for much of the way.

Jim Lester continued to monitor the team for signs of mental stress. Paradoxically, when highest on the mountain and in the most isolated circumstances, the climbers had seemed most at home. The background anxiety of the approach march—the hum of questions and arguments about *how* and *when* and *if*—produced the most stress he'd observed, but receded the higher they went. This wasn't surprising, Lester concluded, considering that climbers head to the mountains specifically to take refuge from worldly stress.

Tom Hornbein felt not so much stressed as mentally exhausted, "with no desires or urges beyond eating, watering, soaking in the beauties of the scenery—and falling asleep almost every time I sit down." For months he had been intensely engaged and focused. Like the others, he had grown comfortable with a simple life, dedicated to the quotidian tasks of survival and upward progress. He began to ruminate on what Everest meant and how it might affect the next chapters of his life. The return to America promised complications and uncertainty, beginning with immersion in a career at the University of Washington.

Hornbein also felt saddened—and guilty—about Unsoeld's toes. *Why wouldn't I have known better,* he asked himself, *when Willi said that his toes felt perfectly fine? Why couldn't I have reciprocated after Willi warmed my toes?* But no one was keeping track of such things— least of all Unsoeld. Besides, Hornbein had helped revive Bishop and Jerstad, who may have otherwise drifted off into a permanent sleep on the Southeast Ridge. They had all been in it together.

And now they weren't. Unsoeld's ascension, by helicopter, had elevated Hornbein's loneliness. They had taken spiritual nourishment from the mountain together, a shared communion.

That was it. That was what made the great enterprise of mountaineering meaningful, after all. It was about friendships, even more than about the mountains themselves.

The helicopter bearing Willi Unsoeld and Barry Bishop skimmed over the eastern rim of the Kathmandu valley and set down in an open field across from Shanta Bhawan, the Methodist missionary hospital to the south of the capital. "Barry and Willi looked like wild people," Bishop's wife, Lila, said. "We were told their feet had been frostbitten, but we didn't know what this entailed."

The doctors fashioned a rudimentary whirlpool bath, and Unsoeld and Bishop greeted visitors while sitting in their therapy tub. CBS Television sent a TV crew from Hong Kong, and the two climbers appeared on the evening news with Walter Cronkite.

Gradually, over almost a month in the hospital, their toes autoamputated.

"The soggy saga of the toes is now approaching its dénouement," Unsoeld wrote to Jim Lester, "and it looks as though they have decided to go their separate ways. My young daughter Devi came into the hospital room and took one look at the blackened, shriveled things, and said, 'But Dad—those are *wizard's toes.*'"

Gradually, nine of Unsoeld's ten toes loosened and began to detach. "In a fit of boredom one day, I found an old pair of scissors and, for a truly unique experience, I snipped some of them off." But he hadn't really lost them, he explained: His kids collected them, put them in a jar, and filled it with formaldehyde. They especially enjoyed bringing out the jar to show to luncheon guests.

On July 8, 1963, the sunburned, freshly shaven team members—minus Unsoeld, who was still languishing in the missionary hospital in Kathmandu—gathered in the Rose Garden of the White House. They stood self-consciously in suits that had grown too large because of their weight loss. Dyhrenfurth and President Kennedy had been chatting in the Oval Office, and when they emerged the president said a few words and awarded each of them the National Geographic Society's Hubbard Medal. Until that time, the medal had only been awarded to single individuals. Dyhrenfurth had insisted that they *all* receive it as a team—including five of the Sherpas—or none.

When Gombu stepped up, he pulled from his pocket a long white *kata* scarf—momentarily startling the Secret Service, some of whom felt for their guns. With effort (because of his short stature), Gombu reached up and draped the *kata* around the young president's neck.

"I hear the Sherpas are very strong," Kennedy laughed, then gently squeezed Gombu's arm.

"You should feel his *leg,*" Jim Whittaker remarked. The president promptly reached down and squeezed Gombu's thigh. Gombu was momentarily transfixed.

"Even if I am reborn as a worm, I will remember the president squeezing my leg," Gombu later told his son—who was born within weeks of the Rose Garden ceremony.

The president's interest in strength and conditioning wasn't idle. Dr. Hans Kraus—who'd spent his summers climbing in the Tetons with some of the Everest team—was Kennedy's physical therapist, and he had helped alleviate the president's chronic back problems. Kraus also coauthored a study that showed that more than half of American children failed simple exercise tests at which Europeans excelled. The Selective Service had also found that half of the men reporting to draft boards during World War II and the Korean War were considered "physically unfit." Kennedy had issued a challenge, and Americans responded. In the first half of 1963, people of all ages began doing "fifty-mile hikes," and a physical fitness craze swept the nation.

Climbers had always been regarded as misfits and losers—fringe characters, at best. Now, here in the Rose Garden, stood the very Americans the president had in mind when he'd spoken of leading a vigorous life: men made of brilliant teeth and lean muscle, men who could "climb to the hilltop," as his speeches often exhorted Americans to do.

The U.S. State Department had invited five of the expedition's Sherpas and a liaison officer to visit America on an eight-week goodwill tour, with Jim Lester as their guide. The motive for the Sherpas' junket wasn't clear, but the public relations value—for both Nepal and America—of hosting six curious citizens from a small developing country wasn't lost on Lester. Sandwiched between India and China—with the Soviet Union not far away—Nepal was just the sort of nation in which America might want to have a long-term strategic interest.

In reality, the United States was mainly concerned about China. Perhaps the Sherpas—or their relatives or friends—might like to help the United States and India gather intelligence on Nepal's northern neighbor. In 1963, the high-altitude U-2 spy plane was no longer a secret, and the art of satellite surveillance hadn't yet matured. But ground-based monitoring held some promise. Might the mountain-wise Sherpas be useful accomplices in the placement of American spy devices at locations high enough to peer into the middle of Chairman Mao's Middle Kingdom?

Chapter 25

The Bliss-Giving Goddess

*The path we have chosen for the present is full of
hazards, as all paths are. The cost of freedom is always
high, but Americans have always paid it. And one path
we shall never choose, and that is the path of surrender
or submission.*

— President John F. Kennedy

*The best journeys answer questions that you didn't
even think to ask.*

— the documentary adventure film
180 Degrees South

In the 1960s, Barry Bishop was known within the Washington, D.C., Beltway as both an adventurer and a researcher—for his work on Greenland's glaciers and with Admiral Byrd's expedition in Antarctica. Now Bishop was an Everest summiter, too. He'd come home without his toes, but with a cover story for *National Geographic*. He took on another assignment, too, but not for a magazine. It was something he would never write or converse about.

At a D.C. cocktail party, Bishop spoke with General Curtis LeMay, the severe-looking chief of staff of the U.S. Air Force. LeMay, a National Geographic Society trustee, had extended the air force's support and some funding to the Everest expedition, and he was curious about

Bishop's views on that part of the world. Specifically, he wanted to hear more about the view from its highest point, looking north. But it wasn't the scenery that intrigued him.

LeMay, the reputed inspiration for General Buck Turgidson—George C. Scott's unforgettable role in *Dr. Strangelove*—was a ringleader of America's missile program. He was increasingly nervous about China's developments in nuclear warfare and technology, a blind spot in U.S. intelligence. The CIA was aware that China was building a nuclear test facility at Lop Nur, a ten-thousand-square-kilometer dry lake bed a few hundred miles north of the Himalaya. Beyond that, they had little hard information.

In October 1964, China conducted its first nuclear test at Lop Nur. Among other concerns, the CIA feared that China's ability to launch a thermonuclear bomb-laden missile could raise the stakes in the expanding Vietnam War.

India was also keen to gather as much intelligence as it could on the Chinese threat. The Indian military had been beefing up its northern borders ever since the Sino-Indian War of 1962, when the Chinese Army (with its better-acclimatized and better-equipped troops) stormed through a string of border outposts in northeast India.

At the same time, Indian prime minister Jawaharlal Nehru was hesitant about partnering with America. The legacy of British colonial rule had made India distrustful of the Western world. India was also offended that the United States was providing military support to Pakistan, their mortal enemy. The United States had previously been conducting overflights of China with the U-2 spy plane, based out of an airfield in Pakistan. But Pakistan withdrew the use of its airfield in 1960 when a U-2 piloted by Francis Gary Powers was shot down over the Soviet Union.

Spy satellites offered a partial alternative, but they weren't yet perfected. *Ground-based* sensors, however, were powerful enough to intercept radio signals between China's military technicians and their missiles. There was one rub: These sensors needed a direct line of sight.

A Himalayan peak just might offer this. From an elevated perch, a spy transceiver would be able to peer into the test site at Lop Nur. It could then relay the data to a listening station, allowing the CIA and

Indian intelligence to monitor the range, speed, and payload of China's missiles.

Such a surveillance system would need a reliable source of power. The government had successfully used small plutonium-powered units to run weather stations at the North and South Poles. While raising funds for the 1963 climb, Norman Dyhrenfurth had proposed installing such a station on Everest's South Col as part of the expedition's research program.

General LeMay was confident that Bishop was the right man to help concoct a clandestine surveillance operation. *National Geographic* granted Bishop leave, and the CIA recruited him.

First, Bishop needed to select a reasonably high peak that didn't share a border with China, which eliminated Everest (and many other summits). But Kanchenjunga—at 28,169 feet, the world's third highest mountain—was situated on the border between Nepal and Sikkim. It might be ideal.

Next, Bishop needed climbers. The 1963 Everesters were obvious candidates for such an innovative and risky mission. They formed the largest known pool of American climbers with Himalayan experience. Bishop's first choice for this *Mission: Impossible* team was Lute Jerstad, his partner on Everest. Jerstad quickly signed on. Another was Tom Hornbein, then working at the University of Washington in Seattle. When Bishop called, Hornbein told him that his boss had already been wondering why "all these FBI guys have been coming around to talk to me." But Hornbein was at the start of what would become a long career on the UW faculty, and wasn't interested in joining.

Willi Unsoeld was likely viewed as being off limits because of his employment with the Peace Corps, which went to great lengths to distance itself from the CIA. This was to avoid suspicions, in countries where the Corps operated, that its volunteers were agents or spies.

The surveillance operation would be executed jointly with Indian intelligence. In the early spring of 1965, Bishop flew to New Delhi to seek out naval captain Mohan Singh Kohli, one of India's best-known climbers. In addition to being a military man, Kohli was a veteran of the nearly successful 1960 and 1962 Indian Everest expeditions. Kohli had been appointed leader of India's third attempt on Everest and was leaving for the mountain in several days. He and his fellow climbers would be able to join the Kanchenjunga team only during the fall climbing season.

On May 14, 1965, the Chinese detonated another nuclear explosion at Lop Nur, this one dropped from an airplane.

The Indian climbing team was on Everest at the time. On May 20, two of their climbers reached the summit, and within the next nine days seven more tagged the top. But when Captain Kohli returned to New Delhi he was given little time to celebrate. Indian intelligence spirited him to the United States, where he joined Bishop, Jerstad, and other climbers at the Bishops' home in Bethesda.

Kohli was familiar with Kanchenjunga. The peak, he warned, is scoured by frequent, deadly avalanches. Only six climbers had ever reached its summit; three others had died trying. A serious attempt would require bottled oxygen and a carefully designed pyramid of logistics.

Bishop and the others agreed to choose another mountain. That was fine with the CIA. Their technicians had already confirmed that a lower summit—Nanda Devi, for instance, the 25,645-foot peak that Willi Unsoeld had admired in 1949—could provide a line of sight across Tibet to Lop Nur.

In the fall of 1965, a team of Americans and Indians—including Lute Jerstad and nineteen Sherpas—were choppered in to Nanda Devi Base Camp. Only here were some of them informed that the "special load" they would be carrying—five porter loads, really—would require assembly near the mountain's summit, under unpredictable conditions.

What surprised the Sherpas, some of whom had climbed on Everest with the Americans, was that one of the nondescript boxes they were carrying *seemed to emit heat*. This was the SNAP generator (for "System for Nuclear Auxiliary Power"), a thermoelectric energy system fueled by plutonium. The Sherpas, eager to absorb warmth from the degrading plutonium, vied over which tent would shelter the SNAP generator at night. They named the device "Guru Rinpoche," after the eighth-century patron saint of the Sherpas: a legendary Buddhist sorcerer whose supernatural powers included the ability to provide protection and sustenance.

On October 16, 1965, the climbers and Sherpas reached Camp 4, within 1,900 feet of Nanda Devi's summit. It began to snow—heavily—and they hunkered in their tents. The drifts grew as their stockpile of provisions and supplemental oxygen shrank. It would be difficult and dangerous, they finally decided, to attempt the summit, especially with five loads of cargo. They radioed for permission to retreat, then waited again while word of their stalled mission worked its way up and down the Indian intelligence ladder. The authorities deferred to the climbers' judgment and allowed them to retreat.

Before descending, Jerstad and the Indian and Sherpa climbers at Camp 4 anchored their loads to the side of the mountain with ropes and pitons. Another team could return the following spring, they figured, to take the thing to the top and finish the job. There was little chance of the surveillance gear being discovered in the meantime; Indian officials wouldn't be granting climbing permits to Nanda Devi.

The American CIA operatives at Nanda Devi Base Camp were not pleased that the climbers were about to leave the device on the mountain. They were powerless to intervene, however, due to a strict injunction against American voices speaking over the radio. The Chinese might be monitoring their exchanges.

Over the winter, the Chinese conducted two more nuclear tests at Lop Nur.

The following spring, in 1966, a team of Sherpa and Indian climbers returned to Nanda Devi's slopes. The CIA had already revised its plan for the surveillance system: Instead of moving it higher up the mountain, they decided, it should be retrieved and then placed on a lower, more accessible peak. But when the small recovery team arrived at Camp 4, they were dumbstruck: The SNAP generator and other loads they had secured in October were gone. What they found instead was a scoured-out depression. An entire section of the mountain had slid away.

The possibility that the SNAP generator had been damaged in the landslide—and that highly radioactive plutonium might be leaking out—was not lost on either the Indians or the CIA. Fortunately, a fresh team of four American climbers had already been trained and was en route to India. *They* could be assigned to find the thing; they'd have a larger team, with helicopter support.

Another American Everest veteran, Dave Dingman, had been recruited for the 1966 team. Early that year Dingman had been drafted for service in Vietnam—an inconvenient development falling right in middle of his medical residency. Just before being shipped out, he received a mysterious phone call.

"Dr. Dingman . . . Would you like to work for the government on a special project?"

"Well, I've already been drafted," he responded with wry resignation.

"We can fix that," said the caller, who claimed to be with the CIA.

Dingman's curiosity was piqued, and he returned to Baltimore for a meeting. He said that he'd consider the Nanda Devi mission, but only if the CIA interceded with the draft board and allowed him to complete his final year of medical residency. The agency agreed.

Early in the summer of 1966, Langley phoned back, saying that they needed him in India right away. They signed him up and gave him an alias. In June, Dingman and his colleagues—all clueless as to where they were going—were flown in a twin-engine Aero Commander with blacked-out windows to a location in the American Southeast. From there they continued to an unnamed island for "bomb school."

"The teachers were soldier of fortune–type characters," Dingman recalled. "About ten of us recruits gathered around a large table and fashioned charges from C-4 plastic explosives and duct tape. The instructor observing our progress said something I have never forgotten: 'Remember, gentlemen: *A neat bomb is a happy bomb.*'"

The cloak and dagger chapter of the operation was about to begin. From the island they were flown to Delhi and lodged in a "safe house" for the better part of a week, and were barred from touring the city. Dingman knew little about the mission, except that it was being kept under tight wraps while Indian prime minister Indira Gandhi's political campaign was building steam. The opposition party had already accused her of collaborating with the CIA.

Taking a series of aircraft, the climbers flew north. Once in the mountains, they were transferred to American helicopters operated by U.S. Air Force pilots and were ferried the final leg to a base camp at about sixteen thousand feet. Then Dingman was informed that the mission for which they had earlier been briefed—to place listening equipment on the southwest side of Nanda Devi—had already been completed a year earlier. Except that a snag had occurred: A "key part" of that surveillance gear had gone missing. Their new assignment was to find the lost device and transport it to the neighboring peak of Nanda Kot. Once it was set up there, at a more manageable altitude of twenty-two thousand feet, they could all go home.

At the time, Dingman was unaware that his Everest buddies Bishop and Jerstad had been drawn into the same project the previous year—along with a handful of other wildcat mountaineers handpicked from the American climbing scene. Like Dingman, they were all oddly patriotic, despite most mountaineers' temperament of being iconoclastic loners. They quickly deduced that climbing exotic, beautiful mountains and getting paid for it—$1,000 a month wasn't bad in the 1960s—was a fine way to serve their country. They could be James Bonds in crampons.

The SNAP generator could have slid thousands of feet down the mountain, but surely it would be found in the scree and landslide debris below Camp 4. To calculate which direction it might have gone, a helicopter dropped some empty butane canisters as it hovered over the camp while spotters watched where they fell.

For days, Dingman and the other climbers scrambled up rocky, frozen couloirs while being pummeled by monsoon rain and rockfall. A search from the air might be faster and safer, they decided, so they shifted gears and began flying helicopter missions. Their chopper was a HH-43B Huskie, a boxy-looking aircraft able to climb as high as twenty-four thousand feet. They removed the rear door of the helicopter to reduce the weight, and sat in the back with a neutron counter—their legs hanging out as if they were perched on the tailgate of a pickup truck.

"At one point the American pilot—a guy on leave from the air force—wanted to shoot a spiral-horned Marco Polo sheep," Dingman said, aware that Marco Polo sheep can be found at elevations over sixteen thousand feet. "This involved flying on a 'search mission' along high ridges, looking for the animals, while I sat in the doorway with a loaded .44-caliber revolver. The HH-43B is an agile helicopter, and we spotted some sheep and chased them—but we were no match for a sheep running for its life. We didn't bag a sheep—but we *did* return alive."

For Dingman, himself a licensed pilot, the flying was the scariest part of the operation. "There are two types of helicopters," he remarked. "Those that *have crashed*; and those that *will crash*."

The recruits were energetic and adventure-starved, but they knew "dangerous and futile" when they saw it. "You can't let a bureaucracy run a mountaineering expedition," one of them commented.

"The Indians clearly didn't care if the thing was found in our lifetimes," Dingman observed. Weeks of searching turned into months. They found no missing device and heard nary a peep from the radiation detectors. Some speculated that India had retrieved the device early that spring in order to dismantle the SNAP generator, remove the plutonium, and use it to fashion a nuclear bomb. "I'm not the first to speculate that the Indians found the generator and took it away—before we even arrived on the scene," Dingman said.

Though this theory was never proved, there remained a symbolic irony to the caper. Nanda Devi is regarded by Hindus as the abode of the goddess Nanda, a consort of Shiva, the Destroyer. She could, at turns, be kind—or wrathful. The nuclear device placed on her flanks had become an inadvertent offering—a double-edged gift of almighty energy, potentially beneficial, possibly harmful.

The CIA recruits were tired of the obfuscation and lack of direction, and Dingman had a fellowship in cancer surgery to return to. In late September 1966 he snagged a helicopter ride from the Nanda Devi base camp to New Delhi and left India. By abandoning the mission he courted disfavor from Indian and American intelligence, but his motivation had been humane: Had they continued, he felt, someone was likely to be killed. Shortly afterward, the rest of the team disbanded, and the mission was terminated. For that year, at least.

When Dingman returned to the United States, he was snatched

up by the draft board. The CIA had promised him credit for military service—but his contract had been signed by his alias. He had no way to appeal, much less to prove where he had been.

The CIA and the Indians were still desperate for intelligence on the nuclear testing at Lop Nur. In 1967, American Everest veterans Barry Prather, Barry Corbet, and two other American climbers were recruited for another surveillance mission to the Indian Himalaya. The two Barrys—a superb handyman and a brilliant, frustrated scientist—were attracted as much by the technical and research elements of the operation as by the climbing. They had both dropped out of Dartmouth, and perhaps could continue at least part of their education on a challenging assignment with the government.

A new surveillance unit and SNAP generator had been brought to the mountains. The team carried it up Nanda Kot, spent a day assembling it, and anchored it to a relatively level shelf not far below the summit. They turned the device on and received confirmation from below that it was working fine.

China performed more nuclear tests while the Nanda Kot device was operational. The intelligence gleaned indicated that the People's Republic did *not* have the capability to deliver a warhead over a long distance. Three months later the surveillance unit was buried in winter snow and ceased functioning. The device and its plutonium-powered core were retrieved the following spring and never replaced.

Within a few short years, satellite surveillance technology made ground-based sensors obsolete. In the 1970s, details of the secret Nanda Devi operation—and the loss of the first SNAP generator—were leaked to the press. A scandal erupted across India, fueled by accusations that plutonium-laced water was contaminating the headwaters of the sacred Ganges River. The Indian government responded by closing Nanda Devi and its surrounding peaks to climbing and tourism for almost a decade. After it reopened in 1976, Willi Unsoeld and his daughter—Nanda Devi—were among the first climbers to attempt to climb her namesake peak.

Chapter 26

Transitions

Important things happen in life that aren't the drama that we see.

—Link Hibbard, U.S. National Women's
Kayak Champion, 1979–80

The line between success and disaster is razor thin, and only seen clearly in hindsight.

—Nick Clinch

The first National Geographic Special to be shown on television, *Americans on Everest*, premiered on September 10, 1965, on CBS. Twenty million people viewed the program, narrated by Orson Welles in his familiar stentorian tones. The *New York World-Telegram* gushed that the color broadcast had a "strange, savage beauty"—even though most viewers watched on flickering black-and-white TV sets.

Norman Dyhrenfurth's dream had been fulfilled: He had transported his team into the living rooms and consciousness of Americans. The program offered an exhilarating alternative to the standard prime-time fare of shows like *Wagon Train* (though a few nights later, the Beatles made their fourth appearance on *The Ed Sullivan Show*).

America got its heroes. Here were gentleman climbers, driven and passionate, who showed us that with enough gumption, anyone could envision—then find and touch—their own version of Shangri-la. Here was proof that the United States had prevailed. For most Americans, the story of the 1963 expedition was tidily concluded.

The story of Dan Doody, Dyhrenfurth's filming assistant, was also concluded—prematurely so. He would never see the film he helped shoot. In the spring of 1965, Doody was ice climbing with a friend on New Hampshire's Mount Washington. Roped together, they worked their way up a solidly frozen couloir known as Pinnacle Gully. Both climbers fell, plummeting hundreds of feet down the gully's length. Doody died almost immediately, and his partner shortly after.

For many members of the team, Everest was a beginning. Some were able to slingshot careers from it. Barry Bishop leapfrogged up the ladder at *National Geographic*. And two years after Everest, Jim Whittaker climbed Alaska's Mount Kennedy with the president's brother Robert Kennedy, then went on to become CEO of Recreational Equipment, Inc.

In the case of several others, Everest was a prelude to challenges more daunting and complicated than even the world's tallest mountain could inflict.

For Jake Breitenbach, Everest had been both a beginning *and* an end. In the autumn of 1969, the Khumbu Icefall relinquished Breitenbach's body. Members of a Japanese Everest expedition found him on the margin of the glacier near their base camp. They placed his remains in a box and carried it to the Tengboche monastery.

At the time, Barry Bishop was living in a remote village in far western Nepal, doing research for his PhD in cultural geography. The U.S. Embassy asked him to return to Kathmandu, then fly to Khumbu to identify Breitenbach's body. At the same time, Norman Dyhrenfurth was leading a trekking group to Everest Base Camp. When he learned that Bishop would be arriving, he made his way to Tengboche.

The helicopter landed atop the monastery ridge, and Dyhrenfurth greeted Bishop. They hardly needed to examine the contents of the box: the expedition-issue sweater, camera, walkie-talkie, and ice ax confirmed that it was Jake Breitenbach.

The abbot of the monastery led a Buddhist memorial service, with clashing cymbals, booming horns, and resonant chanting from sacred texts. On the ridge behind the monastery, the monks dug a grave and laid Breitenbach to rest. Dyhrenfurth and Bishop built a stone chorten reliquary and placed on it a marker that reads LONG LIVE THE CROW. It was a double reference: to the *gorak,* the Himalayan raven that flew from the crevasse where Breitenbach was entombed; and to his favorite beverage, Old Crow bourbon.

Over time, more monuments and markers would be planted at Tengboche, to enshrine the ashes of three other team members. The next would be for Barry Bishop himself, who was killed when his car overturned near Pocatello, Idaho, in 1994—a month after he retired from the National Geographic Society. Bishop's wife, Lila, was in the car but was unhurt. "Two weeks before the accident," she recounted, "Barry stood in the doorway and said to me, 'When I go, I want to go quickly.' Then he was gone."

A memorial service was held for Bishop on their property near the rim of the Gallatin Valley, overlooking Bozeman, Montana. While tributes were being spoken, the mourners were startled by a roar that came over the ridge behind them. Four of Bishop's fellow U.S. Naval Air Corps pilots had flown their vintage fighter planes across the United States to give him a traditional airman's farewell. They streaked through the bluebird Montana sky in a V formation. As they made a broad turn above the mourners, one lone plane peeled away, leaving a gap in the formation.

The following year, Lila Bishop trekked toward Everest with their daughter, Tara, and son, Brent. She carried with her an urn. At Tengboche the monks chanted prayers, and they mixed Bishop's ashes with clay to create small, conical offerings. Some of these would remain at the monastery. The family took the remainder to place on high passes and at sacred sites. In 2002, Brent Bishop—who had already climbed Everest once, several months before his father died—climbed the mountain again. He scattered some of the ash-embedded offerings on the summit.

By 1998, only half of the original team remained alive. That fall, Lute Jerstad was trekking with his twelve-year-old grandson when he suffered a heart attack and died—within a day's walk of Everest Base

Camp. His body was transported to Kathmandu and cremated on the banks of the sacred Bagmati River, which flows through the city.

Fearing that they might lose a few more before their next anniversary, Dick Pownall gathered nine survivors in 1999 for an early fortieth reunion. The men relaxed in the Colorado Rockies for three days, becoming reacquainted in a way they hadn't before—fixing meals together, washing up, talking around a table, hiking. Jim Lester, ever the observant shrink, noted that the tense atmosphere that had suffused the climb—the wariness, hidden concern about one's abilities, and evaluation of one another—was absent. For the first time since the West Ridge and South Col days, Tom Hornbein remarked, he felt he was part of *one* expedition, rather than two.

They remembered Jim Ullman, the expedition scribe, who had died of cancer in 1971. And Dick Emerson, who had died of a heart attack in 1982, after being appointed chairman of the Department of Sociology at the University of Washington in Seattle. Farm boy Barry Prather had continued his glacier research with Maynard Miller in Alaska until 1987, when an oncoming car collided with his one early morning in a town along the Columbia River in Oregon. Prather's eighteen-year-old son Eric was killed with him.

Two years after the reunion, Gil Roberts died of melanoma, following a successful medical career. Soon, memorials for Roberts and Jerstad joined those of Barry Bishop and Jake Breitenbach behind the Tengboche monastery. Relatives and fellow climbers refer to the four men and their chorten reliquaries as "the Boys on the Hill," camped forever in the sacred valley refuge known as Khumbu.

In 1967, Barry Corbet and a climbing partner made a first ascent of Mount Tyree, Antarctica's second highest peak. He seemingly could have climbed anything, but in 1968 he came up against a challenge arguably far more staggering than Tyree or Everest.

After Everest, Corbet had become despondent. He'd lost his best buddy, Jake Breitenbach, and following an informal parade in his honor through Jackson Hole, he had separated from his wife, Muffy.

Filmmaking provided a lift. Corbet partnered with a college classmate to produce innovative adventure films, such as *Yoo Hoo, I'm a*

Bird (for an airline company), and *The Moebius Flip*. Enough income rolled in to hire Norman Dyhrenfurth as a mountain cinematographer.

In the winter of 1968 while filming with Dyhrenfurth on a mountain near Aspen, Corbet climbed into a helicopter to shoot footage of skiers making turns through fresh, powdery snow. Flying behind the skiers, only a few feet above the surface, the chopper suddenly snagged on a hump and lurched forward. The helicopter slammed into the slope, and in an apocalypse of tearing metal, Corbet was thrown through the Plexiglas bubble.

Dyhrenfurth saw Corbet's nose sticking up from the snow, and kept him alive while the skiers raced down the mountain to find help. Corbet lived—but he was paralyzed from the waist down.

Out of the hospital, Barry Corbet grasped at any hope for a cure, while fighting off tenacious and frightful inner demons. By whatever means, Corbet decided, he would reclaim his athletic outdoor life. He began by perfecting what he called "ballistic transfers," in which he could move from a wheelchair to a car or bed in a single explosive yet fluid motion. He also returned to filmmaking. And while shooting a movie from a raft in the Grand Canyon in 1976, he discovered kayaking. At that time, virtually no paraplegics had ever kayaked; he nearly drowned trying.

But Corbet was hooked, and he soon became a "Super Crip"—a new breed of radicalized hero. "Super Crips leap curbs in a single bound," Corbet said, describing how some wheelchair-confined daredevils careen around cities and suburbs with a combination of finesse and unruly abandon.

No longer did Barry Corbet wish to be characterized as a climber. "Sure, climbing a peak has mythic connotations," he wrote. "Though these days, I attach more importance to getting into public buildings or onto buses." Advocating for the disabled brought him a new sense of direction. The Americans with Disabilities Act was more than a decade away, but Corbet and other wheelchair activists had rolled out of the starting gate and were gathering momentum.

The ADA was passed in 1990, and in late 1991 Corbet took the reins as the editor of a magazine called *New Mobility*. His irreverent, intelligent writing set a tone that resonates in the award-winning, high-circulation magazine even today.

In the early 1990s, Corbet drove to the Tetons, where he had been a favorite climbing guide. He pulled into a turnout. The most majestic peaks of the Tetons—the Cathedral Group—rose above the far bank. His second, disabled life was confronting the immutable icons of his first life. "But with the benefit of hindsight, it's easy to see that there is no first life, no second life," he wrote. "There's *this* life, and it's everything we ever hoped for. Life is complete and terrifying and drop-dead gorgeous, and I have just as big a piece of it as anyone else."

Corbet's approach to life as a Super Crip had worked, but he wore out his shoulders. Then he developed incurable bladder cancer, and was losing what little mobility remained. In the fall of 2004, ready for a final adventure, he discontinued taking fluids and food. Tom Hornbein joined Corbet and his family at his ridgetop home in Colorado.

"With his family and other loved ones tied into the metaphorical rope, a climber one time more, he started up that final pitch," Hornbein wrote. Corbet was again leading the way, just as he had when he'd cut steps in the ice for Hornbein and Unsoeld up the Hornbein Couloir, en route to Camp 5W.

His breathing stopped. Hornbein took his hand. "You made it," Hornbein said quietly. Corbet had been a legendary climber and a beloved spokesman for the disabled. He had led two lives, after all. He was a guide in both.

At the American Everest team's 1999 reunion, the missing members weren't entirely absent: It was as if they'd merely reached higher camps on a new route they all were ascending. Willi Unsoeld had been gone twenty years, but strains from his buoyant harmonica seemed to drift down to the reunion's convivial base camp in the Rockies.

Shortly after the expedition, in 1963, Jim Lester had handed out a survey to the team members. One of its follow-up questions asked with whom they would most like to climb on a future expedition. Willi Unsoeld was the most popular choice among the South Col and West Ridge climbers alike.

The West Ridge debate had forced Unsoeld into the role of diplo-
mat. He had listened thoughtfully, spoken compellingly, and instilled
trust. Unsoeld also ranked high on scales of maturity, sensitivity to
one's impact on others, and complexity of personality: the qualities of
a leader.

And of a sincere, seasoned performer. "He was a bit of an actor,"
Lester said. "Except that he didn't *play* a role. He *was* the role."

Beginning in the Tetons in the 1950s, Dick Emerson had watched
"the Willi Unsoeld Legend" grow around him. He wondered if the
myth blurred the edges of the Unsoeld he knew. "I have been trying
for years to 'figure Willi out'—but every time I thought I was getting
close, he changed before my very eyes."

With degrees in physics, philosophy, and theology, Unsoeld naturally became one of the founding faculty of The Evergreen State College, a forward-looking educational experiment in Washington State.
Students flocked to his courses, lingered in the hallway outside his
office, and feasted on his boisterous chortle and cackles of laughter.
At the same time, Unsoeld was the most serious teacher they knew—
demanding their best intentions and effort.

Unsoeld had embarked squarely on a search for meaning. For him,
power and mystery and unimaginable energy could be found in the
natural world—"forever-hidden realms we can only glimpse or intuit,
but where answers to the ultimate questions lie." Mainly, he wanted
his students to build a more ethical and moral world, to leave the
shelter of the ivory tower, go hungry, get angry, and learn to be competitive. Many of his classes, such as Sermon on the Mountain and
Outdoor Education from Hoboken to Humptulips, adjourned to the
mountains.

In 1976, Unsoeld and his daughter, Nanda Devi Unsoeld—Devi—
fulfilled their shared dream. They made an attempt on her namesake
mountain, Nanda Devi, *the Bliss-Giving Goddess*—the peak in northern India that Unsoeld had laid reverent eyes upon in 1949. Devi, at
twenty-three, was an effervescent free spirit, with flowing hair and an
easy smile—a young, female version of Willi Unsoeld.

The route to Camp 4, the last camp below the summit, was steep
and technically challenging. Ecstatic to finally be on "her" mountain,

Devi climbed with rapturous determination. Arriving at the tent platform of Camp 4, at over twenty-three thousand feet, she and Unsoeld were close to touching the sacred summit.

But Devi began to suffer acute abdominal distress. She spent a sleepless night in the tent, belching sulfurous gas. The next morning was snowy and blisteringly cold. Unsoeld and the other climbers agreed that Devi should descend. But her stomach distress worsened. Calmly, Devi announced, "I'm going to die." Within minutes, she expired in Unsoeld's arms.

Shock turned to anguish and confusion. With his stunned teammates, Unsoeld sealed Devi in her sleeping bag, and in a "horrible shove," released her over the edge of the precipice into a steep couloir—committing her body to the mountain.

By the time he returned to the United States, Unsoeld's hair and beard had turned a few shades toward white. In his grief, he was confronting the reality—a raw and personal version of reality—that he had wanted his students to taste but never ingest.

At age fifty-two, Unsoeld had both hips replaced, and he endured a labored gait from his toeless feet and artificial joints. But his spirit remained strong, and by late winter of 1979 his strength recovered sufficiently to lead twenty-one students and another Evergreen professor on an early spring climb of Mount Rainier. Some colleagues opposed the trip as too dangerous. But Unsoeld's confidence inspired trust.

Over four days, the party ascended slowly through fog and falling snow. When the group was finally staged for a summit attempt, they were turned back by a new blizzard. In a whiteout at nearly twelve thousand feet, they hunkered in their tents and snow caves for another night.

In the morning, they decided to descend. Unsoeld headed off with three students on the first rope, down a steep slope below Cadaver Gap. Suddenly, the slope began moving—becoming an avalanche that carried away Unsoeld and his three rope mates. Unsoeld and the student roped closest to him, Janie Diepenbrock, were buried.

The surviving students managed, with remarkable luck, to free the other two on Unsoeld's rope and to find their way to safety. Just as remarkably—in a testament to Unsoeld's effect on students, which carries forward to this day—the students arrived at the base of Mount Rainier literally singing their praise to Unsoeld.

Willi Unsoeld, the Old Guide, died on a mountain he had climbed many times. He had traveled full circle—from the Mount Rainier training ground where the 1963 team had gathered more than sixteen years earlier, to Everest, and back.

Unsoeld's lifelong dedication to philosophical ideas, ethical actions, and the restorative value of nature nourished him. Ultimately, what he learned took him farther—on a quest to unravel the riddle of inner peace. He found it precisely where he had started: in the mountains, among friends and flock.

Unsoeld led his own life in the manner of a dragon, while leading others with the attention and patience of a shepherd. He spent his life elevating the gaze of those around him—friends, fellow Everest climbers, and students—from the ground beneath their feet to the mountains above. And higher still, toward the heavens, into the vast unknown.

Afterword

*I have come to feel that one of the deepest attractions
of mountaineering is its potential, for a time at least, to
allow us to feel whole, pulled together, undivided,
undistracted—in a word, ourselves.*

—Jim Lester

Norman Dyhrenfurth—aged ninety-four in 2012—still has a full head of wavy hair, now silvered. His memory is vivid, and minor injuries have barely slowed him. He springs from his chair and looks prepared to join, or lead, the next Himalayan mountaineering expedition.

But the styles, equipment, ethics—even the purpose and meaning—of Himalayan climbing have changed around him. Dyhrenfurth's style on Everest was democratic: He convened meetings, aired opinions, and shared decision making. He also insisted that the members work as a team. They were professionals, and he was counting on all of them to contribute to the goal of getting *any* climber to the summit.

Over the past two decades, mountaineering on Everest has evolved into an individual sport. Merely by making a phone call and answering some questions—and coughing up $50,000 or more—a reasonably fit person can sign up for a guided climb to the summit. Everest clients can buy their gear after arrival in Kathmandu, fly to the Lukla airstrip, and hike to Base Camp while staying in comfortable inns. At the foot of the Khumbu Icefall, they apply sunscreen, check the charge levels on their digital cameras, then clip in to fixed ropes that lead virtually to the top, while breathing oxygen from lightweight long-lasting bottles.

Some sections of the standard South Col route have become so congested that the Sherpas fix parallel ropes: one for upward travel, the other for downward. "Nowadays, it's like going to the gym or running a marathon," said Dave Dingman. "It's not a tactical challenge, nor an aesthetic experience. Obviously, it takes a lot of stamina, but there's no route finding, no strategy, and very little need for preparation."

David Shlim, who ran a medical post at Pheriche and a clinic in Kathmandu, has marveled at the bonds of friendship that developed in 1963—contrasted with what he saw in later years. "The members of one American Everest expedition, in 1993, had such difficulty getting along on the trip that they couldn't even sit at the same table at a dinner 'celebrating' their expedition in Kathmandu. Some members had summited and some had not. The transition from being able to appreciate group success to only being able to celebrate an individual success was complete. Nowadays, it's as if those going to Everest don't really want to *climb* it, they want to *have climbed* it."

Dave Dingman is saddened by this mindset. "People sometimes say to me, 'Oh—it's too bad you failed to summit Everest.' But I went to nearly twenty-eight thousand feet, and provided help to those who were struggling to get down. I felt fulfilled with my role. In a way, reaching the summit would have distracted me from my medical career and international service work. And to have that kind of success when you're twenty-six or twenty-seven is not necessarily a good thing."

Since Everest was first scaled by Hillary and Norgay in 1953, the mountain has been climbed almost 6,150 times by at least 3,750 people (Whittaker and Gombu were the seventh and eighth). The summiters include 321 women, a seventy-six-year-old Nepalese man, a thirteen-year-old American boy, a blind person, and a double amputee.

The mountain has also become a venue for "splat sports"—parachuting, hang gliding, wingsuit diving, extreme skiing, and snowboarding. In 2005, a high-performance helicopter set down on the summit for four minutes.

At least 240 people have died on Everest's slopes. That's 1 death for every 25 successful summits—which is not a bad ratio, compared to what it used to be. Although the average number of deaths on Everest is increasing year by year, the *chances* of dying have declined (at least on the standard routes via the South Col and the North Col in Tibet). In 1963, the number of people who had died on her flanks was twice the number of those who had reached its summit. Even to the present day, the West Ridge route has seen more deaths (at least 16) than it has successful summits (14).

In the spring of 2012, commercial sponsors staged two American "legacy" expeditions on Everest, as tributes to the 1963 expedition. Both groups hoped to simultaneously climb the mountain via the West Ridge and the South Col. Jim Whittaker's son Leif and Barry Bishop's son, Brent, were members of the team sponsored by Eddie Bauer; Jim Whittaker, at age eighty-one, trekked in toward Base Camp to join them, but was turned back by illness.

"Conditions this year were treacherous," West Ridge climber Jake Norton said. "In place of the solid snow that you'd find in a normal year, we encountered bulletproof, glassy ice—as if everything had melted back to the ancient ice of the Cretaceous."

Jake Norton and Brent Bishop have long been awed by Unsoeld and Hornbein's ascent and traverse; they also appreciate, as Hornbein had, the role that luck plays in the mountains. Neither of the 2012 legacy teams reached even the shoulder of the West Ridge. And the Hornbein Couloir—photographed from a helicopter—appeared to be a deadly shooting gallery: 2012 was a dry year in the Himalaya, and as the ice melted in the sun below the West Shoulder, loosened rocks blasted down on the climbers with frightening regularity.

Before Norton and Bishop and the other West Ridgers turned back, they looked across the Western Cwm, peering over the top of Camp 2. On the Lhotse Face, a conga line of hundreds of people trudged, single file, up the fixed rope. Members of more than twenty expeditions—including a handful of climbers on the '63 tribute teams—were climbing toward the South Col. All had waited for the typically narrow window of clear weather to make their attempt on the top.

"It had the makings for a tragic summit day—and it was," Norton said. "Even in perfect conditions, that many people simply can't move safely and efficiently up the summit ridge."

The next afternoon, May 19, the South Col climbers faced a human traffic jam, just as Norton and Bishop and their teammates had quietly predicted. In a remarkable procession, 244 people tagged the top in a single day, ascending from both sides of the mountain. But six climbers ran out of strength, or bottled oxygen, and died— all of them during the descent, above their high camps. The hopes of capturing a moment of glory—or, for some, a bullet point on a résumé—had carried them onward when it may have been prudent to turn back. Increasingly, the Sherpas find themselves in an awkward position. They perform well at altitude, but are often obliged to coax their highly motivated but less capable clients safely to the top, and hopefully get them back down.

"If they do collapse, it's the Sherpas who are there to try to pick up the pieces," said David Shlim. "There are many sad stories of Sherpas who stuck it out in the death zone for hours trying to get a client to descend, but finally had to go down in order to save their own lives."

The possibility of dying on Everest didn't deter 517 people from reaching the summit during the spring of 2012—out of 659 making the attempt via the South Col. Another 110 reached the top from the north side—for a total of almost 627 summiters that season. The summit was reached on only six days, over the season, for an average of more than 100 ascents per day.

In 1963, still and movie cameras were the team's only connections to media—and the afternoon ham radio call to Kathmandu. For entertainment, they listened to shortwave radio, and Willi Unsoeld played his harmonica.

Present-day guides now wear digital audio players and plug in earbuds—partly to tune out their clients. Everyone is linked to the Internet and international press via cellphones, satellite, live video feeds, and blogs—a scene ready made for "reality" television. One series called *Everest: Beyond the Limit,* which aired on the Discovery Channel for three seasons, highlighted the outsized personal ambitions that can push team members into dramatically dangerous situations.

"When you mix media pressure with life-and-death decisions," Jake Norton said, "it gets scary. I compare the scene on Everest to the frenzies we've seen on Wall Street. When people are motivated only by money, or by summits, they're going to make bad decisions. Everest has become a magnified version of our modern world."

"Something extraordinary happened to Mount Everest after 1963," Jim Lester noted during a return visit to the mountain in 1997. "It has turned from an exotic locale—with overtones of Mount Olympus and Shangri-la—into a rite of passage for everyman. There's reason to believe that our American expedition, in an indirect way, had something to do with that—for better or worse."

Indeed, it might have. On their approach to Base Camp in 1963, the American team skirted a yak pasture known as Lukla, at nine thousand feet in the Dudh Kosi valley. While the team was climbing on the mountain, Edmund Hillary and members of his Himalayan School-house Expedition had paced across this terraced meadow, measuring it for an airstrip. Hillary hoped to fly in supplies for construction of a hospital and more Sherpa schools. The Lukla site looked attractive—except that it sloped downward at an eight-degree angle. The survey team wondered if an inclined runway might be an asset—by helping to decelerate landing planes, and boost their speed on takeoff.

The following year, Hillary's colleagues and a Peace Corps volunteer returned to the Lukla pasture. They used a tree trunk as a roller to level the site while line-dancing Sherpas compacted the surface. Test flights by Swiss pilots confirmed that an uphill landing at Lukla was indeed possible, bumps and all.

The airstrip wound up transporting more than project supplies. Over the ensuing decades, Lukla became the landing zone and launch pad for a whole new socioeconomic order for the Sherpas.

Colonel Jimmy Roberts would play a key role in the transformation. When the American team vacated Base Camp, Colonel Roberts and one of the Sherpas inherited the expedition's lightweight tents, tables, folding chairs, sleeping pads, and cookstoves. Roberts was familiar with the pre-war techniques of outfitting for travel in the Indian

Himalaya, which relied upon squadrons of bearers to transport army tents, sheets and blankets, wooden furniture, and china cups and plates.

It made sense to put the '63 expedition's modern, highly portable gear to good use. In early 1964, Colonel Roberts wrote a letter to Barry Bishop. "For $325 per person, I aim to offer a Kathmandu-to-Tengboche, 35-day round trip 'trek' for a party of four. This includes camping equipment, food, a Sherpa, two kitchen boys, eight coolies, etc."

Bishop was intrigued and offered encouragement. Roberts soon registered the country's first "trekking agency" with His Majesty's Government of Nepal. He named the company Mountain Travel.

At first, government officials had difficulty understanding the concept. Even in America and Europe, the terms "trek" and "trekking" weren't well known. But Colonel Roberts was ready to educate the masses. He placed a small, expensive advertisement in *Holiday* magazine and received five responses. In the early spring of 1965 his clients—"a sporting trio of enthusiastic and appreciative ladies"— arrived for the first Everest trek. In the first year of operation, eight clients signed on.

A decade later, more than twelve thousand people visited Nepal for "trekking or mountaineering." Roberts sold the company in 1975, but the industry continued to mushroom, and at its peak in the early 1990s, Mountain Travel supervised as many as thirty-two outfitted treks at a time. Their roster of leaders included Lute Jerstad, Gil Roberts, and Barry and Lila Bishop. As demand grew, other trekking agencies joined the fray—most of them owned and operated by Sherpas who had learned the business from Colonel Roberts.

In 2011, more than twenty-five thousand trekkers and climbers visited the Mount Everest region, and most of them flew in and out through the former yak pasture at Lukla. Today, during the height of the trekking season, as many as thirty flights a day take off and land (the record is almost sixty). Himalayan weather, though, remains as unpredictable as it was in 1963. In November 2011, nearly three thousand trekkers were stranded in Lukla for days, awaiting fog-grounded planes.

Colonel Roberts likely never guessed that the style of trekking he pioneered—relying on Sherpas to escort clients between Himalayan camps and serve them meals—would eventually extend to Everest's summit.

Perhaps the mountain itself is all that remains unchanged. Or maybe not. Today we are learning—thanks in part to the baseline science conducted in 1963—that Himalayan glaciers are retreating, overall, as a result of climate change; their total surface area has decreased by one-fifth over the past fifty years.

Even as the glaciers recede, a tide of humans continues to surge toward the mountains, seeking livelihoods and chasing dreams. And as more foreigners trek through the Sherpa homeland, the Sherpas head off to pursue aspirations of their own.

In 1963, Sherpa houses were constructed of stacked stone, with clunky wood shutters for windows. Shaggy-haired men and women fashioned their boots by hand from water buffalo hide, and they bathed once a year. Now, many Khumbu Sherpas are wealthy and well educated. They no longer need to carry loads or guide trips, nor even do their own farm work. Increasingly, they have come under pressure to sell their ancestral tracts of land to the Nepalese outsiders who already lease their lodges and till their crops. The Sherpas who remain in Khumbu compare the climbing and lucrative trekking industry to livestock husbandry: If you feed your charges well, they produce more "milk"—tips and benefits—though they demand one's constant attention lest they fall off the steep trails.

A growing number of Sherpas are finding their futures in America, especially in the greater New York City area, where they drive taxis, wash dishes, and work as (much coveted) nannies. But these are entry-level jobs—waypoints, typically, for higher destinations on the socioeconomic scale. Sherpa professionals now include doctors and airline pilots, academics and long-haul truck drivers. For Sherpas nursing lofty ambitions, Everest provided an elevated head start.

With an animated smile, one innkeeper in Namche Bazaar offered an idea. "All of you Americans seem to love our mountains and our houses and culture. Why don't you all come here to live—you can have our houses—and we'll all move to America and live in your houses?"

Nepal, as a whole, hasn't fared as well as the Sherpa community. In 1963, the country's population was only nine million; it has more than tripled since then. The capital, Kathmandu, has traded one medieval theme for another, morphing from a preindustrial enclave into a pollution-choked, infrastructure-challenged city swamped with internally displaced refugees and volatile Maoist party cadres. Unemployed youths from hill villages queue up at scores of "manpower" agencies to pay dearly for the privilege of working as manual laborers in the steaming cities of the Middle East and Southeast Asia. Facing political tension and few opportunities at home, they are happy to step onto the bottom rung of the foreign labor ladder, where they are prized for their willingness to engage in "3-D" work: Difficult, Dirty, and Dangerous.

For the members of the 1963 American Mount Everest Expedition, a return to modern Nepal might well tarnish their memories of a genuinely enchanted time and place. For most of them, though, this opportunity has passed. By the fall of 2012, only seven of the twenty-one 1963 Everest climbers remained.

Dick Pownall had been badly shaken by Jake Breitenbach's accident; his own climbing ambitions, post-1963, were modest. He returned to teaching in Denver and became a high school principal. He's now retired in Vail, where he lives in a house he built with his own hands.

Dave Dingman thrived for more than four decades as a plastic and reconstructive surgeon, and was recruited by Interplast, a charitable organization that does surgeries in developing countries. For Dingman, acrobatic flying now supplants climbing as his source of risk and excitement. In his late seventies, he designed an aerobatic airplane that he calls the *Dingbat*—then built it from scratch. Most days, he takes it for loops and rolls over the Sawtooth Range of Idaho.

At age eighty-one, Tom Hornbein laces up his vintage rock climbing shoes and sure-footedly pads up the steep, smooth rock above his home in Estes Park, Colorado—not far from where he'd climbed as a youth. He makes it look easy, negotiating routes that would stump beginning climbers.

Like Dingman, Hornbein feared that their success on Everest might distract him from his medical and academic career. But distancing himself from the climbing world wasn't easy, considering that his West Ridge traverse with Willi Unsoeld is still regarded as one of the most impressive feats in Himalayan mountaineering. (Hornbein once handed his credit card to a climbing store clerk in Copenhagen. "Were you named after the couloir?" the man asked.)

"As I aged to the point where I could accept my accomplishments as well as my limitations," Hornbein wrote, "I was able to understand and acknowledge that mountains and medicine were the warp and weft of a single piece of cloth." It may be no coincidence that Hornbein would specialize as an anesthesiologist. In the operating theater—as on the mountain—risk and uncertainty are a constant presence, and situations arise that demand near-instantaneous life-and-death decisions.

Glaciologist Maynard Miller continued to build his post-Everest career around mountains and ice. He taught college, directed the Juneau Icefield Research Program for sixty-three years, and found time to serve for eight years in the Idaho legislature. He's now retired in Moscow, Idaho.

Jim Whittaker lives in Port Townsend, Washington, after a successful career in the outdoor equipment industry. He led the first American ascent of K2, in 1978, and returned to Everest to lead the Earth Day 20 International Peace Climb in 1990.

Radio whiz Al Auten went on to become chairman of the Colorado Mountain Club and built a career in the publishing world. He now lives near Denver. Nawang Gombu, the first man to climb Everest twice, became director of the Himalayan Mountaineering Institute, in Darjeeling, and remained energetic and helpful to the end; he passed away in Darjeeling in 2011. And psychologist Jim Lester, beloved and feared by the team members, died of ALS—Lou Gehrig's disease—in the spring of 2010.

On a crisp fall day that year, Tom Hornbein scrambled up a Colorado peak with Jim Lester's widow, Valerie. They sat together on the summit. Hornbein pulled out his iPod and tapped the wheel. Valerie recognized the recording: It was Jim Lester on the piano, playing a jazz classic—"Prelude to a Kiss." As the music surged and flowed, a white butterfly began swooping around them. They could feel Lester's presence. It seemed more than coincidence. The Greek word for "butterfly," Valerie noted, is also the word for "spirit": *psyche*.

Spirit. *That* was what united the members of the 1963 American Mount Everest Expedition. Independent and individualistic, they shared a subtle but luminous spirit, one that endowed them with vision, passion, and purpose. It was the spirit of excellence, of commitment, of teamwork, and of vigor that President Kennedy had invoked when he urged Americans to take on challenges "not because they are easy, but because they are hard."

A half century ago, this spirit—incarnated in a handful of tough men—coincided with the aspirations of a still-young nation. From competing objectives and differing opinions they forged compromises while suspending personal desires for the sake of common goals. With supreme effort, fortified by dreams and bonded by cooperation, America and its mountaineers climbed to the hilltop that President Kennedy spoke of. And there, for at least a moment, they found greatness.

ACKNOWLEDGMENTS

This project wouldn't have been possible without the warm-spirited and generous help of a large number of people. I envision you all as tied together in a familial and literary brotherhood of the rope.

Throughout, the project has been blessed by the patient and attentive insight of Thomas F. Hornbein. He has acted as inspiration and guide, counselor and consoler—and even editor. This book would not have come together in its present fashion without Tom.

It was an honor to meet and work with the six other survivors of the '63 Everest expedition. Al Auten and Maynard Miller told stories of adventure, not just on Everest. Dave and Barbara Dingman were generous hosts, and Dave flew over me in his aerobatic plane. Dick Pownall, in his eighties, came to the Tetons (with his beautiful wife, Mary) to climb the Grand Teton. "Big Jim" Whittaker is still big, and youthful, buoyed by his exuberant wife, Dianne Roberts; I was impressed to see Jim fairly leap from his chair in Port Townsend, at age eighty-one. Norman Dyhrenfurth is equally spry and sharp, at ninety-four, and appears all the more youthful when walking hand in hand with his lovely partner, Moidi (Maria Sernetz). They are an inseparable, eternally gracious couple.

Wives, widows, and a wide range of relatives of the team members were abundantly helpful, especially Valerie Lester (and her son, Toby) for sharing Jim's files, for encouragement, and for reliving memories of a brilliant and soulful man; Barry Corbet's former wife, Muffy Moore, provided background on Barry and that era in the Tetons, as well as photographs. Their children Jonathan, Jennifer, and Mike Corbet were supportive and helpful, as was Barry's brother Burke. Many thanks also go to Lila Bishop (and her son, superb climber Brent Bishop) for all they shared and offered. And thanks to Lou Breitenbach for enlivening stories from Jake's tragically short life. Dick Emerson's wife, Pat, and their daughter, Leslie, were cordial, as was the late Susan Jerstad. Gil Roberts's wife, Erica Stone, president of the American Himalayan Foundation and Rani Supreme, was exuberant and supportive.

Additional thanks go to Barry Prather's daughter Liesl Andrico (especially for stellar editing and guidance, and excellent questions) and to Barry's sisters, Judy Ferrari and Barbara Beede. Maynard Miller's sons, Lance and Ross, were helpful, and ably answered difficult questions about glaciers. Thanks also to Jane Lester, Lynne Breitenbach, Kursung (Phinjo) Gombu, Jolene Unsoeld, and the indomitable Agnes Doody, Dan's sister.

Special mention goes to Rand Chatterjee, for material on Woodrow Wilson Sayre; Miriam Chotiner-Gardner for shepherding everything along; Tom Claytor, for his disquisition on the Himalayan Mountaineering Institute; Charlie Conrad at Random House, for his patience and superb editing; Thomas Dewell, friend and editor; Dave Dornan, for his stories, historical acumen, and friendship; Jim Fisher for his account of the Lukla airstrip construction and background on Willi Unsoeld; Roberts French for his intelligent view of the 1960s in the Tetons; Jeff Greenwald for his guidance and good cheer; Kenny Hosack and Craig Hospital; Jeff Huestis for his support and for access to his father's rich archive; Renny Jackson, for his remarkable grasp of Teton climbing history and details (and recollections of climbing in the Hornbein Couloir—one of three living people who have been there); Joe Kelsey—Vulgarian Emeritus and authority on the Tetons; Frances Klatzel, Canadian author and publisher working in Nepal and student of Sherpa culture, for clarifying details of Sherpa life; Sarah Lazin, my agent, for her patience, friendship, and support; Jeff Long, for his inspiration and guidance; David Peterson for stories about Corbet and Unsoeld; Al and Susan Read, for stories from Kathmandu and the Tetons; Ron Rosner, for his historical perspective and recollections of Nepal; Amy Schneider and Dane Loomer, for the welcoming New Hampshire refuge; David Shlim, for his help on many fronts; Warren Smith Jr., for his Tibetan scholarship, his relief map of Everest, and his comic relief; John Wasson (on the team that made the second ascent of Ama Dablam) and Jocelyn Slack, for their friendship and support; Dave Vrabec for his encyclopedic recall; Scott Wood, who was generous with his time and resources, and who I commend for inspiring a generation of Idaho students with the wisdom of Unsoeld and Corbet. Also, many thanks go to Robert "Brownie" Schoene, Gary and Veronica Silberberg, Jonathan Stevens, Steve Stokes (for the vintage reel-to-reel tape deck), Bill Sumner, Mikel Vause, and Ang Phurba Sherpa of Lukla—now a long-haul truck driver based out of New York. Mainly, thanks to my wife, Didi, for her patience and support, and near-countless hours of assistance.

My highest Himalayan regards go to the following librarians, archivists, and scientists, who generously offered materials on climbers, family, and history: Sheila Berry, Unit Chief, Nepal, Sri Lanka, Bangladesh, at the Department of State; Barbara Brower, for previews of her father Dave Brower's archive of team members' photos from 1963; Julie Carrington and the Library of the Royal Geographical Society; Helen Cherullo, Mary Metz, and Margaret Foster of the Mountaineers Books; Lynda Claassen and Heather Smedberg of the Mandeville Library, UCSD; Kristin Elliott and Eddie Bauer; Richard Ewig, Associate Director of the American Heritage Center at the University of Wyoming; Maryrose Grossman, of the Audiovisual Archives of the John Fitzgerald Kennedy Library; Dennis Hagen, Archivist of the Tenth Mountain Division Resource Center at the Denver Public Library; Beth Heller, Brendan MacDonald, Alex Depta, Erik Lambert, and all the folks at the Henry S. Hall Jr. American Alpine Club Library, for superb research assistance; Katie Ives, Editor-in-Chief of *Alpinist*; David Kessler and the Bancroft Library at the University of California, Berkeley; Monte Later, for his photos and stories, especially of Willi Unsoeld; Robert W. Levenson, Director of the Institute of Personality and Social Research in Berkeley, California; and the well-known IPAR veteran and scholar Harrison Gough; Rosemary Macray, Media Unit Chief of the Office of Policy Coordination and Public Affairs, of the Bureau of Consular Affairs, U.S. Government; Mele Mason for her illuminating videos of Nawang Gombu, Norman Dyhrenfurth, and others; Jim Milledge, veteran of the 1960–61 Silver Hut Expedition, regarded as an authority on high-altitude medicine and physiology; Jack Reilly and Dorothea Sartain of the Explorers Club, New York City; Richard Salisbury and Elizabeth Hawley for their scrupulous data collection and recall; Randolph Stilson, in charge of The Evergreen State College Archives and Special Collections, and curator of the Willi Unsoeld Collection; and mountaineering and Everest historian Ed Webster.

Special thanks go to the National Geographic Society, for reference to the transcripts of audiotaped interviews recorded by Matt McDade following the expedition, and specifically to Renee Braden, Mimi Dornack, Wendy Glassmire, Joergen Birman, Susan Hitchcock, Rebecca Martin, and Susan Welchman; to Carroll Dunham, a tantric *devi* of good cheer and brilliance, for her Nanda Devi material; and to my daughter, Phoebe Coburn, who established and maintained an invaluable cross-generational, multimedia link to the world at large.

Others who freely offered stories, encouragement, good cheer, and resources include Mari Abercrombie, John Adams, Len Aitken, Burt Angrist, Conrad Anker, Stan Armington, Richard Armstrong, Pete Athans, Dick and Barbara Barker, Christian Beckwith, Bonnie Berg, Joe Bieganek, Gerry Birch, Lorraine Bonney, John Borstelman, Jesse Brandt, Suzi Brandt, Bill Briggs, Roger Brown, Arlene Burns, Lester Butt, Deanna and Dann Byck, Alton Byers, Peter Byrne, Alfie Campbell, Gabriel Campbell, Martha Carlson, Lisa Choegyal, Liesl Clark, Winfield "Binny" Clark, Nick Clinch, Bob Craig, Charlie Craighead, John Byrne Cooke, Ed Cooper, Judy Cornish, Marcus Cotton, Chris Devlin-Young, Dick Dorworth, Fred Dunham, Colin Dye, Jim Elder, John Evans, Beth Exum, Roger Ewy, Judy Ferrari, Claude Fiddler, George Fonyo, Jeff Foote, Patrick Freeny, Clark Gerhardt, Mike Gill, Tom Greening, John Griber, Colin Haley, Wayne Hamilton, Ben Harding, John Harlin III, Andy Harvard, Kathy Harvard, Elizabeth Hawley, Kurt Henry and Teton Adaptive Sports, Link Hibbard, Elliott and Frances Higgins, Frances Howland, Ray Huey, Jasper Hunt, Mary Hutz, Paul Kallmes, Lynn Siri Kimsey, Vivian Kurz, Tom Lamb, Peter Lev, Scot MacBeth, John McKinnon, Sam Maddox, Andy Manzardo, Robin Marston, Jim McCarthy, Bernadette McDonald, Bob McLaurin, Rick Medrick, Roger Mellem, Robert Menter, Don Messerschmidt, Denice Mikkelson, Dee Molenaar, Alex Morley, Bruce

Morley, Bruce Morrison, Sterling Neale, Rod Newcomb, Norbu Tenzing Norgay, Jake Norton, Bob Peirce, Peter Pilafian, Matteo Pistono, Sean Plottner, Adina Racoviteanu, Don Reese, Tad Riste, Jean Rodman, Frank Sands, Jonathan Schechter, Fritz Selby, Lynn Sheldon, Ang Rita Sherpa, Ang Tshering Sherpa, Daya Yangji Sherpa, Dorjee Lhatoo Sherpa, Mingma Dorje Sherpa, Namgyal Zangbu Sherpa, Dr. Nawang Karsang Sherpa, Nima Wangchuk Sherpa, Pasang G. Sherpa, Sange Dorjee Sherpa, Dr. Wangdi Sherpa, Yangji Sherpa, Zimba Zangbu Sherpa, Jeff Shushan, Sam Silverstein, Michael Smithson, Marvin Spiegelman, Fred Stanley, Ben Steele, Paula Stout, Herb Swedlund, Tashi, Daniel Taylor, Norbu Tenzing, William Thompson, Jerry Tinling, Roberta Treischman, Jack Turner, Jan Sacherer Turner, Robert and Sally Uhlmann, Jay Ullin, Brian Weirum, Jed Williamson, Gordon Wiltsie, Fred Wright, and Lauri Yablick. Thank you all.

NOTES

NOTES ON PRIMARY SOURCES

One of the more engaging sets of documents referred to during research for this volume were the "Expedition Newsletters" that leader Norman Dyhrenfurth crafted and sent out to the members, beginning with Newsletter No. 1, on July 31, 1961. Businesslike in their approach to the challenges of fund-raising, equipment procurement, and composition of the final team, they also capture Dyhrenfurth's sense that the American spirit would not rest until Everest was secured in the country's lexicon and treasure chest. Dyhrenfurth's last letter before departure, dated December 15, 1962, evokes the excitement of an era when international travel alone demanded scrupulous attention to passports, visas, vaccinations, mail forwarding, banking arrangements, letters of permission, baggage allowances, cameras and film, as well as maps, medicines, and a means for dealing with media inquiries. On the mountain, Dyhrenfurth suffered laryngitis for part of the expedition, yet he tape-recorded a daily account of events, and sent the tapes out by mail runner to Kathmandu. The transcript of these recordings (February 21–June 1, 1963) presents an invaluable record, and Dyhrenfurth deserves accolades for his attention to detail and sense of the historical record. The correspondence resumed with Norman's postexpedition letters, which continued to the end of 1965.

James Ramsey Ullman's tome, *Americans on Everest: The Official Account of the Ascent Led by Norman G. Dyhrenfurth* (Philadelphia: Lippincott, 1964), covers the expedition as a whole, and does so comprehensively and judiciously. Its occasional hyperbole is balanced by humor, and its relentless good-spiritedness nicely captures the many moments of teamwork and excellence on the mountain. Brief passages from pages 28, 67, 169, 178, 179, 181, 184, 187, and 191 are quoted or referred to.

Tom Hornbein's *Everest: The West Ridge,* 4th ed. (Seattle: Mountaineers, 2013) is a classic of mountaineering literature—written about a still-classic climb. In addition to a gripping tale of near-obsessive dedication, total commitment, and survival against all odds, this book soulfully conveys the essence of mountaineering. The 2013 edition contains a new preface, foreword, and photos. Brief passages from pages 30, 136, 138, 142, 143, 163, and 164 are quoted or referred to.

Two accounts that provided background to climbing in the Tetons of Wyoming, from the 1930s through the 1970s, include an endearing book edited by Charlie Craighead, *Glenn Exum: Never a Bad Word or a Twisted Rope* (Moose, Wyo.: Grand Teton Natural History Association, 1998) and the poetically written *We Aspired: The Last Innocent Americans* by Pete Sinclair (Logan: Utah State University Press, 1993).

Some mountain details and expressions have been drawn from audio- and videotape-recorded lectures by Willi Unsoeld, including a Feburary 13, 1979, lecture at The Evergreen State College; a lecture in Westtown, New York, on June 17, 1979; a lecture to Grand Canyon rangers; and a 1974 lecture sponsored by the Colorado Outward Bound School called "Spiritual Values in Wilderness," for a conference in Estes Park on experiential education. Additional details were drawn from a videotaped lecture given in 2003 by Tom Hornbein as part of the annual Unsoeld Lecture Series at The Evergreen State College. "The West Ridge of Everest," a typed sixteen-page paper by Willi Unsoeld, also formed a useful reference. A lecture that Willi Unsoeld delivered at Keene State University can be viewed on YouTube at http://www .youtube.com/watch?v=MvowGvmY-KE.

The seven survivors of the 1963 expedition and their relatives and acquaintances provided stories of the expedition, its members, and the periods before and after. Much of the deceased climbers' correspondence and documents have been archived, along with the expedition diaries (which Dick Emerson insisted they fill in); these proved a rich source of material. (These sources are listed in the acknowledgments.)

Parts of the South Col and West Ridge climbing narratives are drawn from the transcripts of audiotapes recorded by Matt McDade while on assignment with the National Geographic Society. During the march out from Base Camp to Kathmandu in May and June 1963, most of the climbers reviewed events on the mountain in detail with him, and the transcripts were typed up and cataloged in five volumes. (Barry Bishop was recorded at greatest length; vol. 4 and sections "P. wood 2-" and "wood 3-" in vol. 5 were especially informative.)

From the Thomas Hornbein Papers at the University of California, San Diego, handwritten letters to his wife, Gene, and letters to Willi Unsoeld were informative. The transcript of Hornbein's diary, digitally recorded by Tom and transcribed by Didi Thunder, is thoughtful and insightful.

Jim Whittaker's book, *A Life on the Edge: Memoirs of Everest and Beyond,* 2nd ed. (Seattle: Mountaineers, 2013), tells the story of a man who has journeyed farther and climbed higher than most of us could ever aspire; quotes are drawn from pages 11 and 103. And Dick Emerson's "The Traverse of Mt. Everest" (*Sierra Club Bulletin,* 1965) is an especially concise account of the West Ridge climb and the particular challenges they faced.

Jim Lester's notes and text from his unpublished manuscripts have provided important reference points throughout, and his clear writing highlights his observant, scientific eye and his artistic temperament. At the time of his death, Lester had compiled notes and draft text for books on the history and philosophical underpinnings of mountaineering, on the 1963 Sherpas and their historical arc, and for a young adult volume on the 1963 expedition.

National Geographic magazine's seventy-fifth anniversary issue of October 1963 featured the summit of Everest on its cover, with the American flag blowing from the top. This iconic issue featured three articles on the expedition: "Six to the Summit," by Norman Dyhrenfurth, "How We Climbed Everest," by Barry Bishop, and "The First Traverse," by Tom Hornbein and Willi Unsoeld.

Wikipedia was used to confirm some names, places, elevations, and figures.

1. A Vertical Playground

Wayne Hamilton provided stories about his Dartmouth classmate Barry Corbet and how they developed a challenging learning method for rock climbing that involved downing a beer before each attempt on a route until they finally got it right. After their first winter ascent of Mount Katahdin's Knife Edge, Corbet wrote an account that ran in a local newspaper titled "Inexperienced College Student Snowshoes Out 20 Miles in Socks," referring to Hamilton's self-evacuation method after he dried his double leather boots over a fire and they shrank.

Classmate Sam Silverstein provided background, and recalled when Corbet and Breitenbach were doing a new route in the Tetons, and the wind picked up. "Jake led on a difficult pitch as Corbet belayed him from below. The rope stopped moving up, but over the wind noise he thought he heard Jake say, 'On belay!' He started climbing, and several times shouted 'Up rope,' indicating that Jake should take up the slack. Eventually Corbet negotiated the crux move. He found Jake around the corner, still fiddling with the rope. 'Okay—*now* you're on belay,' Jake said to him."

Some of the details of climbing in the Tetons were drawn from a March 1990 interview with Barry Corbet, recorded and transcribed by Scott Wood. Dave Dornan and Jim Elder, elder statesmen of Tetons climbing history, contributed useful information, as did Renny Jackson, Dave Dingman, and Charlie Craighead.

Willi Unsoeld recounted a version of his "guide's badge" story in the television program *American Sportsman*, produced by Scott Ransom and shot with a young actor named David Ladd. Additional details were drawn from a piece by Willi Unsoeld, "The Life of a Teton Guide," in the 1960 *American Alpine Journal*.

2. From Dartmouth Dorms to Teton Tents

Jack Durrance's mother moved him and his brother, Dick, from Florida to Garmisch-Partenkirchen in Germany, where the boys could learn mountain sports and attend high school. They returned to the States in 1935—Dick a champion skier, and Jack a climber. Jack Durrance worked as a Tetons guide during the summers of 1936–41, and was on the 1938 K2 expedition with Fritz Wiessner. He received an MD from Dartmouth and practiced medicine in Denver until he died in 2000 at the age of ninety. Frank Sands, Joe Kelsey, and Pete Sinclair also contributed stories.

In 1958, Dave Dingman organized an expedition to Mount McKinley, and with Tetons guide Dave Dornan climbed it via the West Buttress; they made the first ascent of both summits in the same day.

Guide service co-owner Glenn Exum praised Dick Pownall's exceptional route-finding ability. They made the first ascent of the East Face of Thor Peak together with Mike Brewer in 1950, and with Bob Merriam, Pownall did the first ascent of Red Sentinel. After the climb of the Grand with two dogs, they returned to Jenny Lake, where some members of a dubious religious group called the "I Ams"—said to have a million followers at its zenith in 1938—had spent the day observing the mountain. They regarded the Grand Teton as vibrating on a sympathetic wavelength to Mount Shasta, and believed that caverns (known only to Grand Master St. Germain) linked the two sacred peaks. When they learned that a pair of dogs had pranced around on the summit, Pownall said, the I Ams acolytes became incensed.

Regarding the Yosemite Standards, Dave Dornan said that in 1960, Royal Robbins and Joe Fitschen came to the Tetons from California, and Layton Kor from Colorado, for the first time, and climbed all of the hard routes in the Tetons without difficulty. "This opened our eyes to what was happening elsewhere, and especially in Yosemite. Robbins and Kor in particular set new standards for climbing and changed the culture." Climbing was no longer just a part-time recreation for gentlemen; it became a sport for dedicated athletes.

Additional sources include *Skiing Heritage,* the journal of the International Skiing History Association.

3. A Distant Vision

The Winter Olympics in 1936 were in Garmisch-Partenkirchen.

Tibet scholar Warren Smith, Jr., points out that when British troops invaded Tibet's capital of Lhasa in 1904, seeking trade concessions, the Chinese responded unfavorably to what they viewed as another British colonial takeover. In 1910, the thirteenth Dalai Lama escaped to India and sought refuge in Darjeeling. There, he developed a close relationship with Charles Bell, a well-educated official of the British Government of India. The Dalai Lama returned to Tibet in 1912, and two years later invited Bell to Lhasa as British India's first representative in Tibet. The British kept a representative in Lhasa until Indian independence, in 1947.

Nick Clinch reiterated that Switzerland had little presence on the Himalayan climbing scene in the first half of the twentieth century, and that Germany had selected Nanga Parbat in Pakistan as their "national project." Thirty-one people had died on the mountain before it was first climbed, in 1953.

In the United States, one example of an educated, leisure-class underpinning to mountaineering can be seen in the names of the "Collegiate Peaks" in the Sawatch Range of Colorado—Mounts Harvard, Yale, Princeton, Columbia, and Oxford—which were named by the elite students and instructors who first climbed most of them.

Norman Dyhrenfurth wrote a stirring foreword to *Americans on Everest* by James Ramsey Ullman (pp. xv, xvi, xx, and xxi are referenced here), and some material is drawn from *Mount Everest: 1952,* Dyhrenfurth's report on the fall 1952 expedition to Everest, submitted to the Swiss Foundation for Alpine Research, Zurich. He also prepared a concept paper for the creation of an American Foundation for Mountain Exploration, dated December 1954, White Plains, New York.

Nick Clinch said about the 1960 Masherbrum expedition, which he led: "George Bell was the Climbing Leader, though I never used the term, as I felt it was derogatory. He was the Leader, and I was the Director. I also call myself Leader. I can live with ambiguity. People asked what the difference was and I said, 'He turned down my friends, and I turned down his.'"

Tetons guide and ranger Dave Dornan pointed out that the European alpine climbing clubs were open to all, and these clubs were part of the fabric of countries that shared the Alps—and thereby enjoyed a substantial base for fund-raising. The American Alpine Club was more insular at that time, and had fewer members to approach for funds.

4. Entering the Arena

In July 1962, *National Geographic* issued a press release implying that they were "sponsoring" the expedition. For some time, this scared off other potential sponsors and contributors, who assumed that the expedition's funding needs had been provided for.

The program *I've Got a Secret* was co-created by comedian Allan Sherman, who would also win national fame as a folksinger.

More information on the largest nuclear bomb, "Big Ivan," can be found at http://www.nuclearweaponarchive.org/Russia/TsarBomba .html.

5. Acceptance and Invitations

Glenn Exum's guides drove north to Colter Bay Village for showers, to Jackson Lake Lodge for milk shakes, and to the Stockade Room for evening drinks. In the 1960s, outsiders from both coasts were beginning to move to the area, bringing with them the biases and demands that come with schooling and wealth. The town newspaper quipped that "the most commonly overheard phrase in Jackson Hole is: 'This place started to go to hell in (insert the year you moved here).'" The term "beatnik" was coined by San Francisco columnist Herb Caen, who adapted it from "Sputnik."

High-altitude physiologist and Peace Corps India director Charles Houston was a member of the 1938 K2 climb. In the 1940s and '50s, Bob Bates, his counterpart in the Nepal Peace Corps, was a cheerful, animated English instructor at Phillips Exeter Academy in New Hampshire. "He opened me up to possibilities for greatness," student and Tetons guide Bill Briggs said of Bates. "I figured that if mountaineering had anything to do with the making of his character, then I wanted a part of it." Few students were aware of Bates's thoroughly exciting second life in the highest mountains of the world. The story of Bates and Willi Unsoeld being recruited for the Peace Corps is told by Donovan McClure, Sargent Shriver's public relations officer, in *Come as You Are: The Peace Corps Story*, by Coates Redmon (San Diego: Harcourt Brace Jovanovich, 1986), p. 4.

Willi Unsoeld recounted the tale of his first climb in the Himalaya in "Nilkanta, Garhwal Himalaya, 1949," in the *American Alpine*

Journal, 1950. The story of Unsoeld's return to the Indian village from the attempt on Nilkanta is largely from Daniel Taylor and J. Gabriel Campbell, who have lived and worked in South Asia for most of their lives, and from Alfie Campbell, Ernie Campbell's widow, now living in Wooster, Ohio. Missionary Ernie Campbell's life in northern India included an interlude in the United States in 1964, when he marched for civil rights in Hattiesburg, Mississippi—a natural segue to America from picketing in northern India, in the late 1940s, in favor of Indian independence.

While studying at the Pacific School of Religion in Berkeley, Unsoeld made the first ascent of the East Buttress of El Capitan with Al Steck, Will Siri, and Bill Long, in June 1953.

A number of students, most of them from The Evergreen State College, took Willi Unsoeld's teachings to heart; Jonathan Stevens and Jeff Shushan are two of many who credit Unsoeld with shaping their characters, their worldviews, and their later careers.

6. Beyond the Tetons

An Italian man named Vitale Bramani invented Vibram soles for climbing boots after several friends slipped and died while climbing.

Toward the end of Sir Edmund Hillary's 1960–61 Silver Hut Expedition, Barry Bishop climbed Ama Dablam with Dr. Mike Ward of the United Kingdom, and two New Zealanders, Wally Romanes and Mike Gill. The peak wouldn't be climbed again for eighteen years, though it is routinely climbed today.

7. Scientists and Shrinks

Once Maynard Miller could determine trends in the accumulation and ablation of snow and ice (which are used to calculate a glacier's annual "mass budget"), along with the glacier's lineal advance or recession, he would be able to compare the Khumbu Glacier to similar types of glaciers in Alaska and the Andes. He was curious whether glaciological trends in the Himalaya might correlate with trends on other continents and regions, which would have profound implications in the nascent science of identifying global climatic patterns. In 1956, Fritz Müller, cartographer and glaciologist for the Swiss Everest expedition that year, set up a baseline transect to measure the speed at which the Khumbu Glacier was moving down valley. Miller was keen to reestablish and measure this transect, seven years on. He also planned to gauge the density, hardness, and firmness of the snow and firn (melted and refrozen snow from the previous year), and extract samples from deeper layers by drilling into the glacier with an auger. Subsequent to 1963, studies of the Khumbu Glacier have shown that it has lost considerable mass, and that dozens of small meltwater ponds have formed on the surface—as a result of rising temperatures within the region, particularly during the past thirty years. Some of Miller's proximal conclusions, written shortly after the expedition, are summarized in an addendum chapter to *Americans on Everest,* "Geology and Glaciology," pp. 401–12.

The description of Jim Lester meeting Norman Dyhrenfurth and eventually being recruited for the American Everest team is partly drawn from Lester's unpublished manuscript on the expedition. Jim Lester and Dick Emerson jointly authored an informal paper, "Group Performance in Remote Environments: Some Reflections Based on the Ascent of Everest," a copy of which is in the Richard M. Emerson archive at the Suzzalo Library, University of Washington, Seattle.

Chuck Huestis's son Jeff provided access to an archive of his father's voluminous correspondence on the expedition.

8. A Trial Run . . . or Hike

Fred Maytag, who supported development of the "Hornbein mask," died in November 1962, three months before the team was to depart. Hornbein took the mask that he designed to the Naval Air Station in Coronado, California, and connected it—along with the Indian, Swiss, and British masks—to a piston ventilator that measured resistance to air flow, and he plotted the results on a graph. Hornbein's design was found to be superior.

Dr. Gil Roberts's biographical information was partly drawn from two interviews conducted by John Rawlings in April and August 1997 ("Gilbert Roberts," Stanford Oral History Project, 1999) and from his widow, Erica Stone, who is president of the American Himalayan Foundation.

As part of the trial run on Mount Rainier, the climbers descended into crevasses to practice self-evacuation with the newly developed Jumar ascenders. These indispensible tools for ascending a rope (as contrasted with rappelling) replaced Prusiks: short lengths of manila rope knotted around the climbing rope with a friction hitch.

Jim Lester summarized his findings from the expedition and from the Institute of Personality Assessment and Research studies in "Wrestling with the Self on Mt. Everest," *Journal of Humanistic Psychology* 23, no. 2 (1983): pp. 31–41. IPAR is now the Institute of Personality and Social Research (IPSR). In the study, team members submitted to a variety of sociometric tests, such as the Thematic Apperception Test, the Edwards Personal Preference Schedule, the Bass Orientation Inventory, the Allport-Vernon-Lindzey Study of Values, the Strong Vocational Interest Blank, the California Psychological Inventory, the Myers-Briggs Type Indicator, Rorschach tests, the Minnesota Multiphasic Personality Inventory, the Witkin Rod and Frame Test, and after the expedition, the Gough Adjective Checklist (in which each member selected descriptive adjectives for every other member). Barry Bishop also recounts the testing in "Everest: In Respect and Retrospect," in the *Explorer's Journal,* December 1963.

For the early high-altitude physiology studies at the Donner Lab of the Lawrence Radiation Laboratory, hypoxia was a useful "stressor" for studying the chemistry and physiology of red blood cell production, hormonal regulation, and gas exchange between the lungs and the bloodstream. Will Siri was also interested in the production of aldosterone, a steroid hormone that affects blood pressure and volume. Siri's addendum chapter "Physiology," in Ullman's *Americans on Everest* (p. 379), summarizes his research.

9. To the Other Side of the Earth

Charles Houston's experience with the Peace Corps in India is recounted in Redmon's *Come as You Are,* pp. 92–93. Cameraman Dan Doody was similarly captivated by Asia, and wrote several articulate and descriptive letters to his sister, Agnes, and other relatives, particularly before they arrived on the mountain.

10. Convergences and Close Calls

Dynasties often demand concubines, and when on procession, before 1950, noblemen in Nepal's Rana family oligarchy would scan the crowd and single out consorts for their palaces. This resulted in the architectural touch of adding portholes below the eaves of houses, from which women could observe the parades without being seen.

The former prime minster quoted was the late Kirti Nidhi Bista, to B. Coburn.

The Nepali Congress Party was in power for eighteen months during 1959 and 1960; B. P. Koirala was the country's first democratically elected prime minister. The account of Koirala's meeting with Chairman Mao is told in *Palace, People, and Politics,* by Bhola Chatterji (New Delhi: Ankur Publishing House, 1980). "Chomolungma," the widely recognized Tibetan name for Everest, is likely the name that Chairman Mao invoked. Koirala's Hindu biographer may not have previously heard the Tibetan name and perhaps added the suffix *-lingam*—a phallic symbol linked to the Hindu god Shiva—to create the conflated transliteration "Chomolingam."

Norman Dyhrenfurth prepared a formal statement describing the chronology and implications of Woodrow Wilson Sayre's bootleg attempt on Everest (dated July 25, 1962, Santa Monica; in the James Ramsey Ullman archive at Princeton), and attached it to a letter to President Kennedy. An article on Sayre and his three colleagues' adventure appeared in *Life* magazine (March 13, 1963), and Sayre's book, *Four Against Everest* (Englewood Cliffs, N.J.: Prentice-Hall, 1964), gained some public readership. One of the members was a student from Sayre's philosophy class at Tufts who had been inspired to join the expedition by his teacher's dynamic personality. "The first day of class," the student wrote of Sayre, "he ran up the aisle of the lecture hall in the snowshoes and parka he had used on Alaska's Mount McKinley, vaulted over the lecture table, and landed on the chair standing up. As the class stood and applauded, he bowed deeply and grandly." A climber named Rand Chatterjee met Sayre in 2001 and was able to restore and digitize the expedition's deteriorating 16 mm film.

Nepal's hills are dissected with trails that morph into stairways as they steepen. Most of the new Peace Corps volunteers wouldn't face climbing obstacles, but at the Outward Bound training site in the mountains near Marble, Colorado, enlistees were taught rope work and survival techniques by Willi Unsoeld himself. Unsoeld coaxed them into rappelling off what was dubbed "Willi's Rock," which caused quiet gulps and raised eyebrows when a rumor passed among them that Unsoeld had fallen off it (as described by Jesse Brandt).

Much of the expedition's research grant funds and contributions from the National Geographic Society were disbursed in Indian rupees. The United States had a surplus of rupees as a by-product of Public Law 480 ("Food for Peace"), which provided for government-to-government sales of American grains to developing countries, with payment made in local currencies. The United States then repurposed these funds to support humanitarian aid projects. Nepalese merchants accepted Indian currency and typically asked if a customer was paying in *kampani*—a throwback to the currency of the East India Company—or in *mohar,* the silver coins of Nepal.

11. Treading a Path Between India and China

Adjacent to the lighthearted item on James Ramsey Ullman's New Delhi hospital visit in the *Times of India* sat the provocative headline CHINA CANNOT BE TRUSTED, SAYS NEHRU. "The entire nation must be mobilized to meet the threat on a long-term basis," said India's prime minister. Before approaching the United States for military support, India had been flirting with the Soviet Union and with the policy of nonalignment. Today, maps printed in China that are sold in Nepal come with hand-stamped disclaimers saying that India does not recognize the borders as depicted.

Tibet's border with Nepal had been demarcated by treaty in 1960, and China didn't regard Nepal's frontier as an issue. But China wasn't happy that Nepal was providing soldiers to the Gurkha regiments of the British and Indian armies. This system of mercenary service—driven by its attractive pay—had been a tradition for almost a century and a half.

The Sino-Indian War unfolded, in late 1962, on dual venues separated by a thousand kilometers, with Nepal in the middle. In India's remote northeast, skirmishes broke out in the Tibet-India border region known as the North-East Frontier Agency (or NEFA, now part of the Indian state of Arunachal Pradesh). To the northwest, troops rallied in the remote salt pan known as the Aksai Chin, a thirty-three-thousand-square-kilometer wasteland adjacent to Ladakh, India. China claimed the Aksai Chin as part of its Xinjiang Uygur Autonomous Region. Pushed back as far as they could go while still retaining some honor, India relinquished the Aksai Chin. China granted to India much of the NEFA (which was inhabited by ethnic Tibetans who had maintained a long association with India). In the Sino-Indian War, the Indians were woefully under-armed and underequipped, with British WWII automatic rifles and bulbous-toed "Mickey Mouse" army boots. Unfortunately, a number of the Indian troops suffered sickness and death from high-altitude pulmonary edema and cerebral edema when they were quickly transported to Himalayan border posts—underscoring the need for high-altitude physiology studies.

An account of the 1960 Chinese Everest expedition can be found in "The Conquest of Everest by the Chinese Mountaineering Team," by Shih Chan-chun, in the *Alpine Journal* 66 (1961): pp. 28–41. Early skepticism following China's claim of success has since shifted to acceptance among many international climbers, though little new supporting evidence has emerged. Tibet scholar Warren Smith Jr., author of *Tibetan Nation* and *China's Tibet?*, said that "such was the pressure on local officials to fulfill Mao's unrealistic goals of vastly increased agricultural production that many of them reported huge increases, when in fact the chaos of collectivization caused huge reductions. This resulted in a famine in which an estimated 30–40 million people died. There were likely similar pressures on the 1960 expedition leaders to report success."

A Tibetan refugee named Ngodup prepared a written statement, "Statement of Ngodup," in *Tibet Under Chinese Communist Rule: A Compilation of Refugee Statements, 1958–1975* (Dharamsala, India: Information and Publicity Office of His Holiness the Dalai Lama,

1976), saying that the Chinese expedition didn't reach higher than seven thousand meters. The climbers, he explained, had remained snowbound in the high camp and suffered frostbite before retreating.

Sydney Wignall's account is drawn partly from his unusual and fascinating book, *Spy on the Roof of the World: A True Story of Espionage and Survival in the Himalayas* (Edinburgh: Canongate, 1996), pp. vii, viii, 256. To protect his friends in the Indian Army, Wignall abjured writing about their excursion until 1996. Minya Konka and Mustagh Ata were two of the other peaks that the Chinese attempted before staging the expedition to Everest in 1960. (In 1975 the Chinese climbed Everest, and left a large survey tripod on the summit.)

In 1960, the Chinese may have been unaware that—two hundred miles to the west of Everest, in Nepal's trans-Himalaya border area known as Mustang—a clandestine anti-Chinese operation was under way. By August of that year, a motley band of two thousand Tibetan guerrillas, armed and outfitted by the CIA, were hatching plans to cross high Himalayan passes and stage raids on Chinese army convoys.

12. Goals and Roles

Jim Lester's evocative writings on the landscape of Nepal inspired him to quote John Muir, describing his first visit to Alaska: "Never before this had I been embosomed in scenery so hopelessly beyond description." (Muir: *Travels in Alaska*. 1915: Houghton Mifflin, p. 13.)

Willi Unsoeld was not a prolific writer—his commanding voice and theatrical gestures were his primary forms of expression. "The West Ridge of Everest," a sixteen-page manuscript on the climb, is a marvelous exception, and it succinctly describes key elements of the expedition.

13. Intersecting Worlds

Charles Houston had been invited to approach Everest from the south, via the Dudh Kosi river valley, by his father, Oscar Houston. In the spring of 1950 their party was joined by the legendary climber Major H. W. Tilman and two others. Houston's account of the trip, "Towards Everest," *Himalayan Journal* 17 (1952): pp. 9–18, describes Sherpas as living subsistence lives, untouched by modern amenities.

Anthropologist Don Messerschmidt described his experiences with smallpox as a Peace Corps volunteer in "The Scourge of Smallpox: Nepal 1964," *ECS Nepal*, January 2008, pp. 52–54. In a variation on similar anecdotes heard from rural villages in Nepal, Messerschmidt recalled an arthritic, elderly man who appeared with an empty bottle with a corncob stopper and asked the pilot for a bit of engine oil to rub on his knees. Oil from such a powerful machine, he reasoned, would surely ease the stiffness and pain in his joints more effectively than the mustard oil he usually used.

14. Words from on High

The depopulation and looting of Tibet's monasteries, and some of the destruction (mostly of interiors), took place beginning immediately after the 1959 revolt and continued until about 1962. Physical destruction of the buildings continued during the Cultural Revolution, beginning in 1966. It is believed that the Rongbuk monastery was an empty shell by 1963. For further background on this period of history, see *China's Tibet,* by Warren Smith, Jr., especially the chapter "Confiscated for the Benefit of the People."

Remarkably, across the valley from Pheriche, a Swiss pilot had landed a Pilatus Porter airplane several times in a yak pasture called Mingbo—at fifteen thousand feet, directly below the west face of Ama Dablam. He off-loaded Red Cross relief supplies for Tibetan refugees and building materials for one of the Hillary schools. Pieces of the plane tended to break off each time he landed, and the field was abandoned in 1961, the year after it opened. A civil aviation official flew in and upon landing promptly closed the airstrip. When he saw that he would then have to walk out, he just as promptly reopened it.

The British Raj holdover term "sahib" (from an Arabic word, usually contracted to "sah'b") traditionally connoted a servant-master relationship. The Sherpas are not students of semantics, however, and the term has been mainstreamed as the simplest at hand, an easy one for distinguishing locals from foreign climbers. Nowadays, educated Sherpas often use it when addressing a foreigner whose name they don't know. As language and culture change and adapt, multiple connotations can arise. Nowadays, "Sah'b" can be used as a respectful title when addressing someone of any race.

Radio reception was generally good in both directions, but afternoon electrical storms generated more interference as the season progressed.

The glacier's rough surface was heavily burdened by churned-up rock and rubble, and the glaciological work on the lower part of the Khumbu Glacier took several days. Above them, massive and menacing, loomed the peak of Nuptse, with its nine-thousand-foot wall of granitized sediments and migmatites, not unlike what Barry Prather had studied during expeditions to the Juneau Icefield.

15. Long Live the Crow

The seven rescue climbers were Barry Bishop, Willi Unsoeld, Nawang Gombu, Girmi Dorje, Jim Whittaker, Lute Jerstad, and Dave Dingman.

Spark Schnitzer, a friend of Norman Dyhrenfurth, had trekked in to Base Camp with the expedition. On the trail while returning to Kathmandu, he met a government official. "When I told him I had been with the American Mount Everest expedition," Schnitzer reported, "his face assumed a shocked expression and he informed me that all members of the team had been killed, which he had learned over the radio." The official insisted the story was true, and as Schnitzer continued on his way he pondered the capacity of rumors to get out of hand. He was partly relieved to learn that only a single climber had died.

16. Taming the Beast

"Jim and Willi are really strong," Jerstad wrote in his diary about Whittaker and Unsoeld. "I wondered if I could have mustered the strength to do fifth and sixth class climbing over a long day at that altitude. It was a little humbling, and I guess good for me."

The only available photo showing what would be called the Hornbein Couloir was published in the 1954 edition of *The Mountain World*. The grainy image, taken from some distance, seemed to ask as many questions as it answered.

Tom Hornbein felt that being in on the discussion and decision about focusing on the West Ridge may have resulted in them being granted a small amount more load-carrying power, in the form of Sherpas, so that both endeavors could proceed simultaneously, but with the emphasis clearly on getting the mountain climbed by the South Col. "I did not feel so much personal antagonism as *issue* antagonism," Hornbein said.

Tom Hornbein pointed out that clots from thrombophlebitis can lodge in the lung and are often fatal. High altitude presents an increased risk factor because of the higher concentration of red blood cells that are produced in response to hypoxia.

17. Uncertainty

As Jim Whittaker and Nawang Gombu prepared to leave Camp 6 for the summit, Edmund Hillary was climbing a nearby peak called Tawoche. Hillary remarked that he had never seen Everest's snow plume boiling more wildly, and assumed that the Americans wouldn't dare an attempt in such conditions.

Some details of Whittaker and Gombu's summit day were drawn from Whittaker's compelling memoir, *A Life on the Edge,* and from the *National Geographic* accounts of the expedition. Some background about Nawang Gombu was drawn from an interview that Norman Dyhrenfurth conducted on May 21, 1963, and videotaped interviews with Dorje Lhatoo and Phinjo Gombu conducted in 2012 by Mele Mason. After the expedition, Gombu gave the crucifix that he found below the South Summit to Jim Whittaker, and it is now on display at the library at Seattle University (a Jesuit Catholic institution).

18. Retreat in Victory

Lute Jerstad's notes, dated April 30, 1963, from Camp 5, contributed to this account, and chronology was drawn from Matt McDade's audio-tape transcripts (vol. 2, "cynthia 1-1").

The drugs that Dave Dingman administered were digoxin and aminophylline. The amount of oxygen remaining in the tanks was difficult to gauge, because a partially full bottle weighs nearly the same as a full one.

The account of Project Crater on Mount Rainier is drawn partly from Dee Molenaar, *The Challenge of Rainier: A Record of the*

Explorations and Ascents, Triumphs and Tragedies on the Northwest's Greatest Mountain (Seattle: Mountaineers, 1979), and from the 1961 issue of *Harvard Mountaineering.*

19. Synchronized Climbing

Kalden, Nima Tenzing (of Pangboche), and Pemba Tenzing were the Sherpas who accompanied Bishop and Jerstad toward Camp 3. Accounts in this chapter were drawn partly from Barry Bishop's and Barry Corbet's recorded re-creations of the expedition (Matt McDade interviews), Willi Unsoeld's paper ("The West Ridge of Everest"), and Unsoeld's 1979 recorded lecture at The Evergreen State College, as well as from Hornbein's book *Everest: The West Ridge* (pp. 136, 138, 142). The radio conversation is from "The Traverse of Mt. Everest" by Dick Emerson (pp. 32, 33, 35). Tom commented that Emerson's bivouac "was meticulously planned in a manner typical of Dick's mountaineering efforts."

20. A Wild Idea

Thirty-five years after the expedition, Tom Hornbein gave a lecture titled "Lessons from on High," saying, "Though the West Ridgers managed to keep their motivation charged by sustaining near maximum uncertainty, the South Colers, looking at us, increasingly began to doubt our ability to pull it off. The message here? Uncertainty is an essential ingredient to motivation, to accomplishing any difficult task or goal."

21. A One-Way Round Trip

Tom Hornbein's musing about the strange attraction of the West Ridge is drawn from an intriguing essay he wrote for *Washington University Magazine* (Spring 1964), "The Inevitable 'Why?'"

Interviewed in Golden, Colorado, Al Auten clearly recalled events on the West Ridge. For him, this formed the dramatic highlight of his experience on the expedition—following hours and days spent operating the radio and trying to get the winch to function.

Some of the Barry Corbet material is drawn from an interview he gave to Scott Wood; Tom Hornbein's reflections are partly from a taped interview with climbing veteran Nick Clinch.

22. *The Vast Unknown*

Some of Tom Hornbein's musings on the summit are from *Everest: The West Ridge,* pp. 163–64 and 168–69, and vols. 2 and 3 of the McDade tape transcripts.

This count of Everest summits—number nine and number ten for Barry Bishop and Lute Jerstad—does not include the claim that three Chinese climbers reached the summit in 1960.

23. *A Biblical Calm*

Part of this is drawn from Unsoeld's sixteen-page paper and Barry Bishop's and Maynard Miller's transcribed accounts, as well as a letter that Lute Jerstad sent to Jim Lester on June 5, 1964.

Tom Hornbein doesn't recall needing to find a junction to turn left; they were mainly concerned, he said, that they pick the correct gully to descend.

24. *The Vigorous Life*

Some material in this chapter was drawn from Jimmy Roberts's audiotape transcripts (vol. 5); a December 18, 1963, letter from Will Siri to James Ramsey Ullman; Jim Lester's notes; Norman Dyhrenfurth's taped diary transcripts; Tom Hornbein (Unsoeld Lecture Series); and a letter from Tom Hornbein to his wife, Gene, among other sources.

President Kennedy's words to the team, "Remarks Upon Presenting the Hubbard Medal to the Leader of the American Everest Expedition," July 8, 1963, are online at the American Presidency Project, http://www.presidency.ucsb.edu/ws/?pid=9337.

Nawang Gombu's family gave his son, Kursung (Phinjo) Gombu, the nickname "Jimmy," in honor of Jim Whittaker, though the name didn't stick.

The goodwill tour for five Sherpas and the liaison officer, Noddy, was organized through the Bureau of Educational and Cultural Affairs of the U.S. Department of State.

25. The Bliss-Giving Goddess

Pete Takeda's *An Eye at the Top of the World: The Terrifying Legacy of the Cold War's Most Daring CIA Operation* (New York: Basic Books, 2007) is a well-written account of the CIA-funded caper on Nanda Devi in the mid-1960s, and it provided background to this chapter, along with M. S. Kohli and Kenneth Conboy's *Spies in the Himalayas: Secret Missions and Perilous Climbs* (Lawrence: University Press of Kansas, 2002). Jim McCarthy, who offered valuable advice to the operation in its early stages, was especially helpful, as was Dave Dingman.

Indian intelligence was officially known as the Research and Analysis Wing of the Cabinet Secretariat. Tibet scholar Warren Smith, Jr., believes that the island where Dingman and others went for training was Tinian in the Northern Mariana Islands, which was captured from the Japanese during WWII, used as a B-29 base to bomb Japan, then repurposed as a CIA base. The first CIA-trained Tibetan guerrillas were trained there, and Radio Free Asia's largest transmitters are now located on Tinian.

The Sherpas dubbed the two smaller surveillance devices—the sensor and transceiver—as "big lama" and "little lama." Dave Dingman spent the two years following his clandestine tour of duty at Ellsworth Air Force Base near Rapid City, South Dakota, as chief of surgery at a hundred-bed hospital. "At that time, my peers in surgery were wearing military uniforms in Vietnam, and some were being shot at," he said. "Continuing with military service in a medical setting seemed the right thing to do."

Barry Corbet and Barry Prather installed their surveillance unit on Nanda Kot, then may have waited through a storm cycle. Corbet told Tom Hornbein that he cleared some snow from the device, though the heat from the generator had largely melted a hollow space around it.

26. Transitions

It was rumored that Orson Welles needed to fulfill a tax obligation to the IRS, which he was able to do by narrating *Americans on Everest*.

The 1999 reunion of the '63 Everesters was held at Vail and Denver, and points in between, the weekend of September 25.

The helicopter carrying Barry Corbet had been flying close to the ground. They were above the treeline, and the lack of shadows on the snow offered little definition and likely affected the pilot's depth of field.

Barry Corbet's close friends Len Aitken, a kayaking buddy, and Binny Clark, a Buddhist paraplegic, shared stories of Corbet's struggles with disabled life. A poignant and thought-provoking summary of Barry Corbet's wisdom and teaching can be found in the transcript of his John S. Young, MD, Lecture presentation in 2003, an annual event at Craig Hospital in Englewood, Colorado. The November 2000 issue of *New Mobility* magazine (http://www.NewMobility.com/) has a sampling of some of Corbet's pieces. Tom Hornbein wrote an especially moving obituary for Barry Corbet in the *American Alpine Journal* ("In Memoriam," 2005), quoted here.

John Roskelley wrote about Unsoeld and the death of his daughter Devi in *Nanda Devi: The Tragic Expedition* (Harrisburg, Penn.: Stackpole, 1987). Two biographies of Willi Unsoeld have also been written: Robert Roper, *The Fatal Mountaineer: The High-Altitude Life and Death of Willi Unsoeld, American Himalayan Legend* (New York: St. Martin's, 2002), and Laurence Leamer, *Ascent: The Spiritual and Physical Quest of Willi Unsoeld* (New York: Simon and Schuster, 1982).

Afterword

Mountaineering statistics were confirmed by Richard Salisbury, who has worked closely with Elizabeth Hawley on exhaustively compiling, tabulating, and cross-referencing Himalayan climbing records. Ray Huey, chair of the Biology Department at the University of Washington, has also studied Everest statistics, with special attention to determining where and how deaths have occurred. The double amputee who summited Everest in 2006 is a New Zealander named Mark Inglis.

China began to curtail and delay the granting of Everest permits in 2008, during the Beijing Olympics, apparently out of fear of political activism among foreign climbers. The unpredictability of the permitting process has led outfitters to be wary of booking climbs from Everest's north side, though a sizable number still make attempts from the Tibet side each year.

In the mid-1960s, before sleeping bags became generally available, Colonel Jimmy Roberts fashioned crude versions of them for the porters by placing two or three blankets inside large jute rice bags.

More information on glaciers can be found in "The Status of Glaciers in the Hindu Kush-Himalayan (HKH) Region," and a number of related publications from the International Centre for Integrated Mountain Development (ICIMOD, http://www.icimod.org/), based in Kathmandu.

FURTHER READING AND REFERENCES

Adams, Vincanne. *Tigers of the Snow and Other Virtual Sherpas: An Ethnography of Himalayan Encounters*. Princeton, N.J.: Princeton University Press, 1996.

Anker, Conrad, and David Roberts. *The Lost Explorer: Finding Mallory on Mount Everest*. New York: Simon & Schuster, 1999.

Bishop, Barry C. "Everest: In Respect and Retrospect." *Explorer's Journal*, December 1963.

————. *Karnali Under Stress: Livelihood Strategies and Seasonal Rhythms in a Changing Nepal Himalaya*. Chicago: University of Chicago, 1990.

Craighead, Charlie. *Glenn Exum: Never a Bad Word or a Twisted Rope*. Moose, Wyo.: Grand Teton Natural History Association, 1998.

Davis, Wade. *Into the Silence: The Great War, Mallory, and the Conquest of Everest*. New York: Alfred A. Knopf, 2011.

Dunham, Mikel. *Buddha's Warriors: The Story of the CIA-Backed Tibetan Freedom Fighters, the Chinese Invasion, and the Ultimate Fall of Tibet*. New York: Tarcher, 2004.

Dyhrenfurth, Günter Oskar. *To the Third Pole: The History of the High Himalaya*. London: W. Laurie, 1955.

Elmes, M., and B. Frame. "Into Hot Air: A Critical Perspective on Everest." *Human Relations* 61, no. 2 (2008): pp. 213–41.

Emerson, Richard M. *Mt. Everest: A Case Study of Communication Feedback*. Report under NSF Grant GS14, February 1965.

Fürer-Haimendorf, Christoph von. *The Sherpas Transformed: Social Change in a Buddhist Society of Nepal*. New Delhi: Sterling Publishers, 1984.

Gillman, Peter, ed. *Everest: The Best Writing and Pictures from Seventy Years of Human Endeavour*. Boston: Little, Brown, 1993.

Hawley, Elizabeth. *Seasonal Stories for the Nepalese Himalaya*. Annual reports, 2004–11.

Heil, Nick. *Dark Summit: The True Story of Everest's Most Controversial Season*. New York: Henry Holt, 2008.

Hillary, Edmund. *Schoolhouse in the Clouds*. Garden City, N.Y.: Doubleday, 1964.

———. *View from the Summit*. London: Doubleday, 1999.

Hornbein, Tom. *Everest: The West Ridge,* 4th ed. Seattle: Mountaineers, 2013.

Isserman, Maurice, and Stewart Weaver. *Fallen Giants: A History of Himalayan Mountaineering from the Age of Empire to the Age of Extremes*. New Haven, Conn.: Yale University Press, 2008.

Jones, Chris. *Climbing in North America*. Seattle: Mountaineers, 1997.

Klatzel, Frances. *Gaiety of Spirit: The Sherpas of Everest*. Kathmandu: Mera, 2009.

Launius, Roger D., John M. Logsdon, and Robert W. Smith, eds. *Reconsidering Sputnik: Forty Years Since the Soviet Satellite*. Amsterdam: Harwood Academic Publishers, 2000.

Lester, James. "Spirit, Identity, and Self in Mountaineering." *Journal of Humanistic Psychology* 44, no. 1 (2004): pp. 86–100.

———. *Too Marvelous for Words: The Life and Genius of Art Tatum*. New York: Oxford University Press, 1994.

Lester, Valerie. *Fasten Your Seat Belts! History and Heroism in the Pan Am Cabin*. McLean, Va.: Paladwr Press, 1995.

Logsdon, John M. *John F. Kennedy and the Race to the Moon*. New York: Palgrave Macmillan, 2010.

Mason, Kenneth. *Abode of Snow: A History of Himalayan Exploration and Mountaineering*. New York: Dutton, 1955.

McCallum, John D. *Everest Diary: Based on the Personal Diary of Lute Jerstad, One of the First Five Americans to Conquer Mount Everest*. Chicago: Follett, 1966.

McDonald, Bernadette. *Brotherhood of the Rope: The Biography of Charles Houston*. Seattle: Mountaineers, 2007.

———. *I'll Call You in Kathmandu: The Elizabeth Hawley Story*. Seattle: Mountaineers, 2005.

McDonald, Bernadette, and John Amatt, eds. *Voices from the Summit: The World's Greatest Mountaineers on the Future of Climbing*.

Washington, D.C.: Adventure Press, National Geographic Society, 2000.

Potterfield, Peter, ed. *Everest*. Seattle: Mountaineers, 2003.

Ramsay, Cynthia Russ. *Sir Edmund Hillary and the People of Everest*. Kansas City, Mo.: Andrews McMeel Publishing, 2002.

Salisbury, Richard. *The Himalayan Database: The Expedition Archives of Elizabeth Hawley*. Golden, Colo.: American Alpine Club, 2004.

Sherpa, Lhakpa Norbu. *Through a Sherpa Window: Illustrated Guide to Traditional Sherpa Culture*. Kathmandu, Nepal: Vajra Publications, 2008.

Sinclair, Pete. *We Aspired: The Last Innocent American*. Logan, Ut.: Utah State University Press, 1993.

Smith, Warren W., Jr. *China's Tibet? Autonomy or Assimilation*. Lanham, Md.: Rowman and Littlefield, 2008.

———. *Tibetan Nation: A History of Tibetan Nationalism and Sino-Tibetan Relations*. Boulder, Colo.: Westview, 1996.

———. *Tibet's Last Stand? The Tibetan Uprising of 2008 and China's Response*. Rowman and Littlefield, 2010.

Ullman, James Ramsay. *Americans on Everest: The Official Account of the Ascent Led by Norman G. Dyhrenfurth*. Philadelphia: Lippincott, 1964.

Unsworth, Walt. *Everest: A Mountaineering History*. Boston: Houghton Mifflin, 1981.

Whittaker, James. *A Life on the Edge: Memoirs of Everest and Beyond*, 2nd ed. Seattle: Mountaineers, 2013.

INDEX

About the Author

Broughton Coburn is the author or editor of seven books, including two national bestsellers, *Everest: Mountain Without Mercy* and *Touching My Father's Soul: A Sherpa's Journey to the Top of Everest* (with Jamling Tenzing Norgay). He has worked in environmental conservation and development in the Himalaya of Nepal, Tibet, and India for two of the past three decades. He lives in Wilson, Wyoming, with his wife and two children.